Praise for

FUTURE FILES

"Provocative, entertaining, and full of surprising facts. A book to help you decide whether the world is going mad or possibly becoming more intelligent."
Theodore Zeldin, author of *An Intimate History of Humanity*

"I found myself warming to his (Watson's) intense curiosity about what is going on in the world and I appreciated the absence of academic snobbery."
Simon Caterson in *The Age*

"The book… is fascinating, frightening and strange."
Esther Van Doornum in *Bookseller & Publisher*

"Fascinating reading for anyone who considers themselves forward thinking."
MX

"A snappy look at possibilities and a timely dose of reality."
Boss Magazine

For PBW & RRW
(a marriage of art and science)

FUTURE
FILES

5 trends that will shape
the next 50 years

Richard Watson

NICHOLAS BREALEY
PUBLISHING

LONDON • BOSTON

First published by
Nicholas Brealey Publishing in 2008

3–5 Spafield Street
Clerkenwell, London
EC1R 4QB, UK
Tel: +44 (0)20 7239 0360
Fax: +44 (0)20 7239 0370
www.nicholasbrealey.com
www.nowandnext.com

20 Park Plaza, Suite 1115A
Boston
MA 02116, USA
Tel: (888) BREALEY
Fax: (617) 523 3708
www.futuretrendsbook.com

© Richard Watson 2008
The right of Richard Watson to be identified as the author of this work has
been asserted in accordance with the Copyright, Designs and Patents Act 1988.

Illustrations by the author.

ISBN: 978-1-85788-514-9

Library of Congress Cataloging-in-Publication Data

Watson, Richard, 1961-
   Future files : 5 trends that will shape the next 50 years / Richard
Watson.
     p. cm.
   Includes bibliographical references and index.
   ISBN 978-1-85788-514-9
   1. Twenty-first century--Forecasts. 2. Technological forecasting. 3.
Economic forecasting. I. Title.
   CB161.W378 2008
   303.49--dc22

2008023356

British Library Cataloguing in Publication Data
A catalogue record for this book is available from the
British Library.

FSC

Printed in Finland by WS Bookwell on
Forest Stewardship Council certified paper.

Contents

The 5 most important trends for the next 50 years   1
Introduction   5

1   Society and Culture: why we'll take longer baths
        in the future   15
2   Science and Technology: the rise of the machines   38
3   Government and Politics: us and them   60
4   Media and Entertainment: have it your way   90
5   Money and Financial Services: everyone is a bank   116
6   Automotive and Transport: the end of the road
        as we know it   145
7   Food and Drink: faster *and* slower   168
8   Retail and Shopping: what we'll buy when
        we've got it already   191
9   Healthcare and Medicine: older and wiser   214
10   Travel and Tourism: "sorry, this country is full"   238
11   Work and Business: the new right-brain economy   258
12   Conclusions: where to next?   277

5 things that won't change over the next 50 years   285
Sources   289
Acknowledgments   293
Index   295

I was a peripheral visionary.
I could see the future, but only way off to the side.

Steven Wright

The 5 most important trends for the next 50 years

This book is about looking out of windows and making maps. It is also about making connections. What they don't teach you at Harvard Business School is that focusing on core competencies or specializing in a particular industry at the exclusion of all others can result in you knowing an awful lot about next to nothing. Equally, a laser-like focus on immediate issues and priorities can mean that you are well equipped for next week but hopelessly unprepared for anything more than about 18 months out.

Hence the book concerns itself with the longer view. It is shamelessly about breadth not narrowness, and explores what happens when one frees one's mind and starts to synthesize large quantities of disparate information into plausible scenarios. In other words, it's about now and what might happen next.

I mention more than 200 trends, which some people would say is too many. I'd agree. Then again too much information, twinned with not enough time, is something we'll all have to get used to in the future. I have tried to help simplify matters by placing a summary of 5 key trends before each chapter, but even this adds up to 55 trends. Therefore it will be useful to start by highlighting what I believe will be the 5 most significant and enduring drivers of change over the next 50 years.

Ageing It's someone's 50th birthday every 8 seconds in the US but companies are still obsessively focused on young people. In Japan the percentage of people aged 75+ is forecast to increase by 36% between 2005 and 2015; the percentage increase in taxation required to maintain current benefit levels for its next generation is +175%. The implications of this demographic shift include higher expenditure on pharmaceuticals, which is already at record levels, plus a general interest in issues such as wellbeing, medical tourism and healthcare planning. The type of diseases and surgery we'll see in the future will also change. We've had voicelifts and other forms of anti-ageing surgery already and we can expect to see more R&D dollars put behind areas like memory recovery and the replacement of worn-out body parts. At a mundane level there will be a boom in industries such as travel and companies will employ older people to design packaging that those with old hands and poor eyesight can actually open.

Power shift eastwards   The centers of economic, political and military power are shifting from West to East. For example, consumer spending in China is predicted to hit $2.2 trillion by 2015. Meanwhile between them, Saudi Arabia, UAE, Kuwait, Bahrain, Qatar and Oman have US$1 trillion of capital investments in the pipeline and this could double or even treble over the next decade. The point here is that emerging markets like China and India are no longer just sources of cheap supply and demand. They are increasingly global hubs for capital and will become important centers of upstream innovation. Equally, we'll see companies from the CHIME nations (China, India and the Middle East) buying Western companies and infrastructure; the same could happen with companies from Russia and Brazil or from the so-called N11 Nations (Bangladesh, Egypt, Indonesia, Iran, South Korea, Mexico, Nigeria, Pakistan, the Philippines, Turkey and Vietnam). One further consequence of growth in these regions is that demand for natural resources will continue to grow, outstripping supply in many instances. This is, of course, assuming that these nations don't take an economic nose-dive or self-destruct for other sociopolitical reasons.

Global connectivity Greater connectivity, brought about by technology, deregulation, globalization, low-cost travel and migration, is changing how people live, how people work and how people think. For example, one billion of us are already online and this figure is expected to double within a decade or so. There are also 2.5 billion talking to each other on cellphones and 13% of the world's population is now living somewhere other than the country of their birth. Implications? There will be information anxiety (too much information being passed too quickly around the world causing widespread insecurity and panic) and capital will travel to and from places where it probably shouldn't (to or from dictators with suspect ethics, for example). Similarly, the networked nature of interbank lending will increase risk and workforces will become highly mobile. GPS, RFID and "smart dust" will mean that inert physical objects (and people) will know where they are and will be able to communicate with each other. The bad news, perhaps, is that technologically speaking, privacy is dead or dying. The good news is that all this connectivity is increasing transparency and hence our behavior may actually become more honest. We may even get smarter at making decisions, because our connectivity will allow instant polling and the wisdom of crowds is nearly always greater than the intelligence of any single member. We will thus see a subtle shift from "me" to "we".

GRIN technologies Machines will be a dominant feature of the future. Computers will eventually become more intelligent than people, at which point humanity will be faced with something of a dilemma. If machines are more intelligent than their makers, what's to stop them taking over? This, of course, requires an element of self-awareness, but impossible is nothing in the future. The other intriguing aspect of this issue is the convergence of computing with robotics and nanotechnology (GRIN refers to Genetics, Robotics, Internet and Nanotechnology), which could give rise to self-replicating machines. Add to this the possibility of not only downloading human intelligence into a machine but adding human consciousness too, and you are faced with the question of whether it is better to live for ever in a machine or for a limited time as a carbon-based biped. And to think that in 2008 we were worried about getting too much email.

The environment   It is hard not to mention environmental issues like climate change and global warming in the context of important trends for the next 50 years. While climate is influencing — and will continue to influence — how governments, corporations and individuals think and act, I would suggest that it won't be the only game in town. Climate change is a present concern but this could change very fast if a more immediate threat — like an economic collapse or a global flu pandemic — comes along. Equally, we are facing other issues including peak oil, peak coal, peak gas, peak water, peak uranium and even peak people (a severe shortage of workers in many parts of the world). The finite nature of natural resources is not necessarily a problem, although it will require a profound shift in attitudes and behavior (and technology) to overcome. Hence sustainability in a more general sense and the mantra of reuse, recycle and reduce will be something we'll be hearing a lot more of in the future. Perhaps the answer to the question "What will the future look like?" should be Copenhagen and Amsterdam as much as Mumbai, Dubai, Shanghai, Tokyo or Las Vegas.

Introduction

I have seen the future, and it's very much like the present, only longer.
—Woody Allen

Above my desk is a faded newspaper cutting that reads "Insurers want a map of the future". I've been tearing interesting articles out of newspapers and magazines for over 20 years. And for over 20 years I've regularly lost them or put them somewhere I can't find them. So eventually I had an idea. Why not pull out the key points from these cuttings and then start to look for patterns and connections that make sense to me and hopefully to others too? Better still, why not archive these key points and connections online where they would be easy for me and other people to find? That, in a nutshell, is how I ended up having a website about trends that nobody except myself ever looked at. I didn't care. If nobody else wanted to look out of the window at the distant horizon so be it. But I was curious. Moreover, I was curious about how I could get people to stop what they were doing for just a second and take a proper look around.

The answer, it turned out, was pictures. People are short of time and our new digital culture means that the information universe is becoming almost infinite. Hence people seem to relate best to information when it's been filtered and delivered in short, snack-sized bites or when a picture replaces a thousand words.

Maps are one way of doing this. In late 2006 I was playing around with a written list of trends and thought that it would be interesting to try to draw the trends in the form of a map. Being from London I immediately thought of the iconic Underground map. Obviously using the actual map was out of the question — an artist tried it once and got sued — so I started to play around with the lines, putting them in different places to make the connections between the various trends come to life. It worked up to a point but was very much a doodle in progress. For example, digital cash appeared at the end of the "money" line but I couldn't quite make this "station" relate to the death of coins, banknotes and paper bills. Nevertheless, I liked the map enough to incorporate it into my annual hard-copy trend report that was duly sent out to various people across the world.

I don't know whether you've noticed, but life sometimes has a habit of sneaking up and surprising you when you're busy making other more strategic plans. That map is a case in point. Unbeknown to me it turned out that one of the people I'd sent the report to with the map inside lived with a commissioning editor of a publishing company. Consequently I got an email out of the blue asking me whether I could stretch my 8,000-word report into a book of around 90,000 words. The rest, as they say, is history.

But that was only the beginning. I decided to release the map on the internet and people started linking to it and talking about it. One site even referred to it as "The best trend map in the world — ever". This was a bit unfair because there have hardly been any trend maps in the world, ever. Nevertheless, things started to snow-ball. I added a clipping of the map to the homepage of my website and the average time visitors spent on the site went through the roof. I started doing talks and the one thing everyone wanted me to talk about was the map. One other thing I did was to say that the map was published under a Creative Commons Attribution — ShareAlike 2.5 License. This effectively says that I don't own the map and anyone is free to use it or revise it just so long as they attribute where it came from. Although this seemed to be a major factor in the map's cybersuccess, I think the main reason was simply that we live in a visual culture and people seem to relate best to information when it's presented in an aesthetically pleasing way.

The "Trend Blend" on the cover thus highlights some of the main trends that are referred to in this book and shows their connectivity using industry or sector lines. But please don't take it too seriously. It's still a work in progress and there'll be a new Trend Blend along shortly. The illustrations overleaf are not maps but timelines, but their purpose is similar. They are attempts to visualize information and to start conversations about the future. One is an innovation timeline showing possible inventions between now and the year 2050, while the other is its opposite, an extinction timeline showing some of the things that are expected to disappear over the same period. Again, they are not comprehensive and shouldn't be read as gospel. Incidentally, all of these can easily be found on the internet or on my website (www.nowandnext.com) under "trend maps".

So is the aim of this book to predict the future? Yes and no. Anyone who says they can do this is either a liar or a fool. My intention is simply to reinterpret the present. Hopefully you will see familiar things in a new light and unfamiliar things with greater clarity. My objective is to broaden perspectives and widen horizons; to make as many individuals and organizations as possible think twice about where they are going and to consider whether, once they get there, it will be worth staying. The book should therefore appeal to business analysts, strategists and anyone else who is curious about the future or who needs to stay ahead of the game.

This is not easy. To achieve it you must first observe what is already happening and then make an educated guess as to where some of what is happening may lead. This in turn inevitably means putting your hand up and making the odd statement, which, for all practical purposes, is the same as making a prediction. However, most of these "predictions" are in fact simply references to general patterns rather than definitive statements about specific events. Having said that, it is sometimes just too tempting not to stir things

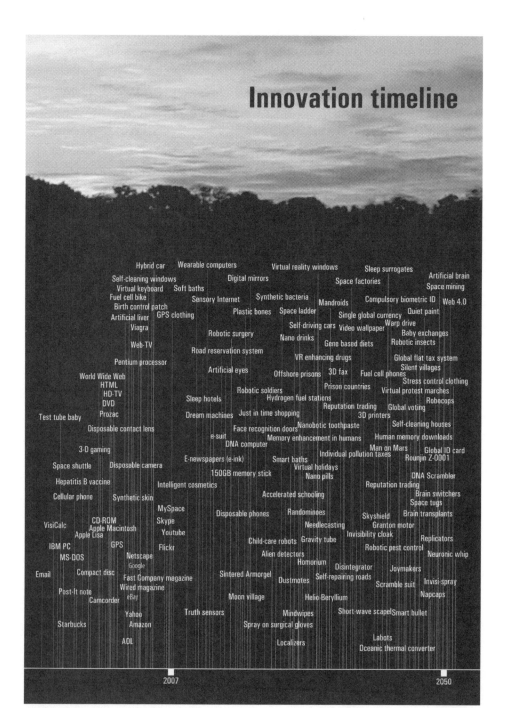

Innovation timeline

Hybrid car   Wearable computers   Virtual reality windows   Sleep surrogates   Artificial brain

Self-cleaning windows   Digital mirrors   Space factories   Space mining

Virtual keyboard   Soft baths

Fuel cell bike   Sensory Internet   Synthetic bacteria   Mandroids   Compulsory biometric ID   Web 4.0

Birth control patch

Artificial liver   GPS clothing   Plastic bones   Space ladder   Single global currency   Quiet paint

Viagra   Self-driving cars   Video wallpaper   Warp drive

Robotic surgery   Nano drinks   Gene based diets   Baby exchanges

Web-TV   Robotic insects

Road reservation system

Pentium processor   VR enhancing drugs   Global flat tax system

Artificial eyes   Offshore prisons   3D fax   Fuel cell phones   Silent villages

World Wide Web   Stress control clothing

HTML   Robotic soldiers   Prison countries   Virtual protest marches

HD-TV   Sleep hotels   Hydrogen fuel stations   Robocops

DVD   Reputation trading   Global voting

Test tube baby   Prozac   Dream machines   Just in time shopping   3D printers

Disposable contact lens   Face recognition doors   Nanobotic toothpaste   Self-cleaning houses

e-suit   Memory enhancement in humans   Human memory downloads

3-D gaming   DNA computer   Man on Mars   Global ID card

E-newspapers (e-ink)   Smart baths   Individual pollution taxes   Rounjin Z-0001

Space shuttle   Disposable camera   Virtual holidays

150GB memory stick   Nano pills   DNA Scrambler

Hepatitis B vaccine   Intelligent cosmetics   Reputation trading

Cellular phone   Synthetic skin   Accelerated schooling   Brain switchers

MySpace   Space tugs

Disposable phones   Randominoes   Skyshield   Brain transplants

CD-ROM   Skype   Needlecasting   Granton motor

VisiCalc   Apple Macintosh   Invisibility cloak

Apple Lisa   Youtube   Child-care robots   Gravity tube   Replicators

IBM PC   GPS   Flickr   Robotic pest control

MS-DOS   Netscape   Alien detectors   Neuronic whip

Google   Homorium   Disintegrator   Joymakers

Email   Compact disc   Sintered Armorgel   Dustmotes   Self-repairing roads   Invisi-spray

Fast Company magazine

Post-It note   Wired magazine   Scramble suit   Napcaps

Camcorder   eBay   Moon village   Helio-Beryllium

Yahoo   Truth sensors   Mindwipes   Short-wave scapel   Smart bullet

Starbucks   Amazon   Spray on surgical gloves

AOL   Localizers   Labots   Oceanic thermal converter

2007   2050

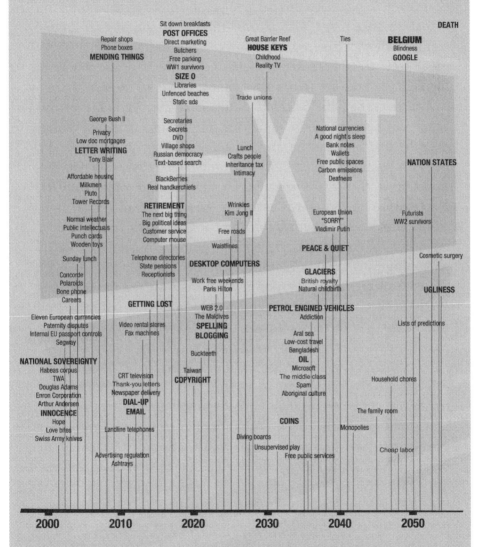

Extinction timeline 2000-2050

Note: Extinction refers to things that are insignificant beyond this point.

up a little. Thus you will find the odd — and sometimes the very odd — prediction in this book.

It was tempting to write in chronological order, but I have opted instead to start with broad societal trends and then dig down into a series of specific disciplines and industries, without putting dates against anything unless this helps to paint a more vivid picture. You will also notice that I have allowed the trends and ideas from one sector or chapter to bleed into others, which, in my opinion, is very much how trends are disseminated generally. It is also a way of highlighting how key trends have almost universal impact.

I have chosen the 5 trends outlined at the beginning of this chapter as being the most significant accelerators of global change over the next 50 years. As you'd imagine, picking just 5 was tricky, not least because different industries and regions have differing histories and throw up specific challenges and opportunities. Nevertheless, the 5 trends I have selected will have an impact globally despite localized opposition and counter forces. In no particular order the key trends are **ageing**, **global connectivity**, **GRIN technologies** (Genetics, Robotics, Internet and Nanotechnology), the **environment** and the **power shift eastwards**. I thought long and hard about including fear and anxiety in this list, but in the end I decided to add them to a list of 5 things that *won't* change over the next 50 years, which appears at the very end of the book.

Why these 5 key trends? Any list is inevitably highly personal and subjective, but ageing is hard to disagree with. Indeed, demographic trends are more certain than virtually anything else because short of a global pandemic, nuclear annihilation or rogue asteroids, we can be pretty sure how many people will be around in 50 years' time based on how many are already here and on current death and fertility rates. Global connectivity is a little less certain, not least because there are some good arguments about the end of globalization and the emergence of (re)localization. For example, resource scarcity plus the rise of China, India and the Middle East (the so-called CHIME nations) could drive economic protectionism in the

West. Nevertheless, I think the connectivity created by everything from deregulation and the internet to low-cost travel and immigration will be a difficult idea to put back into a box marked "Do Not Open". The same argument applies to the GRIN technologies. Once such things get invented it's very difficult to un-invent them and in most cases development significantly accelerates over time.

The environment was a tricky one. The current debate about climate change seems to have got stuck between two extremes and I am starting to suffer from eco-exhaustion. On the one side are some who argue that it's all a huge hoax, while on the other are those who claim that we're all heading for an immediate and irreversible disaster. I think both arguments are unreasonable and that ultimately we'll adjust to anything Mother Nature throws our way. However, the fact remains that the environment in general is a big issue, not least because rapid urbanization and development are creating resource scarcity on a scale hitherto unknown. Again, humanity will cope, but we are in for a period of significant upheaval and change.

Last but by no means least of my 5 trends is the power shift eastwards. At the moment the numbers indicate that this is a no-brainer. Economic power (and with it cultural influence and military might) is moving from the US and Europe to the Middle East and Asia, particularly China and India. This could be a fad (that is, a short-term trend) but I don't think so. Equally, one should not write off the US or Europe quite yet either. They are relatively free and stable politically; apart, one could argue, from a rather angry, dispossessed and potentially radical economic middle class. As a result, they are hotbeds of economic and cultural inventiveness. Whether countries in the Middle East and China can replicate this degree of creativity will be an interesting question.

The date of up to 50 years hence (let's call it the year 2050 for the sake of simplicity) has been chosen because it is sufficiently far away to avoid accusations of incorrectness (who, after all, can tell if I'm right and demand their money back?). Presumably by then most readers will have forgotten about this book entirely or time will have healed any mental wounds created by misjudged ideas or incorrect dates. Having said that, a few years ago I serendipitously stopped in the middle of nowhere in the English coastal county of Suffolk. Opposite me was an old church that had been turned into a secondhand bookshop. I walked in for no particular reason and ended up buying a first edition of *Future Shock* from 1970 for 50p, as well as, for the same price, another book called *Originality* that was written in 1917 about the year 2000. You just never know.

Ironically, it is often easier to make predictions about the distant future than next month or next year because it can take a long time for patterns to emerge or new ideas to replace old habits and conventions. For example, digital wallets and hydrogen-powered cars are definitely coming, but nobody can yet say for sure if and when they will be widely adopted by the majority of society.

In terms of source material for the book, I owe a debt of gratitude to literally hundreds of people working for various organizations such as the *Sunday Times, The New York Times, The Economist,* the *New Scientist* and the BBC, who have done all the hard work by putting various ideas and anomalies onto my radar. It may seem simplistic to some people that my source material is news and media organizations, but I am a great believer in simplicity — as I am in the power of the encapsulating anecdote. Moreover, this methodology of content analysis (or environmental scanning as it's sometimes called) is not dissimilar to the scientific method, consisting as it does of observing what is happening in a dispassionate manner and looking for simple patterns that have some robustness.

In other words, getting your sieve full of information is only the beginning. Next you have to shake the sieve rigorously until the insignificant details fall away. You then need to look at how the small grains of truth that remain are connected, and ultimately seek out convincing explanations in terms of causal factors and key implications.

I do not have space to go into detail about how this process works, but suffice to say that looking at trends involves thinking about issues like the size of a trend and how fast it is moving. From an organizational perspective it is also important to consider whether the key drivers (or forces) behind a trend can be controlled and also to question whether it is really a trend at all. Perhaps what you are seeing is a short-term fad, a subtrend (part of a much bigger trend) or even a countertrend (a reaction in an opposite direction to another more powerful trend). Once you've done this, the handful of trends you've selected can be used as a framework for innovation or as an input into a scenario framework, which is in turn part of a formal scenario planning process.

This might sound a bit dull, but believe me it isn't. Trends, and the frameworks they can produce, are a treasure trove of strategic wildcards and scenarios. They are a smart and sometimes irreverent guide to the future that can be indispensable to anyone who's curious about what's coming next.

And here's the real rub. Much of this process is conjecture, which is precisely why some people have a problem with the future. Large organizations are data driven. A numerical approach works fine when you are dealing with things that have already happened, but obviously the future hasn't. There are no facts about the future because it isn't here yet. The best you can therefore do is employ a fact-based approach to analyze what happened in the past (which would include the present because the moment you observe something it's already history) and use this information to inform your thinking about the future. Parts of the future are embedded in the present but only as a kind of riddle.

A significant proportion of this book is about things that have already happened, which, up to a point, we can assume will continue to happen and thus will shape our future. It examines emerging patterns and developments in society, business, science and technology, government and the environment and makes educated and, hopefully, amusing speculations about where they might take us. This is a dangerous and problematic game because the future is never a linear extrapolation from the present or the past. Totally unexpected ideas and events can conspire to trip up even the best-laid plans and predictions. Indeed, if history teaches us anything it is surely that revolutionary thinking can overturn so-called inevitabilities and impossibilities. Nevertheless, it's better to think about the future in this way than not to think about it at all.

5 trends that will transform society

Globalization Globalization used to mean Americanization, but these days it means exposure to people, products and ideas from everywhere. Globalization has an impact on the sourcing of products and services and on market-expansion opportunities. It also means connectedness and mobility. Everything from countries and computers to gadgets and global banking will be hyperlinked together. In the future this trend will accelerate even faster, thanks to devices such as GPS, RFIDs, sensor motes and smart dust (all essentially tiny wireless transmitters and/or receivers of some kind). Hence privacy will disappear but transparency and risk may increase (the latter due to risks being networked and traded globally).

Localization Localization (or re-localization) is a perfect example of a trend creating a countertrend. Localization will occur because people don't like globalization or homogenization. The European Union could therefore splinter and ultimately collapse. This new tribalism will drive city states, locally tailored products, economic protectionism and the sale of flags. This near-sightedness will also occur because resource shortages (most notably oil) will mean that economic production will be forced to localize due to the cost of transport.

Polarization The future is an either/or kind of place, with most things polarizing in some form or another. First there will be multiple futures, some of them speeding up and others slowing down. Some people will embrace technology while others will reject it. Industrial markets will split between luxury and low-cost options, with access to services like health and education, transport and security similarly polarizing, depending on your ability to pay. The economic middle class will eventually disappear in most developed countries, with people either moving upwards into a new global managerial elite or downwards into a new enslaved working (or not working) class.

Anxiety   If "they" don't get you, a global pandemic or high interest rates probably will. At least that's how many people will feel in the future. Trust in institutions will all but evaporate and the speed of change will leave people longing for the past. This insecurity is to some extent generational, but whether you are 18 or 80 there will be a growing feeling of powerlessness and a continual state of anxiety that will fuel everything from an interest in nostalgia and escapism to a growth in narcissism and localization.

Search for meaning   One of the most fascinating questions about the future is whether religion will be a victim or a beneficiary of change. Some people predict that faith will decline because the spread of information will undermine the mindset necessary to support belief. Physics will produce a theory of everything and this will destroy old-fashioned superstitions such as religion. In other words, science will become our new religion. I'm not so sure. If science, technology and complexity become key ingredients of the future, this will drive change and uncertainty. And the more this happens, the more people will seek out safety, comfort and guidance from religion. This could just lead to an increase in individual spirituality (people searching for the answer to the question of how to live their life), but I suspect that globalization, mixed with a general feeling of powerlessness and anxiety, will drive group actions and beliefs. Hence we will witness an increase in tribalism, nationalism and xenophobia, which at the extreme will fuel Islamic fanaticism and "muscular" Christianity.

Chapter 1

Society and Culture:
why we'll take longer baths in
the future

If you want to know your past, look at your present conditions.
If you want to know your future, look into your present actions.
—Buddhist saying

Early in 2006, a 40-year-old woman called Joyce Vincent was discovered dead in her London flat. There was nothing remarkable about this, except for the fact that she'd been dead for more than two years and her television was still on. How could this happen? Where was everyone? The answer, of course, was that everyone was somewhere else.

London, like most major cities, no longer has neighborhoods; it has collections of individuals leading more and more isolated, selfish and narcissistic lives. Neighbors keep to themselves and people don't ask questions or volunteer information. In an age when everyone is increasingly connected to everyone else through the internet, nobody really knows one another any more. We have lots of friends, but few of them dig deep enough to understand our hopes and fears.

In Japan there is a social phenomenon called *hikikomori*. This roughly translates as "withdrawal" and refers to boys who retreat into their bedrooms and rarely, if ever, come out. In one case a young man shut his bedroom door in his early 20s and played video games, watched television and slept for 14 years. Food was supplied by his mother, who lived downstairs, virtually alone. This is a particularly Japanese condition, although nobody can quite understand who or what is to blame. According to experts there are somewhere between 100,000 and 1 million *hikikomori* in Japan, caused by everything from absent (always-working) fathers to overprotective mothers.

There are a number of simple explanations for problems like this, and most are wrong. Some people blame individualism; others point the finger at urbanization, technology, education or even government. The reality is that it's all of these, but ultimately we have nobody to blame but ourselves. We have let this happen. And if society is like this now, what will it be like in another 50 years?

I'm sitting in a budget hotel room at Miami International Airport. It's 10.30 p.m. My room is basic but I have free access to the internet, either from my own computer or via a giant television in my room. There is a coffee machine, complete with non-dairy creamer, and a small bar of hypoallergenic soap in the bathroom. Outside, on the other side of the freeway, a large neon sign reads "Girls". Unfortunately, inside the hotel humans are rather absent. Indeed, while I can check up on the news in London through my television, I can't order a sandwich because the restaurant closed 30 minutes ago. There is no room service either, presumably due to a focus on "essential services". The hotel is pretty full, but I don't expect to come into contact with anyone else. If I placed the "Do not disturb" sign outside my door (and my credit rating was good enough) I could probably drop dead inside my room and nobody would notice. My email isn't working either because my email provider has thoughtfully "recently completed an upgrade of all services to enhance security and reliability". Believe it or not, I can't access my email because they have sent me a new password but I can't get hold of that because I don't have the password to open my email. Brilliant.

If you want a vision of the future, this is a good one. I could be anywhere. In another 10 or 20 years I will be able to access every film ever made in any language through the television. The room will be personalized too, in the sense that the hotel chain will know where I come from and what I like — so BBC London will be playing on the radio as I enter my room, and decaf coffee and real milk will be in the fridge. A sandwich will still be an impossible request unless I'm staying at one of the company's premium hotels, but I guess I'll be able to order one for 24-hour delivery. In 25 years' time I will enter the hotel by placing my finger on a security panel by the entrance and both the receptionist and the "girls" will be holograms. I will gain access to my room with my worldphone or the chip inserted in my jaw and be able to customize it myself to look and smell just like home — but I still won't be able to get a sandwich from the restaurant at 10.30 p.m. and my email still won't work.

Two big trends at the start of the twenty-first century are urbanization and the increase in the number of people living alone. In 2006, 25% of homes in the UK were single-person households. There are more people living by themselves, or in one-parent households, in the UK than people living as part of a traditional nuclear family; 40% of all British households are forecast to be under single occupancy by the year 2020. In the US it's a similar story. Single-person households have grown to 30% in 30 years (up from 3% in 1950) due to factors such as people staying single later, easier divorces and longer lifespans, especially for women. We have also seen a significant reduction in the number of children being born and a massive increase in the number of old people. In short, there is a lack of both births and deaths, which means that the global population will go into decline around 2050, putting an end to fears of global overcrowding. You can see this already in the statistics: 22% of women in the UK say that they don't expect to have children and 44% of American adults are single (up from 9% in the mid-1950s).

Home alone

The number of urban singles is driving everything from a growth in late-night convenience retailing (for example buying a single portion of chicken fillet at 1 a.m.) to how the tables and chairs are laid out in your local McDonald's. Reasons for this urban renaissance are various.

Twenty years ago it seemed as though everyone was moving out of the cities. In the US the term "white flight" was coined to describe white, middle-class families fleeing inner-city crime and grime to start new lives in the suburbs. Nowadays the reverse is happening. Known as boomerang migration, singles and childless couples are flooding back into cities like New York, London and Melbourne because that's where the action is and the commute isn't. Indeed, by the year 2050 if this trend continues, most inner cities will be made up almost entirely of rich singles, wealthy families and gay couples with high disposable incomes and liberal political persuasions. Some might say they already are. The rural areas that still exist will be populated by rich hobby-farmers interspersed with downshifters, smartisans and digital nomads.

But it's not just the cities that are changing. In 1950, 80% of US households comprised the traditional husband, wife and one or more children. Now it's under 50%. The rest are singles and same-sex couples (increasingly with kids). There are also blended families — mother, father, plus two or more children from different relationships or marriages — and extended financial families, homes with more than one generation living under the same roof.

In other words, shifts in social attitudes (what is considered normal or acceptable), together with changes in demographics, housing stock and even retailing, are making it easier to live however you like. And for many people this means by themselves. Even if you don't live alone you will increasingly be able to do whatever you want unencumbered by family pressure or practical considerations. This is freedom without responsibility. For example, at a recent new home show in the US, a dream house was displayed that allowed each family member to come in via a different entrance. Individuals could watch television or surf the internet in their own room and choose separate kitchen facilities and bathrooms, so as not to interact with other family members. And to think that back in the 1980s people were worried about families not eating breakfast together. In the middle of the twenty-first century the problem will be how to get individual members of the family even to talk to each other.

In Australia in 2005, adults spent on average 3 hours watching television every day — and 12 minutes talking to their partner. In the US over 25% of 2-year-olds have a television in their bedroom, and children aged 2 to 17 spend 20 hours a week watching television versus 38 minutes talking to their parents.

No wonder the fastest-growing reason for women seeking a divorce in some countries is absent (always-at-work or always-working) partners. There is already a growing gulf between the sexes, and this will open up yet further as women become more economically self-sufficient. Even when both sexes are together physically, men are usually emotionally somewhere else. Women just want to talk, while men just want women to be quiet. In the future there will be a law passed in Europe that requires married men to be at home by 9 p.m. on Thursdays or else they will be fined 500 euros. There will also be tax breaks for people who choose not to live alone and pet owners will be taxed if the owners live on their own as an incentive for people to have children rather than child substitutes.

Of course, there is an irony here. We are increasingly leading separate lives and in the future it will become much easier to isolate ourselves physically from other people at home or at work — which, for some people, will be the same place. Simultaneously we are becoming more and more connected.

One of the most popular websites in the UK is Friends Reunited. MySpace (now Rupert's Space) in the US has well over 100 million members globally and regularly receives more hits per month than Google. On the surface both websites seek to put like-minded individuals and groups in touch with one another, but maybe something more profound is happening. To a large degree, the history of the next 50 years will be about the relationship between technology and people. Moreover, there is an inherent instability built into this relationship because technology changes fast and exponentially, while people change slowly and incrementally. What this means, in effect, is that the more technology gets embedded into our lives, the more we will run away from it. As a result, there will be a greater demand for human-to-human physical contact and direct experiences.

There will also be more interest in spiritualism and philosophy — unless, of course, humans and technology merge, in which case things will get very confusing indeed.

By the year 2025 artificial intelligence (AI) will be a real part of life. In simple terms, this means that when you phone your bank and have a 20-minute argument about credit-card charges, you'll be speaking to a computer without realizing it. More spookily, by the year 2050 there will be two highly intelligent species on Earth: traditional, genetically pure humans and technologically aided hybrid humans. The latter will be "people" who have been genetically manipulated by the insertion of DNA segments to prevent certain diseases or to create particular emotions or personality traits. They will also have been robotically and computer enhanced to improve strength, sight, vision or intelligence. Again, one species will evolve very slowly; the other will change as rapidly as technology and ethics permit.

Do we want this to happen? Perhaps the question is whether or not we can stop it.

Some people claim that we will understand the threat and pass laws to prevent such enhancements, much in the same way that human cloning is already outlawed. But if history can serve as any guide to the future, it shows us that humankind is curious. Someone, somewhere, legally or illegally, will be tempted to answer the question "What if?"

In Los Angeles you can already visit a reproductive technologist and choose sperm or eggs based on IQ or appearance: "Blonde hair, blue eyes and an aptitude for tennis, please." If you can't make it to LA, you can always order sperm over the internet. And if we are already doing this, it's only a very small step before we add non-biological elements to our children. Given that companies such as Nike sponsor 13-year-old soccer stars, it's probably also just a matter of time before a company signs up a promising foetus on a 35-year sponsorship deal.

If such experiments simply involved the insertion of technological elements into a human brain or body, they would be almost no threat to the human species. But what if the enhancement involves nanotechnology (that is, the manipulation of structures at an atomic or molecular level) or computers and the machine elements really do start to think for themselves? What happens when we produce machines that are more intelligent than us? What happens if these machines develop some kind of self-awareness (consciousness) and become self-replicating? Once that genie is out of the bottle it will be very difficult indeed to put it back in.

OK computer

Our relationship with objects is going to change. In the past, objects were neutral. They were not intelligent and did not possess a state of mind. If they had a personality, it was given to them by their designers and was entirely skin deep. Otherwise we imbued personality into objects via our imagination. This won't be the case in the future.

Take children's dolls as an example. Historically these were inert, rather poor representations of the human form. They are already becoming more realistic and more intelligent. Owners of "Amazing Amanda" can chat with their doll and "intelligence" is available in the form of facial recognition, speech recognition and accessories impregnated with radio-frequency identification devices (RFID). If you're a bit older (and presumably no wiser) you can even buy a physically realistic, life-sized "love partner" for US$7,000 from a company called realdoll.com. But you ain't seen nothing yet.

In a few years' time you will be able to personalize your doll's face (to your own choice or, more likely, to resemble a celebrity), communicate with your doll by telephone or email, have real conversations and experience your entire life history through the eyes, ears (and nose) of your doll. The latter will be achieved by the doll and linked devices preserving your emails, phone calls and other images and information captured through its artificial eyes, ears and nose. In other words, the doll will become a digital storage device with the capacity to document your entire life. The so-called life-caching industry is already worth US$2.5 billion annually. This will in turn give rise to a debate about the ethics of information, involving questions such as who owns such data, whether or not it can be sold or traded and what happens to the information once the "owner" dies.

Dead, but increasingly not forgotten

In the past, after you died there was very little of "you" left. One hundred years ago you might have left some letters or drawings. Fifty years ago you may have left some fading photographs. Currently you can seek or accidentally attain digital immortality through video clips, sound files, digital photographs and emails on your own website or sites belonging to others. There is even a website called mylastemail.com that promises to send out your last email once you've died; and you can check what date that might be at deathclock.com. But there are already problems.

When 17-year-old Anna Svidersky tragically died a few years ago she had a page on MySpace. She is still there, unaware of her fate in the physical world. And because her MySpace page is protected by a password known only to her, the page — her digital afterlife — will remain, potentially for ever. It's the same with everything in cyberspace. If you upload something it doesn't disappear.

So if as a drunken 18-year-old you post pictures on a social networking site, they could be cut and pasted and appear on numerous other websites and there is nothing you can do about it. They could be there for posterity, for future employers or partners to see. And heaven forbid you post something a little more explicit on YouPorn. Similarly, anything you search for on the internet is captured somewhere and so too are digital data trails from cellphones and credit cards. Maybe this bothers you. Maybe it doesn't. But remember that once you give your digital privacy away it is very difficult, if not impossible, to get it back.

Of course, there are countertrends. Scrapbooking is phenomenally popular at the moment as a low-tech way of preserving memories and engaging in physical contact with other people across generations.

It might not be so low-tech either. Some people believe we are living in the digital dark ages because most of what we are currently preserving will be unreadable by future generations. I already have a stack of floppy discs from the early 1990s that I can't access and it's entirely possible that the photographs of my children (4,753 at the last count) won't be readable or printable in 20 years' time due to "digital evaporation".

You think I'm kidding? NASA can't read some of the records of its 1976 Viking Mars space landing and the BBC can't read the digital copy of the Domesday Book it produced in 1986 to celebrate the

900th anniversary of the original. Of course, the original itself remains perfectly readable.

In the not-too-distant future, everyday objects such as shoes, carpets and toothbrushes will contain technology that collects information. You will then be able to personalize these objects, allowing them to change physical state (like color) or respond to your daily mood. They will also be able to exchange data with other objects and send information to other people. For example, your toothbrush will be capable of analyzing your breath and booking an appointment with your doctor if it detects the smell of lung cancer. In other words, what were once just ordinary objects will be increasingly networked and intelligent. Manufacturers will use the information generated by these smart products to sell you other services or enhance your "ownership experience" — although whether people will want such a relationship with their toothbrush remains to be seen.

In Japan you can already buy school blazers embedded with GPS tracking technology. This means that as a parent, you can elect to receive an email or SMS alert when your child arrives safely at school each morning (or at least when the blazer does). This idea is no doubt linked to the rise in paranoid parenting and apprehensiveness over "stranger danger", but there will be other services linked to similar products in the future. For example, kitchen appliances will monitor their own performance and order spare parts and service calls all by themselves — much in the same way that the McLaren F1 supercar alerts the factory when something goes wrong, thanks to onboard monitoring and GPS tracking.

Equally, ordinary clothes will be able to monitor their condition, arrange for dry-cleaning pick-ups or alert their owner to new design upgrades. But what are some of the likely attitudinal and behavioral implications of these developments?

At the East Sutton Park Young Offenders' Institution and Open Prison in Kent (UK), offenders with low self-esteem are encouraged to do gardening. Even something as simple as raking up fallen leaves has been shown to have an instantly satisfying effect. As 20-year-old Leah says, "If I'm angry I dig." Gardening will enjoy a huge surge of popularity in the years ahead because it will be an antidote to the future. It will deliver the solitude and peace and quiet that will be so lacking in people's lives. It will be a way of dealing with too much technology. Washing dishes by hand and making your own bread will become popular for much the same reasons. They will provide physical results and people will feel that they've achieved something by themselves.

One of the consequences of ubiquitous technology is that some of us will unplug some or, in extreme cases, all of our lives. In theory, new technologies will make our lives easier. Things will move faster, saving us time and money. They will also be more reliable. Technology will make things that were previously difficult or impossible easier and more affordable. But history suggests that the opposite is much more likely to happen. Indeed, in some areas there will be no progress whatsoever.

Do you remember the predictions about the paperless office and the leisure society? Between 1999 and 2002 global use of paper increased by 22% and we now seem to have less spare time than ever. We are also sleeping less than we used to, down from 9 hours per day in 1900 to 6.9 hours today. Indeed, the benefits of the computer age can be seen everywhere except in the productivity statistics, because we are inventing new ways of making ourselves busy.

Comfortably numb

This obsession with "busyness" can be seen in the way the work ethic has invaded childhood. Children must be kept busy at all times. As a result, they are becoming overscheduled and we are creating a cohort that cannot think for itself, a generation of passive, risk-averse citizens and comfortably numb consumers with almost no imagination or self-reliance.

The Japanese word *benriya* loosely translates as convenience-doers. These are people, usually older men, who fix leaking taps, change lightbulbs, remove cockroaches from sinks and generally do things that require an ounce of common sense. Their existence implies that there is a section of Japanese society that is totally incapable of fending for itself.

Another obvious problem is that complex technologies fail. In the past, when something broke down it was relatively easy to fix. If your car wouldn't start there were only three or four things that could be wrong, each readily repairable by the driver. These days breakdowns are more complex and chances are you won't be able to solve the problem yourself. Moreover, as things become smarter and more networked, these failures will become even more catastrophic.

The term "cascading failure" refers to when the failure of one element of a network is able to bring the entire network to its knees. If you lose your house keys today it's a problem but hardly the end of the world. In the future, though, you won't have house keys: you'll have smartcard or biometric entry, and if your card gets lost or the fingerprint reader breaks down it really will be a headache because it will be linked to all the other devices inside your house. So you won't be able to switch on the central heating or make a cup of coffee, since the central-heating settings and the coffee machine will have been personalized and linked to individual smartcards for each member of the household or the biometric door-entry system.

People will therefore seek out older products with less technology or hack into new products to remove the unnecessary features. In the long term, technology may solve this complexity problem itself — but don't bet on it. A more likely scenario is that companies will keep inventing useless gadgets like internet fridges, and some deluded souls will even buy them, but most of us will stick with what we know. Our lives are complicated enough already and we won't embrace technological dreams like smart homes until it can be demonstrated that the new really is superior to the old. This means faster and cheaper, but it also involves taking into account the bigger picture: "Does this make my life easier?" as well as "Does this make the world a better place?"

After all, as a very old friend of mine, Douglas Slater, once reminded me: "Old things become old because they are good. They are not bad simply because they are old." Books (including the Domesday Book), door keys, newspapers, coins and banknotes have survived for centuries because they are extremely well designed for their purpose. Don't get me wrong here: e-books, keyless entry and digital money all exist already, but a great many people will continue to use the original tried-and-tested versions for a number of practical, historical and emotional reasons.

Things cannot get faster or more complicated for ever. Our minds (at least our current minds) won't be able to cope — there is only so much data we can take on board. The trend called too much information (TMI) has a distant cousin, too much choice (TMC). In a nutshell, humankind is producing an excess of stuff. The amount of new information we produce today is estimated to be around 2 billion exabytes annually. That's (very roughly) 2 billion billion bytes or about 20 billion copies of this book. The average large corporation similarly experiences a doubling of the amount of information it produces annually.

Information is no longer power; that comes from capturing and maintaining a person's attention. The problem is so bad that the world's largest bank (Citibank) is testing something called auditory display software as a way of delivering vital information to traders via music because visually based data just isn't getting through.

A Japanese company has already invented a way to move a cursor across a screen simply by thinking about it, so ultimately we may be able to send and receive messages telepathically. Will such innovations make our lives better? It depends. Some people will rush to embrace these developments, while others will seek temporary or permanent solitude in everything from alcohol and countryside pursuits to memory-erasing pills (slogan: "Take one to forget what happened to you today"). There will be a war for peace, including a boom in people buying remote real estate and islands to get away from it all. However, most of us will live somewhere in the middle, or will mentally commute between these extremes.

Hence there will not be a single future because we will all experience the future in different ways; there will be multiple, often contradictory futures. The future will arrive faster if you live in a metropolis such as London, Sydney or New York than if you live in a rural village. Equally, the level of change you will experience will vary according to your age, your income and your occupation.

New theories of time and space

These differences will generate tensions. People living in metropolitan areas will tend to push for the rapid deployment of innovations, while older, more conservative, rural and semi-rural populations will generally seek to limit them. It will also be a battle between the technology haves and the new Luddites (the technology have-nots and want-nots). The first tribe will have money but will suffer from time famine and space anxiety because they won't have either of these luxuries. The second tribe, conversely, will have time and space but little or no income, relatively speaking, because this will be tied up in real estate or spent on healthcare.

So young people will enjoy very high salaries but will be unable to afford the overall standard of living enjoyed by their parents and grandparents because of long working hours, the high cost of real estate and the lack of private space. What was "free" to their forebears (fresh air, public parks, public beaches, libraries, roads and so on) will all cost money. Thus the future will not just be faster, it will be more expensive too.

Overall, while we will cope — just — with the avalanche of change, uncertainty and anxiety, many people will seek refuge in the past. They will escape the present through various nostalgic pursuits, although their love of the new will sit alongside a fondness for the past. Hence almost nobody will live in the present.

We will mentally return to the eras we grew up in, which we will perceive (often incorrectly) as being safer, warmer and more certain than the present or the future. We will covet old cars, old clothes, old music and old technology. Again, this is already happening. Just look at the popularity of old arcade video games (Pong), old car designs (the "new" VW Beetle), old running shoes and "old" food (recipes). Indeed, as people and products become more perfect (humans through surgery and gene modification, products through quality control and innovation), imperfect people and products will be what we seek out.

Patina will be big in the future. Women with facial lines will be highly desirable, while hydrogen-powered cars will be available with used-looking paintwork and worn leather seats as optional extras. Another example is pornography. The fastest-growing segment of the industry worldwide is "amateur" pornography using real people rather than airbrushed or surgically enhanced models. In other words, porn like it used to be. Nostalgic pornography for the over-70s crowd? That will be coming along shortly too.

We will also, where possible, shut the outside world away completely by locking our front doors and turning our homes into either high-security compounds or — more likely — miniature holiday resorts. An interesting fact I came across recently is that the ratio of gated communities to trailer parks in the US is 1:1. People will withdraw into themselves because they will feel impotent in the face of change and believe that their lives lack meaning. This will be a problem, because if the majority withdraw and take refuge within their homes and inside individual obsessions, governments (and companies) will have carte blanche to behave exactly as they like. To misquote Woody Allen, all that future dictators will need to be successful is for nobody else to show up. The opposite of good isn't evil — it's indifference.

Meet mini-me

For the technically minded, doorbells will disappear in favor of proximity indicators. We will continually know where our friends and family are thanks to the descendants of services like FriendFinder and we will be able to screen out the unknown and the unfamiliar. Although this will undoubtedly increase our safety, it will remove the element of surprise from our lives.

Amazon's recommendation software already inhibits chance encounters with totally unrelated books. Other types of software could do the same with people in the future. This is bad news for society and especially bad news for new ideas, which thrive on social interaction, cross-fertilization and serendipity. We will therefore meet more people like ourselves in the future and be protected from people and ideas that are strange or unfamiliar. This is hardly a recipe for global harmony and understanding.

We will also be taking longer baths as an antidote to stress, anxiety and change. However, we will be contradictory. Many of us will embrace natural-looking materials and bath scents rather than authentic ones because we will have so little experience of the real thing. Research conducted by the US Taste Research Foundation recently found that people generally prefer artificial to real aromas, partly because they are nostalgic about fake smells from their childhood. In the future, fake will thus become more real than real. Any (fake) experience we want will also be available via smart drugs, nanomedicine and screen-based products, making reality strange and unfamiliar to most people.

The fully wired smart home will exist for some, while many of us will reject it in favor of its opposite. Even those who fully embrace technology (generally the younger generations) will use it to escape from reality. This will mean further growth in fantasy-related industries, ranging from gaming to virtual sex — the latter becoming increasingly realistic and acceptable to a vast swathe of society. People will take virtual vacations and have serious relationships with real people they never actually meet.

The real will also become almost indistinguishable from the virtual. Again, some of this is happening right now. It has been estimated that Everquest is the 77th largest economy on Earth despite the fact that it doesn't truly exist. Gamers are even spending actual currency to buy virtual currency and virtual real estate. In another example of our escape from reality, the top five worldwide grossing movies in 2005 were all escapist fantasies: *Harry Potter and the Goblet of Fire, Star Wars Episode III, The Chronicles of Narnia, War of the Worlds* and *King Kong*. Why? If reality is too much, escape into a fantasy world. If we were to experience another Great Depression I would expect the entertainment industry to do rather well.

By 2050 Hollywood, the computer industry, neuroscience and the pharmaceuticals industry will have almost merged into one. This will enable people, legally and illegally, to spend days inhabiting what are quite literally (according to all five of our human senses) other worlds — like in the films *The Matrix* and *Logan's Run* — but for real.

What are the implications of this? First, we will become socially and emotionally inept. Relationships will be originated, consummated and terminated digitally. A court in Malaysia recently upheld a divorce that a husband sent to his wife via SMS; while I don't think that this will catch on, relationships will undoubtedly become more superficial and fleeting. People will still get together physically but it will be less common and they will commit to each other through renewable 10-year contracts downloaded from the internet. While divorce will be even more frequent (the rate has hit 60% in the US), when people do finally settle down they will tend to stay together for longer — more out of fear of loneliness than love in many cases. Virtual adultery will become a reasonable cause for a divorce, although everyone will be doing it.

We will also be exposed to more experiences earlier, so childhoods will be compressed, while adults will find it easier to remain "children" indefinitely. Indeed, childhood, adolescence and adulthood will become less distinct: 10-year-olds will want the same birthday presents as 40-year-olds and 60-year-olds will dress identically to 18-year-olds. At least buying gifts will become easier.

Inventing new types of fear

What will we be afraid of in the year 2050? The answer is reality. The refuge we seek in other "places" (holidays, books, films, virtual worlds and so on) due to our disorientation and lack of comfort with the level and speed of change will mean that the entertainment industry will become the biggest game in town. Add to this the natural human inclination to see what's next and you have a society that will refuse to tackle current problems such as debt, education, healthcare and transport, while simultaneously worrying about things that happened in the past or might happen in the future such as asteroid strikes.

We will be afraid of not knowing. We will fear things that are outside our control. We will be frightened of uncertainty. Most of all, we will be afraid of "them" — people who come from somewhere else, and I don't mean the planet Mars. These fears will drive the accumulation of information. We will crave "scientific" data on the statistical probability of everything while simultaneously seeking out personal stories of people, products and organizations as some kind of faux reassurance.

By the year 2020 people, products and organizations will have reliability ratings. These will grade honesty, integrity and transparency and will be created by and available to everyone. We will be able to rank everything from politicians to personal computers based on past claims, actions and performance, much in the same way that buyers and sellers are currently assessed on eBay. Reputations will therefore be actively managed and, in some cases, even traded or stolen.

As an interesting counterpoint, it will be almost impossible to maintain a perfect record because everything we say and do and everywhere we go will be monitored and recorded. Secrecy will be history. People, products and corporations will therefore be assumed guilty until investigated. This will eventually give rise to the idea of ethical bankruptcy, a clean slate for your reputation.

If none of this appeals, we will also see the appearance of disappearance. In the future, people will pay professionals to help them disappear. This will be difficult due to the level of electronic surveillance but not entirely impossible, especially for younger people already familiar with the concept of using multiple identities on the internet or for older folk who have never existed online. For the rest of us, saddled with credit cards, GPS-embedded cellphones and biometric identity cards, it will be just another fantasy.

Many of the institutions and other anchor points in our lives, especially in developed Western societies, have already vanished or had their reputations eroded to the point where people no longer implicitly trust them. The family, the church, government, business, science and even the local bank manager have lost or are losing their ability to unite or be trusted. This cynicism and antipathy will continue in the future. People will focus even more on themselves and a culture of self-reliance — the do-it-yourself society — will emerge. People will live in isolation bubbles and won't trust doctors, hospitals or pharmaceutical companies, so self-diagnosis and self-medication will become commonplace. In 2050 smart software packages will be available to identify what's wrong with us and websites like Genes Reunited will offer genetic histories enabling us to anticipate hereditary diseases and defects. We will also be able to hire or purchase robotic surgeons to perform operations in our own home or office.

At this point, you are probably thinking that most of what you have just read is wishful thinking, more science fiction than science fact. My response to that is simple. Make a list of what exists today and what you are able to do now that didn't exist or couldn't be done 50 years ago. Now add a multiplier to take into account the fact that technology tends to advance exponentially and you may start to see that the future really is "out there".

Having said that, much of what is around today will still be around tomorrow. The basics won't change much. Our fundamental hopes and fears will be exactly the same. We will still want to be acknowledged. We will still want our time on Earth to have made a difference. We will still want to achieve something and we will still crave recognition and respect. We will also still want to know whether our collective existence is anything more than a cosmic accident.

Like Joyce Vincent, alone in her London apartment, we will still want to love and be loved.

Plus ça change, plus c'est la même chose.

14 November 2030

Dear Renée

This will knock you out. I'm sending you something I've just found called "Leaves."™ It's a new product from Past Toyz in Shanghai featuring a giant biodegradable plastic bag containing real farm-grown leaves that have been hygienically dried and treated with an anti-bacterial agent for "safe outdoor fun."™ Can you believe it? Why didn't we think of that? You empty the bag in your backyard and play with the leaves. Either that or you can drive that hygiene- and order-fixated neighbor of yours crazy by placing a single leaf on his plastic lawn every night for the next two years. I suppose the company did some research with trendsetters and early adopters which said that people in urban areas aren't getting as close to nature as they like. Nature deficit disorder, I think they call it.

Back in my day leaves grew on trees but the colors weren't manipulated and the bugs were kept in check by other bugs, not chemicals. I guess that lawsuit last year against the company that developed *Dangerous Holidays for Boys* might have something to do with this too, although if you ask me promoting the idea of playing conkers using real horse chestnuts and without wearing full safety equipment was rather asking for it. Anyway, it certainly made me laugh. You can always send the Leaves™ back if the joke is lost on you.

What's next — aerosol dirt?

All the best

Sing

5 trends that will transform science and technology

Nanotechnology   Nanotech is the hyped technology of the new millennium. It's unlikely to disappoint either, because it's disruptive. Nanotech will affect every industry from aerospace and construction to energy and medicine and will create products that we cannot possibly imagine now. However, public debate about it will be almost invisible until there is a major high-profile nanotechnology accident.

Biotechnology   We had Dolly the cloned sheep in 1996 and since then we've had cloned mice, cows, rabbits, horses and dogs. A human clone can't be far away, although it's unlikely that it will come from a US or Western laboratory. A clone will certainly grab the headlines, but a more threatening concept is perhaps the idea of genetically enhancing humans to strengthen or remove certain traits. There is also the alarming prospect of tests to judge personality or future actions based on genetic makeup and hereditary factors. In the future, everything from careers to relationships will involve genetic issues. Anyone for genetically engineered mosquitoes? How about one that glows in the dark so that you can see it coming? Or what about genetic enhancements and tests for unborn children?

Emotionally aware machines   Much has been written about artificial intelligence, but personally I think that AI in any meaningful sense is a long way off. Having said that, can you imagine the implications if an internet of the future did actually become aware of its own existence? Ohmygawd. As for the foreseeable future, a more immediate driver of change will be emotional intelligence —

or emotionally aware machines. In the future we will see cars that link the emotional state of the driver with various safety controls and mood-sensitive features, computers that can tell whether we are in a good mood and voice-recognition systems that can judge if we are lying. How about therapeutic robots or radios and televisions that tune into happy programs when we're feeling sad? Or what about online retailers tailoring their home pages, product offerings and even product descriptions to the emotional state of individual customers?

Ethics Science and, to a lesser extent, technology have always operated within a political context, but until recently they were more or less left alone. Not any more. Both will come under the microscope as society debates not whether something is possible but whether its consequences are desirable. Top of the list of gatekeepers will be government, with its own national and international agenda based on political philosophy, the economy and defense. Privacy will also become a key issue once people realize that computers are everywhere and almost no place on Earth is free from surveillance. No form of communication will be safe. Other people will know who you are, where you are, what you are doing and perhaps even what you are thinking. Privacy in a digital and connected age is dead. Gen Y knows this and doesn't care. Gen X and the Boomer Generation either don't realize or are horrified. In the future we will even debate questions such as whether it is wrong for an adult to love a machine or whether people should marry robots or have sex with them.

Robotics Robotic soldiers anyone? They're coming, but should such machines feel pain or regret? And if (when) there's an accident, who should be held responsible? Would you trust a robot to administer a general anaesthetic and perform surgery on you? Or what about when someone makes a robot that your child loves more than you? The convergence of a handful of trends is about to transform the field of robotics. First, the cost of computing power (processing and storage) is dropping fast. Second, distributed computing, voice and visual-recognition technologies and wireless broadband connectivity are similarly becoming cheaper and more available. Personal robots will be cleaning floors, dispensing medicine and keeping an eye open for intruders, while industrial robots will operate dangerous machinery and handle hazardous materials. On a smaller scale, robots could carry our bags from the supermarket, work as guide dogs for the visually impaired, or replace care workers in hospitals or nursing homes. Whether a machine will ever fully replace human or animal contact is a big question, to which most people currently answer no. However, attitudes may shift over time.

Chapter 2

Science and Technology: the rise of the machines

We live in a society exquisitely dependent on science and technology, in which hardly anyone knows anything about science and technology.
—Carl Sagan

The history of human civilization is, to a large degree, the history of technology of one kind or another. Hence the history of the next 50 years will largely be determined by what is invented by boffins in Bangalore and nerds in New York. More precisely, the history of the future will be heavily influenced by what we as societies allow to happen in terms of applying science and technology. There will be other key influencers, like climate change or the emergence of an idea that will challenge global capitalism, but it is technology that will dictate change and will be at the forefront of any future paradigm shifts in social attitudes and behavior.

Computers will become more intelligent than people by about 2030. At this point, humankind will be faced with something of a dilemma. If machines are more intelligent than their makers, what's to stop them taking over? We could, of course, design machines with in-built controls (see Isaac Asimov's "Robot Rules" in *I Robot*), but we will face a very strong temptation to see what would happen if we didn't.

The other intriguing, if not outright alarming, aspect of this issue is the convergence of computing, robotics and nanotechnology, which could give rise to self-replicating machines. Add to this the possibility of not only downloading intelligence but also consciousness into a machine, and this leads to the question of whether it is better to live for ever in a machine or for a limited time as a carbon-based biped. Personally I think downloading human consciousness is impossible, but you should never say never. Ian Pearson, head of BT's Futurology unit in the UK, argues that by the half-century mark it should be possible to download the contents of a human brain into a computer. If the human mind is then aware of what has happened this would be a form of immortality and the start of the human race splitting into two halves: the natural and the enhanced.

Singularity is the term futurists use to describe the point at which machines have developed to the extent that humans can no longer fully understand or forecast their capabilities. The idea of artificial intelligence (AI) goes back to the mid-1950s, although Asimov was writing about smart robots back in 1942. The true test for artificial intelligence dates to 1950, when the British mathematician Alan Turing suggested the criterion of humans submitting statements through a machine and then not being able to tell whether the responses had come from another person or the machine.

The 1960s and 1970s saw a great deal of progress in AI, but real breakthroughs failed to materialize. Instead, scientists and developers focused on specific problems such as speech recognition, text recognition and computer vision. However, we may be less than ten years away from seeing Turing's AI vision become a reality. For instance, a company in Austin, Texas has developed a product called Cyc. It is much like a "chatbot" except that, if it answers a question incorrectly, you can correct it and Cyc will learn from its mistakes.

But Cyc still isn't very intelligent, which is possibly why author, scientist and futurist Ray Kurzweil made a public bet with Mitchell Kapor, the founder of Lotus, that a computer would pass the Turing test by 2029. He based this prediction on ideas expressed in his book *The Singularity Is Near*: in essence, arguing that intelligence will expand in a limitless, exponential manner once we achieve a certain level of advancement in genetics, nanotechnology and robotics and the integration of that technology with human biology. The precedent here is obviously the speed at which computing has developed. Sony's PlayStation 3, for example, is 35 times more powerful than its predecessor and has the computing power of a supercomputer dating from 1997 — and at a cost of only US$600.

But while Kurzweil sees computers doubling in speed and power and programmers working feverishly to this end, Kapor believes that human beings differ so totally from machines that the test will never be passed, not least because we are housed in bodies that feel pleasure and pain and accumulate experience and knowledge, much of which is tacit rather than expressed. Other experts such as neurophysiologist Bill Calvin suggest that the human brain is so "buggy" that computers will never be able to emulate it.

Ultimately, though, this might not be the point; as some have suggested — such as James Surowiecki in his book *The Wisdom of Crowds* — the internet is already fostering an unanticipated form of AI, a highly efficient marketplace for ideas and information known as collective intelligence or the "hive mind". In other words, if we connected up all the computers on the planet and asked the resultant network or grid a question like "Is there a God?" the answer may very well be "There is now".

Nothing but the truth

In the same way in which Adam Smith suggested that buyers and sellers, each pursuing their own interests, would together produce more goods more efficiently than under any other arrangement, so too online suppliers of collective intelligence, like bloggers, can create more knowledge with less bias and over a wider span of disciplines than any group of experts could. At least, that's the utopian theory.

If in 1982, for example, anyone had suggested that hundreds of thousands of ordinary people located across the world could together create anything of real value, they would have been seen as either a hopeless romantic or a complete lunatic. Nowadays user-generated content (UGC) is all the rage, especially in new media circles, and empires like YouTube and MySpace have been built almost entirely on UGC; although some would question their value. But then there's Wikipedia, an online collaborative encyclopedia with the modest aim of one day being the greatest and most comprehensive repository of human knowledge ever built.

Wikipedia is "open" in the sense that anyone can contribute and the content is freely available to whoever wants it. It has a benign ruler (a foundation) but no leader. It is huge, too. There are presently 10 million articles on Wikipedia in 250 languages. By contrast, *Encyclopaedia Britannica* online has around 100,000 articles. Wikipedians (the content providers, essentially) agree collectively what is and isn't allowed and multiple users create, edit and link the pages, all of which tends toward content improvement. Interestingly, none of this was really supposed to happen, at least not in this manner.

The original idea behind Wikipedia was for experts to contribute content, but it turned out that they weren't in the least bit interested. You might expect that using amateurs instead of experts to supply, agree on and edit content might be a recipe for anarchy and online vandalism, but a recent study by the journal *Nature* found that the quality and accuracy of Wikipedia articles were almost indistinguishable from those of *Encyclopaedia Britannica.* And vandalism is almost non-existent because the community stops any anti-social behavior as soon as it starts. To my mind, the really interesting thought is what the consequences of Wikipedia might be. For instance, delicious philosophical questions such as "What is truth?" can now be answered by a democratic community rather than an expert elite. The wider use of the internet to bring people together could also be beneficial in the future because questions like "Should we use technology like space mirrors to solve global warming?" could be addressed to most of the planet, thus taking key debates far outside the scientific community.

"Truth" is now whatever Wikipedia says it is. Moreover, truth is whatever Wikipedia says it is right now (which, by implication, may change tomorrow). As a counterpoint Jaron Lanier, who coined the term "virtual reality", has predicted that collective intelligence — or digital Maoism — will have the same deadening and anti-creative effect as political collectivism. In other words, the wisdom of "idiots" will remove any opinion that does not fit with its own; if the online majority decides that 1+1=3, that will be the "truth".

Either way, it's important that we recognize what computers can do already (more than most people realize) and then think about how this may eventually change — and change us. Do we want knowledge to be owned by an anonymous online collective? If we don't, we should be saying so now before it's too late.

If you could read my mind

An obvious achievement of the internet is the retrieval of "spot knowledge", the antidote to memory loss that enables us to clear our minds of minutiae to focus on matters at a higher level. But while some dream of a life where embedded reminders mean we never have to worry about forgetting — and we can forget about worrying — others wonder what will happen to our cognitive functions if first-stage thinking is all but taken care of for us.

If the convergence of computing and communications led to the information age, then perhaps we are on the cusp of another dramatic shift. Natural sciences such as biology are merging with physical sciences such as engineering. In automobiles, engineering is merging with areas like computing, while computing itself is being greatly influenced by biology and neuroscience.

Science and technology are allowing us to look backwards and forwards in time, for example to identify genetic time-bombs inside our bodies. A more controversial idea, perhaps, is that free will does not exist and that our personalities and actions are largely shaped by our genes and are fixed by our ancestry. If proven, this would be an explosive idea because individuals could claim that nothing was ever their fault. We would be able to look inside a young person and forecast with some degree of certainty how their life would pan out in the future. In other words, we would, like the Department of Future Crimes, know what people would do before they did it. This would also open up a Pandora's box of people's personalities being altered through genetic fiddling. Even more contentious is the thought that there is a genetic component to intelligence (and other traits) and that this varies by ethnic group and gender. Even the merest hint of this idea is enough to incite violence, so imagine if there was a total collapse of consensus about all people being the same. The end of free will would also destroy the rule of law. But I'm sidetracking again.

A scientist in Cambridge, UK, has developed a prototype computer that can "read" users' minds by capturing and then interpreting facial expressions, reflecting concentration, anger or confusion, for instance. In experiments using actors, the computer was accurate 85% of the time, although this dropped to 65% with "ordinary" people. The technology raises a number of privacy-related issues, not least of which is the collection of highly sensitive personal data. Toyota is allegedly already working with its inventor,

Professor Peter Robertson, to link the emotional state of car drivers with various safety controls and mood-sensitive features. Other customers might include insurance companies wanting to crack down on dishonest claims, banks targeting identity fraud, teachers trying to teach more effectively (does the student really understand?) or governments wanting to identify terrorists or social-security cheats.

In the future, car companies or local councils could even tailor road maps or signs to a driver's level of aggression. What intrigues me most, however, is whether you could link mood sensitivity to products such as radios and televisions so that they tune into happy music or programs. There is also the fascinating possibility of online retailers tailoring their home pages, product offerings and even product descriptions to the emotional state of individual customers. A future challenge for scientists is thus to create software that develops in response to its environment, building neural nets holding past experiences that will build into something resembling basic consciousness and intelligence.

Sensing the future

One interesting area that's close to my heart is forecasting. In the future, traffic forecasts will be as common as weather forecasts. There will also be pollution forecasts, disease forecasts and even war forecasts.

War forecasting is already a growth industry, involving a number of key players in countries such as the US, Germany and Australia. One of the leading systems used to predict military outcomes is a piece of smart software called the Tactical Numerical Deterministic Model (TNDM), produced by a military thinktank in Washington, DC. TNDM is the mother of all battle simulators and can predict the outcome of future conflicts (especially casualty rates and duration). Its accuracy is largely due to the mountain of historical data and factors available, including everything from rainfall and river widths to foliage cover and muzzle velocities. The result is a mathematical model that predicts outcomes, including, you might think, the likelihood of presidents winning another term. Models such as this will become increasingly common, thanks to the ability of smart devices to collect vast amounts of data in real time and to tag this information with time stamps and geographical locations.

RFIDs, sensor motes and "smart dust" are some of the new ways in which such data will be collected in the future. Smart devices, some no larger than a full stop (0.15 mm square and 7.5 microns thick), will increasingly connect what is happening in the real world to mathematical models, which in turn may be used to alter or influence reality. For example, if the seas suddenly get too hot or there is a tidal surge in a remote region, we'll know about it. Surprises and mistakes will to an extent disappear — although in fact they will simply be replaced by new mistakes and new surprises.

Some of these sensors will be part machine. Wasps, spiders or houseflies may carry small cameras and wireless devices so that scientists can detect abnormal activities. Add a dose of nanotechnology and things could get very interesting and very frightening indeed. It's another nail in the coffin for privacy. If everything becomes intelligent and displays its location to a central network, everyone will be "bugged". Maybe this bothers you, maybe it doesn't. Your attitude to privacy will probably depend on how old you are.

The good news, perhaps, is that our shoes and clothes will contain GPS so that they (or us) will never get lost — and if they did we'd just Google them. Equally, our shoes or clothes will "talk" to our shoe polish or washing machine to ensure that they're not damaged when they're being cleaned.

Technology is also getting smarter in the sense of being able to second-guess what we want or remind us to do things. Unfortunately, at the moment we have to program most devices ourselves for them to second-guess what we want. In other words, we have to adapt our behavior to the technology. However, the next generation of devices will simply "watch" and "listen" to what we say and do (and where we are) and adapt themselves to us. For instance, cellphones will "watch" who we call and when and then remind us to do certain things at certain times. Such "reality mining" will undoubtedly be of great interest to sociologists and epidemiologists (and marketers), who will study how our social networks are created or how diseases spread. But again, are we giving too much away? There is a growing suspicion that this area of science and technology is already running out of control.

Moreover, unlike 25 years ago when most people trusted experts such as scientists, they now feel that many are in the pay of powerful business and government interests and can therefore no longer be trusted.

New technologies and ideas are nearly always resisted at first; the stronger or more disruptive the idea, the more resistance there will be at both a direct level (physical actions) and indirect level through the creation of myths. The cellphone, for example, is one of the most successful innovations of recent times and yet its ubiquity has done little to dispel safety fears surrounding its use. Similarly, the invention of the telegraph created a widespread belief that signals would interfere with the weather, while the introduction of trains and automobiles was predicted to create a variety of physical and mental disorders. I was talking to an 86-year-old man recently about cellphone masts and he pointed out that exactly the same objections were raised when lamp-posts were first introduced.

Too much information

In my experience, the nostalgia bug tends to kick in around the age of 40. Before this everything new is shiny and exciting. Afterwards, everything used to be better in the old days. Older people (and especially people aged over 60, which will be 22% of the world's population by 2050) tend to loathe technological change. Some very old people also struggle to remember who they are, although this problem is becoming more common with all age groups thanks to the growth of multiple identities online.

The average office worker has between six and twenty passwords that he or she is technically supposed to be able to remember. Imagine trying to recall all that at the age of 70. One solution is pictorial passwords (especially faces) or fingerprint IDs. Another is simply to drop out by refusing to buy kettles that know when you're getting up or fridges that reorder milk when you run out, whether you want some more or not.

Many of these devices are liars in the sense that they don't really save you time, or else they make your life even more complicated than it was before. Dishwashers are a case in point. Everyone I know has a dishwasher, but I swear it takes longer to stack and remove the plates than if you washed all the dishes yourself. Plus you can't take the plates out for two hours once a standard cycle has started — and what do you do with all the time you're supposedly saving anyway?

Another way of dealing with too much change is not to grow up. Psychological neoteny is a theory that the increased level of immaturity among adults is an evolutionary response to growing change and uncertainty. This makes a certain amount of sense. Humanity has long held youth in high esteem, originally because it was a sign of fertility and health, which were important for hunting and reproduction. In fixed environments, psychological maturity was useful because it indicated experience and wisdom.

However, some time in the latter part of the twentieth century childlike youthfulness started to have a new function, which was to remain adaptive to a fast-changing environment. In other words, if jobs, skills, scientific ideas and technology are all in a state of flux, it is important to remain open-minded about learning new skills, and the best way to do that is to retain a childlike state of receptivity and cognitive flexibility.

Another fascinating new concept is continuous partial attention. Interruption science is the study of why people get distracted and how best to interrupt them. In the late 1980s, NASA needed to find ways to deliver important information to busy astronauts. If a significant communication is not distracting enough it may get ignored, while anything too distracting could ruin a multimillion-dollar experiment. The timing and style of delivery of communications are vital. NASA found that text-based communications were routinely ignored while visually based communications seemed to get through.

So how is this relevant to people with their feet firmly planted on planet Earth? The simple answer is that many of us suffer from too much information thanks to faster computers and increased connectedness. We are continually subjected to a torrent of interruptions, ranging from email to cellphone calls. Indeed, a recent survey found that employees spend an average of 11 minutes on a task before being distracted by something else. Furthermore, every time employees were interrupted it took almost half an hour for them to return to the original task and 40% wandered off somewhere else. We are so busy watching everything and multitasking that we are unable to focus on or finish anything except after hours or at home. Information is no longer power — getting and keeping someone's attention is.

Given that computers and the internet are largely to blame for this, it's not surprising that computer and software companies are taking the issue very seriously. Part of the problem is that our memory tends to be visual and computers only allow the display of limited amounts of information on a screen. Some people solve this problem by sticking lo-fi sticky notes around the sides of their screen. Another way might be to say no — to unsubscribe and unplug parts of our life.

Technology could also change the way in which information is delivered. For example, if a computer could understand when we are busy (via a camera, microphone or keypad monitor) it could rank emails in order of importance and then deliver them at the most appropriate moment. Information could also be presented in the same way that aircraft instruments are laid out, so it can be glanced at easily. In the more distant future we may even figure out a way of getting rid of computer screens altogether and embedding information we can glance at in everyday objects, or we might deliver important information using pictures, sounds and smells.

Indeed, we do this already. I have spent years talking to companies about important trends and most of the time the information zips in one ear and flies out the other. Last year I decided to do something different. Instead of words I tried pictures — a map on a single sheet of paper, to be precise, like on the cover of this book. The response was extraordinary.

Robot wars

Robots have been a central feature of the future for as long as people have been making movies, particularly the idea of machine intelligence enslaving its creators. It's the same with aliens. Both genres of science fiction are really about what it means to be human and what we fear most about ourselves. The robots and the little green men (nearly always men, interestingly) are a subplot. So what are some of the coming attractions in terms of robots over the next 20 years or so?

Robotic assistants will slowly make their way out of the toy cupboard and off the lawn into our offices and living rooms. The cutting edge of robotics is military applications, but the ageing population (especially in Japan) offers up an alternative future.

Maybe robots, in an ironic turnaround from the script, will become carers and companions for the elderly: therapeutic robots delivering aged-care solutions. This, of course, brings us back to some interesting ethical debates, especially when humans start to profit from the addition of bionic arms, legs and eyes (modeled on dragonfly eyes, probably). In the meantime we will be able to lie back and stare in wonder at snakebots that slither down drainpipes, robotic lobsters (military applications, apparently) and robogoats that look for disaster victims on steep mountainsides.

None of this is very far off. In 2005 the US military deployed armed robots in Iraq. The robots, which looked like small radio-controlled tanks (what a letdown!), were operated by human soldiers up to a kilometer away. Each robo "soldier" was equipped with cameras, laser sights, thermal vision, night vision and either a machine gun or a rocket launcher. The Pentagon has been dreaming about the use of robotic soldiers for 30 years and has just budgeted US$127 billion (that's billion not million) to create what are euphemistically called "future combat systems". This is the biggest military contract in US history and it surely says something about the migration of the robot from a kid's room to a conscience-free combatant.

Meanwhile, in Japan a computer scientist has built what he claims to be the world's most humanlike (and attractive) android. In anticipation of the day when software can emulate human intelligence, Hiroshi Ishiguro has created a human-looking interface to house a computer. The android, modeled on a famous Japanese newscaster, has been painstakingly created to appear human — not only in looks but in mannerisms and movements. The creator has found that some people, especially children and the elderly, have taken it for a real human being. He feels that having a human-looking interface is important for communication. In fact, while people can accept robots that look like they come from central casting, they are quite disturbed by those that look similar to humans but not similar enough.

I think it was the writer Bruce Sterling who once said that in the future all products would be cuddly and he might have been right. While it seems we are threatened by things that look too much like ourselves, if they become too high-tech I expect we will all do a handbrake turn in the middle of the road and rush headlong into the arms of things that are warm, soft and familiar. But that's quite a way off.

Smarter but boring

Future technologies will include airborne networks that allow airliners to fly without pilots (inconceivable now but acceptable in 50 years); silicon photonics (using silicon chips to emit light to speed up data processing); quantum wires (using carbon nanotube wires to carry electricity); biomechatronics (mixing robotics with nervous systems to create new artificial limbs, as has already happened with monkeys controlling robotic arms by thought in the US); bacterial factories; metabolomics (a new medical-diagnosis tool using metabolic information); synthetic biology (the merger of biology and engineering); and nanoelectronics (for example using nanostructures to store more and more data in smaller and smaller areas).

We'll also have wireless battery recharging, new quiet materials (the future is a loud place), electronic camouflage, disposable computers, smart mirrors (that show us what we might look like next year), 3D printers, customized materials (the structure and properties of which can be designed millimeter by millimeter), organic computers, space-ladders, holographic displays and storage, home-use DNA stamps (to identify what's really ours), wearable computers in all shapes and forms, voice-based internet search ("Show me film clips of car chases"), personalization ports in all devices (so we can change them to suit our particular needs), a fully sensory internet (all five senses delivered over the web) and a high level of machine-to-machine communication. Oh, and quantum mechanics and teleportation (hey, I'm an optimist) too. Phew.

There will also be meta-materials that can be programmed to react to light or electromagnetic radiation in controllable ways.

This will allow the control of light flows over or around certain objects so that nuclear power stations (ugly) or military bases (secret) could simply be made to "disappear". In other words, they're there but they're not.

Getting even more futuristic, we might see robotic pest control, smart bullets (that follow bad guys around corners), sky shields (curtains or mirrors in space to stop harmful sunlight), joy-makers (use your imagination), accelerated schooling (everything else is speeding up), scramble suits (so people can't intercept personal communications), neuronic whips (a weapon that stimulates the nerve endings to cause extreme discomfort), randominoes (dominoes that randomly generate new numbers), mindwipes (had a bad day at the office? Simply delete it with a pre-moistened wipe), disintegrators, short-wave scalpels, childcare robots, space tugs, oceanic thermal converters (a device that uses the sea to generate energy), face-recognition doors, spray-on surgical gloves, napcaps (hats that send you to sleep), stress-control clothing, gravity tubes (a way of removing gravity in a specific area), sleep surrogates and self-repairing roads.

Another emerging field is epigenetics, the study of how particular genes act based on chemical and environmental factors. It's significant because previously scientists thought that genes (and the DNA from which they are made) were "fixed" — DNA is destiny. But perhaps not.

The new theory is that environmental factors can influence how a specific gene acts. Moreover, the so-called junk DNA that makes up 98% of all DNA possibly isn't junk at all and can influence cell function. If true, this is revolutionary because if there is a "criminal" or "genius" gene it could in theory be turned on or off, thus making the world a safer and smarter but potentially more boring place. After all, if you get rid of the demons the angels fly away too.

Rage against the machine

Despite the focus on applied science over pure science, it is still one of the very few areas where ideas in their purest form remain prominent. We have discovered a lot over the past 2,000 years (1.8 million other species, for example) but there is yet more to be unearthed. Nevertheless, for every door we open in the future I suspect we may find another that is firmly locked. Moreover, the history of science shows that ideas are periodically reshaped by revolutions in thinking and we are more than overdue such an upheaval.

So what ideas or events could produce another seismic shift?

The big one, to my naive mind at least, would be either the discovery of a parallel universe or hard evidence of life elsewhere within the galaxies. It wouldn't even have to be alive or very intelligent life to transform how people think back on Earth.

Futurist Richard Neville once commented that the question of whether or not UFOs exist is the wrong one. What if the real question were: "Why do people keep seeing them? What if their 'existence' was a cry from the collective unconscious, a plea for magic in a materialistic age?" Good point. As Arthur C. Clarke once said, "Any suitably advanced technology is indistinguishable from magic", so we will be seeing a lot more magic in the future. As I've already said we will also be seeing a lot more religion because, despite arguing logically and scientifically that it's all a fraud, we will need religion as a counterbalance to our increasingly virtual and technological lives. I'm sure that the mere mention of alien spaceships and God in the same breath will stop many readers in their tracks and confine me to the edges of something or other; but to be honest, that's fine.

Actually, mentioning religion brings me to another thought: perhaps science will be the new religion. Historically science and God have been opposing forces. But as we discover more about the universe, science itself may become the higher intelligence that most of us believe in.

There is still the problem identified by Richard Neville that science lacks the ceremony and ritual that form part of most organized religions. There are no cathedrals either.

Personally I'd just love it if a spaceship landed in Central Park in my lifetime, largely because it would call into question every single idea that has ever existed and would, presumably, topple humankind from our egotistical assumption that we are somehow special and at the top of an evolutionary tree. Even a fossil from Mars might do. It would also be great in terms of watching how the individual religions cope with the fact of something else out there. One suspects that Buddhists would be pretty Zen about it, but I'm not sure about some of the others. Knowing for certain that we are totally alone in space would perhaps cause a similar reaction.

There will be a lot more controversy in the future, some of it increasingly hostile. For instance, unless the evidence is immediate, I fully expect the debate about climate change to become more and more polarized between believers (it's all our fault) and skeptics (it's the sun wot did it). Equally, there will be widespread panic about the next pandemic, with a small number of quizzical scientists claiming that a repeat of historical pandemics is unlikely because of changed conditions.

Other possible upheavals would be a collapse in consensus about one of the major ideas of nineteenth- or twentieth-century science. There are lots of contenders to be debunked, but perhaps the most high profile are the theories of Darwin and Einstein. Again, I will probably be labeled a nut for suggesting that the work of such giants could ever be overturned, but this merely demonstrates the strength and power of conventional wisdom and the sheer force required to displace such ideas. As Arthur C. Clarke again observed, "If an elderly but distinguished scientist says that something is possible he is almost certainly right, but if he says that it is impossible he is very probably wrong." Remember, the Earth was once definitely flat.

It is our relationship with machines that will be the defining characteristic of the twenty-first century. Where we draw the line between what we want "them" to know or do or see will set the direction for the next thousand years. For example, do we want machines to feel pain? If we are to imbue them with a basic emotional capacity or understanding, surely they must be able to feel pleasure and pain? This idea immediately transports us back to the supercomputer HAL in *2001: A Space Odyssey*. It's a very important question and one that is difficult to answer with any half-measure. If machines are given the powers of life and death — robotic soldiers, nurses or surgeons, for example — surely they must be taught to understand right from wrong? It's also a case of all or nothing: we can't really give a machine a *bit* of emotional understanding. If we want a machine to feel pride — a very advanced emotion indeed — then we need to install happiness and desire. And for happiness to function properly we have to enable sadness and regret. If we do all this we may end up with another HAL, a machine that's so messed up emotionally it can't function properly.

One of the really great things about machines now is that they don't think. They just do. And even if they can be said to "think" they only really think about what they are doing, which leaves the gates wide open for humans to have empathy, imagination, creativity and ideas. At least that's what I keep telling myself so I can sleep at night.

31 December 2049

Dear Ian

Thanks for the birthday present. To be honest I'm a bit old for a joy-maker but I'm sure I'll put it to some good use (maybe I can wire it up to my old car and we can go for a joy ride, ha, ha). At least it's better than the emotionally aware bathroom scales your brother got me. They're driving me mad.

Anyway, I just can't believe that you'll be 50 next year. Any idea what you want? I thought perhaps one of those new Monopoly holographic editions? By the way, did you see the story about the new jetliner that goes from London to Sydney in two hours? Apparently it just shoots up into the edge of space and sits there waiting for the Earth to rotate before dropping back down (then again I would think that it should take nine or eleven hours not two, but what do I know?). Hope the seatbelts are good.

Personally I'm still working on the space ladder project. We've cracked how to make the cable using carbon nanotubes, so now it's just a matter of putting the cable into a geosynchronous orbit and tethering it to a counterweight in deep space.

Thought you'd like the retro communication. I even managed to buy a real stamp off AmazonBay, which apparently FedPost will still deliver.

All for now — busy as ever.

Cheers

Richard

5 trends that will transform politics

City states Countries, national politicians and national elections are all under threat. People and jobs are becoming more mobile; defense, economic policy and law making are being increasingly influenced by regional or international interests. Corporations are becoming more stateless too, and in the future loyalties may be directed toward one's company first and one's country second. Voters will try to influence international politics through global NGOs and single-issue action groups, although the most significant shift will be back toward city states because this is where economic power, media interests and ideas will be most concentrated. By 2020 the GDP of Tokyo or New York will be roughly similar to that of Canada, a G7 nation.

Tribalism Historically international relations have been forged between nation states, but this is changing. Many conflicts are now between tribal groups inside states and some of these groups are very small indeed. Hence micro-trends and micro-segments may be more important than mega-trends and national consensus in the future. Moreover, the very idea of the nation state is under threat, not only from globalization but from regional politics. Local issues are seen by many voters as more important than national ones, because at least with them they have a chance of influencing the outcomes. This will lead to the rebirth of regional politics, as local patriotism mixes with nimbyism. It will also lead to xenophobia, as nations escape into their glorious (and not so glorious) pasts.

Happiness Materialism and consumerism are starting to lose their appeal. We are working harder and longer — and earning more money as a result — but it's becoming increasingly obvious that money can't buy happiness and that identity is shaped by how we live rather than what we own or consume. To some extent, the focus on happiness and work/life balance is really just an aspiration, a search for meaning in a meaningless world. But it is also a result of the fact that people have too much time and money on their hands. A century or two ago people were focused on survival and just didn't have time for such introspection.

Climate change and the environment The threat of climate change is real enough but the panic reaction isn't. Present solutions are tokenistic, opportunistic and simplistic (like the war on four-wheel drives and flying but not air conditioning or electrical goods) and focus too much on the small picture. Our weather may indeed become more volatile and severe, meaning more bad hurricanes and disastrous flooding in some regions. Extreme heat and lack of water may make other places almost uninhabitable, while rising sea levels could devastate low-lying cities. But the solution isn't symbolic taxation. What we need is a paradigm shift in the global economy, especially in manufacturing efficiencies. We should also focus on the limited future availability of natural resources, including people. Shortages could cause global conflicts, while environmental destruction may trigger the unregulated movement of millions of people from one country to another.

On the other hand, higher oil prices could mean fewer cars on the road, less obesity (as we walk or use bicycles more) and less consumerism. This may trigger a new sense of make-do-and-mend that will rejuvenate local communities and national self-esteem. Climate change plus a shortage of resources will also be a catalyst for innovation, on the basis that crisis and adversity are usually the mother and father of invention. We'll see new biofuel technologies, hydrogen power, starch-based plastics and home-based micro-generation. Even the landfill problem will be resolved when someone realizes that there's money to be made by digging up old refuse sites and converting used plastic bags and bottles into fuel.

e-Action   We can bank online, bet online, date online and watch television online, so why can't we all vote online? In the future, we will. Initially e-voting will involve electronic booths inside polling stations, but ultimately we will be able to vote at home, at work or in the supermarket, on everything from whether teenage fathers should be given compulsory training to whether successful marriages should be awarded tax credits. We will also be able to vote for the American President even if we live in Poland or Patagonia. Global e-action groups and virtual protests will thrive. This won't necessarily change anything, but it will make politics much more interesting and entertaining. Also expect an increase in cyberattacks and cyberterrorism.

Chapter 3

Government and Politics: us and them

The empires of the future are the empires of the mind.
—Winston Churchill

Former British prime minister Harold Macmillan once observed that his biggest problem was "events". Predicting anything is a recipe for failure and frustration, but politics is almost impossible to forecast due to such events. Indeed, the only thing you can say with any degree of certainty about politics is that if you take a long enough timeframe, almost anything is possible.

Predictions about the end of history now seem as ridiculous as Thomas Jefferson saying that "History, by apprising [people] of the past, will enable them to judge the future: it will avail them of experience of other times and nations." If this were true, why did UN officials decide to cover up a copy of Picasso's *Guernica*, which hung outside the entrance to the UN Security Council, on the very day Colin Powell addressed the UN about the case for war in Iraq? We are, it seems, destined to repeat past mistakes.

The field of politics is littered with false prophets whose usual error is to extrapolate past and present ideas and events into the future. This can work in the short term, but sooner or later some totally unexpected event or idea trips up these intricately woven visions. September 11, 2001 provides a recent example and we are still dealing with the aftermath.

The years immediately after the terrorist attack on the World Trade Center witnessed a profound swing toward semi-authoritarian rule and, at the governmental level at least, there was a feeling of solidarity and oneness with the US's response. However, the legacy of September 11 is fading. The eight world leaders who attended the 2005 G8 Summit and posed for a "family photo" are now either history or soon will be. Schröder (Germany), Koizumi (Japan), Chirac (France), Martin (Canada), Putin (Russia) and Blair (UK) have all gone. Bush (US) is going, and Berlusconi (Italy) went but came back for a while. Western leaders are losing their grip, or at least their credibility.

In many cases their departure has been because voters have become disillusioned with the war on terror — which has had precisely the opposite effect from that intended. Voters are feeling less safe and secure than ever, due to everything from the shadow of terrorism and globalization to their inability to influence national or international politics effectively.

The end result is falling membership of political parties (down 50% in the UK since 1980), low voter turnout at elections and a general collapse of confidence in both politics and politicians. In theory, this situation could be reversed with the election of a new US President and a fresh set of other world leaders, although, if anything, the level of anxiety is likely to increase because of the effects of globalization and technology. Anti-globalization and anti-US sentiments could also fuel a swing to the left in many developing nations, which, together with the rapid rise of authoritarian Russia and totalitarian China, could lead to a new world order and cold war dominated by patriotism and protectionism. Autocracy is on the way back too.

Fear, as the sociologist Frank Furedi has pointed out, has become a significant force shaping the public imagination across the globe. In the future it will be used to justify everything from compulsory biometric identity cards to a global persons' database. Our feeling of powerlessness is also driving insecurity that makes us swing from one panic to the next, even when the probability of our worries materializing is almost non-existent. Clever politicians know this and have used fears about crime, immigration, education, jobs and climate change to fan uncertainty, causing many to vote for the devil they know (the incumbent) rather than the one they don't. Historically this has worked, but the world is changing.

Nation-states are also becoming irrelevant. Issues that matter are generally either local or international. National sovereignty is under threat from the increasing mobility of workers and tax systems that encourage global corporations to move their profits elsewhere. There is also the question of what government and countries are ultimately for. For example, if governments increasingly withdraw from providing essential services and public infrastructure projects (education, health, transport and so on) and national security is increasingly delivered through multinational organizations, what exactly are we paying national politicians to do?

Ultimately, I'd expect worldwide voting on all major issues (for example, the US presidency could be voted on globally) and citizens will become more involved partly through convenience (electronic voting in supermarkets) but also because the internet — and future metanets — will make special interest groups and non-governmental organizations (NGOs) immensely powerful. In other words, the internet will effectively be the second chamber in most democracies, with leaderless movements and self-forming networks becoming a major threat to local control and regulation.

War will be a similar story. The idea of inter-state war is increasingly old-fashioned, with most future threats coming from the spilling over of intra-state conflicts or stateless organizations. States will also be less likely to go to war simply because very few people in developed nations will be willing any longer to die for an idea.

There will be exceptions to this, but generally fanatics will have quite an advantage. The causes of war will change too. Oil is currently top of the list, but in a few decades water will be a major source of conflict, as will food. If plants are increasingly used to make fuel (to replace oil), struggles may arise over control of the world's grain markets, which are in the hands of rich Western nations (OPEC in reverse, perhaps).

Equally, an undemocratic regime, possibly acting alone or in conjunction with a terrorist group, could bring the US (and hence the West) to its knees simply by selling some currency. Almost 70% of global currency reserves are now in the hands of developing nations, many of them undemocratic and unstable. Indeed, most of the huge debt owed by the US is "owned" by China, Saudi Arabia and Russia, none of which is exactly a model democracy, to put it mildly. Iran and Venezuela also have substantial holdings of American debt.

A more pressing concern for governments and citizens alike comes with demographic trends and, in particular, the ageing of most populations. For example, more people are likely to suffer from age discrimination than racism and sexism, but government legislation tends to neglect ageism in favor of other forms of inequality and human rights.

An age-old problem

Ageing populations and declining fertility rates are well-known trends, but what is generally missed is that as a consequence there will be a future military recruitment problem. It is possible to solve this shortfall by encouraging more women into the armed services, but most countries are still uneasy about using women in combat roles. Another solution is the importation of soldiers (say through temporary or long-term immigration). To some extent the future shortfall will be made up by the increased use of technology, but in the short term these devices will still need human operatives and the best-qualified people will be young people who have grown up familiar with computer games and virtual reality. The only other solution would be compulsory national service, which seems to be universally unpopular. Mind you, this will be less of a concern in the future because the major voting bloc will be older not younger people.

Population — and more precisely the unregulated movement of population — is a critical element in the future security of nations. It is already looking as if Europe is under threat from growing immigrant communities that have very little loyalty to their host nation. Nationalism will become a defining trend of the twenty-first century and there is a very serious possibility that Europe will disintegrate into the regions from whence it came. Equally, the impact of foreign nationals living abroad is a significant factor influencing the so-called soft power of nations. Much has been written about China and India, in particular the sheer size of their populations, but the 60 million Chinese and 20 million Indians already living abroad who are subtly affecting their host nations are often overlooked.

Instability in developing countries, brought on by environmental degradation, could send further waves of migration into Europe on a par with the movements that led to the collapse of the Roman Empire in the fifth century. The most likely areas to experience mass migration include Africa, the Middle East and Central Asia, which are affected by water shortages, a decline in food production, rising sea levels and radical Islam. The impact would be seen first at the edges of these areas, but would become more problematic as borders disappear and large urban populations become ungovernable.

Population may influence politics in other, more subtle ways. Across the globe, people are having fewer children. The obvious problem this creates is funding retirement (which would thus require higher taxes), but there are some other implications.

Philip Longman, writing in the *Atlantic Monthly*, has pointed out that if a generation has fewer offspring, its genetic legacy is reduced. This means that the beliefs to which a generation adheres weaken over time. Moreover, the people who do decide to have children — especially lots of them — tend to be more conservative than those who don't. For example, in 2004 states that voted for George W. Bush had fertility rates 12% higher on average than states that voted for the more liberal John Kerry. In other words, individualist and libertarian elements of the population will tend to die out while more traditional, patriarchal, patriotic and even fundamentalist elements will inherit countries by default.

Current politicians also don't appreciate that for an increasing number of people it's no longer about the money. Materialism is still in full swing in most countries, with about one billion new consumers ready to join the party in China, India and elsewhere. However, for many people approaching the top of Maslow's hierarchy of needs, money is starting to lose its appeal. We are working harder and longer than ever — and earning more money as a result — but we don't seem to be getting any happier. People are also starting to realize that identity and self-esteem are not shaped by what you own or consume but by who you are and how you live. To some extent the happiness phenomenon is really a search for meaning. But people also have too much time on their hands in which to reflect on the human condition. Nevertheless, the politics of happiness will move increasingly to center stage, partially replacing the debate about work/life balance.

The implications are significant. Traditionally, politicians have been elected on the basis first of security and certainty and, more recently, on their promise to make us better off. Tax cuts have been the currency of politicians for the last 50 years; future voters will demand happiness. Although this is a ridiculous requirement and one that surely says something about the delegation of responsibility in society, it's on the cards nevertheless.

Happiness is largely an aspiration. It is not something you can buy off the shelf and it can never be a permanent condition. Regardless of that, ordinary voters will demand it in the future and opportunistic politicians will pledge to deliver it. Obvious implications will include a focus on green and community issues and various promises of free time and family-friendly policies. Of course, this trend could go out of the window the moment there's a flu pandemic, major war or economic downturn.

Global or national?

Another wildcard is globalization, or perhaps more accurately de-globalization. While most people assume that globalization is here to stay, I'd argue that this is far from certain. Globalization will probably last for at least another decade or two but there are a number of worrying signs. First, the rise of China and India could result in economic protectionism in regions like the US and Europe, putting a few speed-bumps in the road to further globalization. It's interesting to note that in 1990 there were 50 regional trade agreements around the world but by 2005 there were 250.

Equally, most of our international institutions are fragile, to say the least, and nationalism is already clearly evident in regions as diverse as the former Soviet Union, Europe and even Australia and the UK. Ultimately, higher oil prices could also lead to more inflation, higher interest rates and economic turmoil, which could cripple the global economy. Globalization could then come to an abrupt halt because goods, especially perishables such as food, may not be able to be transported cost-effectively around the world. Industry and politics would thus return to a pre-1914 (or perhaps pre-1950) model.

Whether or not globalization ultimately remains a sustainable trend, nationalism will certainly be a feature of the next 50 years. Europeans collectively complain about George W. Bush, but the fact is that they usually want to be governed by his local equivalent. As a result, global provincialism is taking over from global cooperation as a dominant theme of modern politics. This is happening because globalization requires presidents and prime ministers to allow wide-ranging socioeconomic reform if a country is to compete internationally. In contrast, ordinary voters are usually rather attached to the old ways, especially when these brought international prestige (history influencing the future again).

Thus an instinct for identifying and preserving what makes a country, or region, special is a prerequisite for high office and popular support. This may appear ridiculously parochial or superficial to some, but it's increasingly what voters want. This view not only explains George W. Bush and his particular form of "muscular" Christianity, but it also elucidates why Gerhard Schröder was such an enthusiastic defender of the German lifestyle and John Howard was so in touch with Australian values.

From whiter than white to greener than green

Energy has always been a strategic resource and the same will be true of a handful of key resources in the future. Ten of the world's largest oil companies are "nationals", state controlled. Moreover, many of the owners of the world's biggest remaining oil fields are moving to the far left politically and could potentially nationalize all energy and resource production within their borders. Venezuela is frequently quoted as a future trouble spot as it contains some of the world's most significant remaining reserves, but Nigeria (which has the eighth-largest oil reserves), Libya, Bolivia, Peru, Ecuador, Angola and Sudan are other countries that could potentially shut off supplies to foreign nations or become catalysts for conflict.

All this is important because we are about to enter a critical historical period. Resources (everything from oil and water to uranium and grain stocks) are running low, so there will be a headlong rush by energy-dependent countries into the arms of nations that can satisfy this hunger until technology provides them with a more sustainable solution. Energy anxiety will be dominated by the paradoxical need for secure access to future supplies, while at the same time engaging in public rhetoric about the need to cut emissions and reduce dependency. The same will be true of other key materials and future development will be heavily influenced by the cost and regulation of these resources.

Edward O. Wilson calls this the "bottleneck". This is the point at which population growth, economic development and environmental destruction put maximum stress on both the planet and the human race. As a result, the resources trade will increasingly operate on a "no questions asked" basis. In the long term, I believe that energy and general resource-scarcity issues will be solved through technology; but in the meantime, energy (along with climate change and sustainability) will dominate politics.

Most studies predict that we will hit peak oil production by 2015, or 2020 at the latest. Supplies will run out around 2050. This will be followed by peak gas and peak coal. As a result, nuclear power is firmly back on the political agenda, an inconceivable thought 20 years ago. Widescale use of wind and particularly solar power is also being seriously investigated, although it is hard to see how either can successfully replace oil, coal and gas without a substantial change in the way energy is used.

According to Richard Heinberg, a US academic and author of several books on the end of cheap oil, we should all be planning for another 1930s-style economic depression. A report produced for the US Department of Energy says that when peak oil does hit, we will experience abrupt and revolutionary change. The world's appetite for oil is certainly insatiable. Between September 2003 and May 2008 the price of oil increased by almost 500% but demand has not declined at all. Indeed, demand is predicted to rise by 50% between now and 2025. China has already been responsible for 40% of the greater demand for oil since 2001. Meanwhile, demand for electricity there has risen by 700% since 1978 and the country currently consumes 30% of the world's coal, 40% of its steel and 25% of its aluminum and copper. Are we all in denial about the future availability of oil? Probably. When it does run out, we will certainly be in for a shock. Higher fuel prices will drive global change but we will, I think, adjust. The intensity of oil usage is already changing, as are attitudes and behavior surrounding energy creation and consumption.

The end of oil may lead to a renaissance in local manufacturing and consumption and even to the end of the worldwide obesity epidemic. If you think the last point is a bit far-fetched, consider this. In Cuba the average adult lost 9kg after 1992 because the collapse of the Soviet Union increased the severity of the US oil embargo and the country had to rely on 10% of its pre-1992 oil supply. As a result, Cubans started to use gearless Chinese bicycles to get around and this increased the fitness of the entire nation.

What will in fact happen depends on human ingenuity and whether or not technology can provide an alternative to crude oil. Personally, I think that there are tough times ahead and that we will have to get used to consuming less of everything, which may not be a bad thing. Reverse globalization would re-energize local communities. We would become more self-reliant and, just as people did during and immediately after the Second World War, maintain and repair things rather than replacing them. There is indeed a strong possibility of an energy bottleneck to pass through first, but ultimately I believe that future generations will be better off, not worse off, once oil and other key resources run out.

The desire to be green will determine how governments operate, much in the same way that it will affect corporations. However, governments will also tend to pass the buck on to ordinary citizens and use green concerns as a way of increasing revenue. Although the push to become greener started with individuals, it was countries that made the first big moves (the Kyoto protocol is a prominent example). Momentum then trickled down through companies and organizations and has now landed firmly back at the feet of ordinary individuals. The environment will thus create regulation, which will in turn force change.

For example, a broad coalition of politicians, environmentalists and economists believe that green taxes (and carbon taxes in particular) are a solution to the growing problem of energy scarcity around the world. With many of the world's governments facing a budget deficit, green taxes offer a way of building a better environment (or appeasing the environmentalists, if you're of a cynical persuasion). Crucially, they also generate extra tax revenue, which electorates find difficult to argue against without appearing selfish. According to Dieter Helm at New College Oxford (UK), green taxes will be used by most democratically elected governments within the next five years. In British New Labour speak this means that there will be a shift from taxing "goods" to taxing "bads". Give me a tax break.

There is also likely to be a shift from energy- and transport-related green taxation to taxation based on pollution, chemical use and waste production, especially packaging. Many of these taxes will be aimed at individuals and small businesses despite the fact that most of the pollution is produced by a tiny handful of large corporations and countries. Research conducted by the *Guardian* newspaper, for example, says that just six companies in the UK produce more CO_2 than all the car drivers in Britain combined. Meanwhile, until recently Australians were being urged to turn out their lights while the Howard government simultaneously sold millions of tonnes of coal to China and refused to ratify the Kyoto protocol.

The problem of climate change certainly seems to be urgent. Of the 20 hottest summers on record, 19 have occurred since 1980; since 1970 the number of Category 4 and 5 hurricanes globally has doubled. Yet we still currently release 300% more CO_2 than our oceans can absorb. India's CO_2 emissions are also likely to rise by

70% by 2025; between now and 2030, emissions from China are predicted to equal that of the rest of the world combined (it is already the single largest emitter of greenhouse gases, although the US tops the list if you calculate this statistic on a per head of population basis). Nevertheless, we seem to be losing our sense of perspective. The science surrounding climate change is complex and the outcomes are still uncertain.

It remains possible that climate change is part of a natural cycle, although if you say this in most polite circles you will probably be lynched. This is precisely what happened to Andy Revkin when he had the audacity to suggest in *The New York Times* that the planet is not in peril.

A growing number of scientists (but still not very many) believe that the activity of the sun could be linked to the Earth's temperatures, perhaps explaining as much as 30% of global warming. Moreover, periodic environmental crises have been part of the Earth's history for as long as the planet has existed. In fact, there are a few people who think that the odd mass extinction is good because it allows evolutionary processes to start again.

What we forget is that from the Earth's point of view, we don't need ice caps, Brazilian rainforests or any specific sea level. These things ebb and flow with the passage of time and it is arrogant in the extreme to believe that the Earth belongs to us and therefore we should protect it. Our planet will protect itself and, ultimately, bounce back from anything we humans could possibly do to it. In other words, the idea that the Earth is somehow in our care is a complete nonsense.

Water, water, nowhere

However, 6.4 billion people do currently live on the planet and, while a mass extinction is perhaps of no consequence when it happens to other species, it matters very much if it looks like it may happen to us. Thus the climate/carbon/water debate is really about how future change will affect those people who are too poor to adapt. The key consequence of climate change — and one that politicians should worry about — is how higher temperatures, rising sea levels and increasingly severe and unpredictable weather will threaten the food security of millions and perhaps hundreds of millions of people. And remember, this isn't just an altruistic point. If millions have their food or water supplies shut off, they will do what any sensible person would — they will move to the areas where supply is more certain. Such mass migrations would have profound implications for the stability of the entire world.

Water in particular will become a serious problem over the next few years, although not in the way some people expect. It takes 11,000 liters of water to make a hamburger and 83,000 to make a medium-size family car, while the average person uses 135 liters every day (most of it wasted). Water, or more precisely the lack of it, will be a big problem in the future due to growing populations and urbanization.

These problems may be avoided, but I doubt it. We have already seen Coca-Cola criticized for allegedly stealing water in India and Chinese provinces are accusing each other of taking more than their fair share of rain by "seeding" clouds in an attempt to increase precipitation in their area. Water theft is thus set to be one of the defining crimes of the twenty-first century. Half the world's population is likely to be living in water-stressed regions by 2025 and some countries could be in very serious trouble.

What are the consequences? Bottled water has been singled out as ethically unsound because it involves removing water from one region and selling it in another — in Asia's case this can mean shipping it 10,000 kilometers, contributing to carbon emissions. In Canada some churches are urging congregations to boycott bottled water, citing reasons of ethics and social justice. Similar arguments could in theory be used against wine or even bread.

Equally, as the writer Bryan Appleyard has pointed out, eating lettuce may become socially unacceptable because growing the plant is not environmentally sustainable — it uses lots of water (and in some cases heat) — and it has a nutritional value of next to nothing. The same could perhaps be true of melons and cucumbers. Farming irrigation uses 60% of all water taken from rivers and aquifers globally and, while the world grows twice as much food as it did a generation ago, we use three times as much water to achieve that.

A single kilogram of rice requires 2,000–3,000 liters of water, while a kilogram jar of instant coffee takes 20,000 liters. Even a liter of milk needs 4,000 liters of water to produce. People's attitudes to water will therefore shift seismically in some regions; politicians, keen to jump on another bandwagon, won't be far behind. The pollution of rivers and lakes will thus move to center stage along with dam building and the ownership of pipe networks and water companies. The water use of every industry from food to fashion will be in the spotlight and science will be given the task of developing drought-free crop varieties.

Finally, it's worth mentioning the link between water and economic performance. Water could potentially be an Achilles' heel for China in particular. Currently, 400 out of the country's 600 biggest cities are short of water and it has below-average water resources per capita, all of which could potentially put a large spanner in its development model.

Chairman China

By the year 2010 the world's population will stand at 6.8 billion (up from 6 billion in 1999), but 95% of global population growth will come from developing countries, most of them in the East. While India will become a superpower (especially in services), most attention will continue to focus on the potential of its manufacturing-based rival, China.

China is about to become the world's largest exporter (over-taking Germany) and will shortly beat the US as home to the most internet users. It is also due to become the world's second largest importer and to rank as the third largest economy (measured by GDP and subject to exchange rates), behind the US and Japan.

Beyond economics, China is also important politically for a number of reasons, including its sheer size (geographically and population-wise) and its territorial claims. These factors make the country a significant foreign-policy player and ultimately, perhaps, the world's number one superpower. Nevertheless, we shouldn't forget that it is currently a totalitarian state with, some might argue, the seeds of its own destruction already sown. Urban–rural conflict, rampant corruption, a bankrupt state-backed banking system, overdependence on the US economy and environmental problems could all bring China down. (It's a similar story with nationalist Russia, which, I predict, will start looking for enemies both inside and outside its borders the moment things begin to become difficult for the current hard-line regime.)

So what are some of the most likely scenarios for China over the coming years? One possibility, identified by the Global Business Network, is that it will play by the established rules and slowly move toward a recognizable Western democratic model. This would involve enforcing intellectual property laws and opening its doors to foreign companies on a totally level playing field. Ultimately labor shortages could become a problem, but then China could simply contract work to regions such as Africa or use relocation to free up another 10 million workers over the next couple of decades (there are currently 750 million workers in China, of which 375 million work in state-owned enterprises, so the level of government control is significant).

A second scenario is that corruption and urban unrest will continue and the region will simply grind to a halt. A third possibility is that China will grow in economic and political stature but only as fast as its Asian rivals. This could mean intense competition for resources and markets, or it could lead to a series of regional pacts and trade agreements much to the disadvantage of the West, although this in turn could spur increased cooperation between the US and Europe or between North and South America. Either way, globalization — or at least the free movement of goods, services and people — may be in trouble.

The fourth and final scenario is simply that China will keep on growing. With unrest quashed (or peaceably accommodated), the country could end up as the world's dominant superpower. Then, perhaps, China will stop buying US debt, the US economy will collapse and the yuan will become the favored global currency, displacing both the dollar and the euro. I think this is somewhat unlikely, because China and the US are mutually interdependent economically. As a result, it would be in neither country's best interest to allow the other to falter economically.

At least that's the theory. An emerging argument says that the US could collapse economically without taking China or the rest of the world with it thanks to the liquidity of the CHIME nations (China, India and the Middle East). Nonetheless, China could still end up wrecking the global economy on which it also depends. While there is the unfinished business of Taiwan, in the short term I'd expect the focus to be on issues that are much closer to home, such as the booming domestic market and worker shortages rather than international issues like relations with the US. I would therefore expect the power shift to the East to continue, although a key question is whether China can pull off what Japan did so successfully after the Second World War.

In other words, can China move from a manufacturing-based economy that essentially copies what is designed and developed in the West to one in which innovation is at the very core? Moreover, is the shift to an innovative, entrepreneurially led culture possible without full political freedom and can you build a knowledge economy without having a free flow of knowledge? We shall see.

Edukation ain't wurkin

Along with crime, transport and jobs, education is a classic swing factor in politics. In the future this list of voter concerns will increasingly be joined by health, immigration and the environment, but education will remain a top priority — not least because it will have to change fundamentally if countries are to remain competitive in the new globally connected economy.

Education will also alter radically in response to new discoveries and understanding about how the human brain works. Developments in artificial intelligence will ultimately cause education to focus on those areas of human thought and activity that computers and technology are unable to deliver efficiently — namely, the development of new ideas (broadly speaking creativity and innovation) and empathic interaction with other human beings.

Twenty years ago the school gates marked a clear separation between the influence of teachers and parents. Trust was implicit and transparency was unnecessary. Moreover, the values and influence of business hardly got a look in. Not any more. Due to increased competition for university places and jobs (the influence of globalization) and changing demographics (more pressure on individual children because of smaller families), parents are getting more involved in their children's education.

In some cases this has led to a renaissance of private education (also thanks to an increase in disposable incomes), but even in the state-funded sector parents are demanding to be let inside schools and to have a say in what's being taught and how. Parents are thus being given the email addresses of teachers and, in some cases, are suing schools when their expectations (such as exam results and career paths) are not met. In the US there was a 25% increase in the number of teachers buying liability insurance between 2000 and 2005.

A good example of the pressure on students — from both parents and educators — comes in a quote from the head of a preschool in the US. Andi (who clearly can't spell) is of the opinion that afternoon naps for 4-year-old pre-schoolers should be stopped because, "If they get behind (by wasting their time sleeping), by the age of six they have difficulty catching up." Never mind that children of 4 or 5 need 10–12 hours of sleep a day and heaven forbid that they might be allowed a few hours just to be kids and develop a sense of curiosity and wonder. The pressure to perform starts as soon as you are born.

The issue for some parents is their desire for education to be directly linked to the "real world". Subjects studied must therefore have a pound or dollar value career-wise and knowledge for its own sake is taking a back seat to vocational learning. Indeed, the stakes are now becoming so high that some parents are removing the element of chance altogether and doing most or all of their children's homework or school entry assignments themselves. This won't last for long of course, because technology can already be used to identify the writer.

Another issue is what's been termed "cut and paste" education. A survey in *Education Week* claims that 54% of students in the US have plagiarized material from the internet. In the UK the Plagiarism Advisory Service (really!) says that 25% of students regularly pass off downloaded material as their own. There are even websites such as Cheathouse.com to help students do this.

Where there's a threat there's always an opportunity, so teachers can upload suspect material to Turnitin.com. That's assuming their pupils haven't got their retaliation in first by reporting them. Sites like Ratemyprofessors.com allow students to evaluate their teachers publicly. In theory this is a welcome development, but one wonders where the obsession with instant evaluation will end. Could children be rating their parents online in the future, or could private school fees be adjusted on a daily basis depending on the previous day's ratings from students and parents?

In the US the education market is already worth close to US$750 billion, although only 10% of this is "edupreneurial" in the sense that it is for profit. In Sweden a third of all schools are now run by private companies and the sector is also growing fast in countries such as Brazil, South Africa and the UK.

There are many arguments against the privatization of essential services such as education, but the one that will capture people's imaginations in the future surrounds the long-term social consequences of a system where the best brains are creamed off at an early age, possibly by corporate sponsors with little interest in the wider social impacts of their actions. For example, if education becomes too polarized between public and private, this will magnify the creation of a new establishment elite and the corresponding underclass, with each group living, learning and earning in separate bubbles.

I certainly expect to see the development of schools based on the look and feel of companies or hotels. They will open earlier and close later to fit in with the schedules of busy working parents. They will offer breakfast and dinner and in some cases temporary overnight accommodation. They will also teach discipline and values, because parents will be too busy to do either. Unfortunately, these schools will rarely accommodate any talent that falls outside the prescribed curriculum or agenda. Commerce, media studies, accountancy and law will all be well catered for, but anyone with an aptitude for the study of ancient history will struggle to find a home for their talents.

Another big issue in education is how to teach boys. Thirty years ago girls were the issue, since 58% of undergraduate students in the US were male. Now boys account for only 44% and they are failing across almost every benchmark.

There are various explanations for this, including the general feminization of society, but a more likely culprit is continual testing for very narrowly defined outcomes. Another issue that affects boys is the decrease in physical education and sports. This is partly due to urbanization and booming property values (there is less space available because it has become so expensive) and also down to parents withdrawing their children from competitive sport since it is either perceived as dangerous or they don't like the idea of their child losing at something.

Thirty years ago scientists argued that the differences between boys and girls were largely the result of nurture (socialization). These days most think the opposite. In other words, behavior is hard-wired. So if in the future boys are proven to be very different biologically from girls, perhaps we'll see the old idea of teaching them separately come back into vogue. This may also become popular because of the lack of male teachers in the primary (early education) system, meaning that young boys will have fewer and fewer male role models in their lives. In the US 40% of boys currently grow up without their biological father, thanks to high divorce rates and significant levels of single motherhood.

Of course, some of this thinking is not new. John Stuart Mill, writing at the start of our industrial age, was concerned that development — with its speed, stress and shorter attention spans — would cause "moral effeminacy", while a short while later figures like Robert Baden-Powell and Pierre de Coubertin were so worried about the "male malaise" that they invented the scouting movement (due for a revival in popularity, I predict) and reinvented the Olympics as cures.

Here comes the taxman

They used to say that nothing in life is certain except death and taxes. In the future there may be a question mark over death but taxes will remain, although their form may change.

In 1994 Estonia became the first country in the world to adopt what is now known as a flat-tax system, essentially one rate of tax: in Estonia's case 26% for all individuals and companies. There is no schedule of rates and there are no exceptions. The idea proved so successful that a number of other countries have introduced it.

Critics who initially said such a system would be unworkable have now moved on to argue that it is unfair because it is not progressive (that is, everyone pays the same). However, while the amount is fixed, there's nothing stopping a government applying a threshold (exception amount).

The advantage of a flat-tax regime is its simplicity. In the US the cost of running and regulating the current tax system is estimated at between 10 and 20% of total revenue received. That's a sum equivalent to something in the region of 25 to 50% of the country's budget deficit. Thus I'd predict that more and more countries will eventually move to a flat-tax system and ultimately a single rate will apply across the entire world.

Until then we will see a continued shift toward indirect and "stealth" taxes. These may include tax cuts for people who move to unpopular or depopulating regions, low-tax or no-tax incomes for people working in certain industries or professions (teaching and aged care, for example) and conscientious-objection taxes for people who don't want their tax dollars spent on defense or other ethically challenged investments. Zero tax for government employees may sound like "jobs for the boys" but it does make a certain amount of sense. What is the point of a government (generally the largest employer in most countries) paying its employees and then going on to waste administrative time and effort collecting taxes from the very same people? Wouldn't it be simpler just to offer lower, tax-free salaries in the first place?

The sins of the father

A final swing factor is crime. In the US, the Justice Department is funding research to identify and track the leading indicators of lawlessness in order to build a crime-forecasting model. The idea is that if supermarkets can predict sales by the month, or time of day or based on the weather, the police ought to be able to do something similar. Some crime forecasters already believe, for example, that temperature influences criminal behavior. If this is true then in the future crime waves will be anticipated, although there would still remain the problem of knowing who to look for and where to go.

The question of "who" may be solved in the future by compulsory DNA tests (although a more low-tech methodology might be simply to observe or track the children of well-known criminals on the basis that history, criminally speaking, tends to repeat itself through the generations). This is controversial stuff, even suggesting that the sins of the father trickle down due to environmental factors, so imagine the implications if someone eventually proves a genetic component to criminal behavior.

The British government is already creating a national children's database, which will contain the name, address, gender and date of birth of every child in the country up to the age of 18. It is not too much of a leap to imagine that eventually every child in the nation (currently 11 million) will be tagged to record their precise location and their interaction with known offenders — who would also be tagged. And if you think that is too far-fetched, consider the following.

If you are charged with a criminal offense in the UK, a sample of your DNA is taken and added to a national DNA database where it stays indefinitely, even if you are subsequently acquitted. So far the UK database contains the profiles of 4.5 million people, or 7.5% of the entire population. In contrast, the US DNA database incorporates just 0.99% of the country's population, while most other national databases hold the names of fewer than 100,000 people. The technology allows police to create a DNA fingerprint using a single human cell (taken from a print on a broken window, for example). In the future, police officers will carry handheld devices that can instantly upload these samples and test them against the database. They will then be used to create 3D photofits of suspects, giving police officers accurate information on likely height, skin color, hair color and even personality type.

Privacy campaigners are obviously concerned about this, but the technology will be so useful that I'd expect the database to be enlarged as part of a national biometric identity-card scheme. Eventually, every single person in the country will therefore be listed "for their own security", at which point adding some kind of GPS or other location-tagging component would seem an entirely logical idea. The problem with this is that once a government starts to view all its citizens as potential suspects, there will be subtle changes to how everything from policing to law making operates. There are issues here around data accuracy and security.

This discussion of course assumes that in the future people will commit crimes in person. In the UK the number of domestic burglaries has fallen by 45% over the last decade, while identity theft and internet scams are now almost as worrying to people as car theft and muggings. It must only be a matter of time before an underworld avatar successfully commits a crime against a law-abiding avatar walking the street in some virtual world or other.

Globalization is also a factor, in the sense that some products are now so cheap that it makes little sense to steal them. As a result, the new items of choice for burglars are cash (a perennial favorite), checkbooks, laptops and cellphones. The other reason for this shift has to do with drug trends. There is a correlation between the types of drugs someone takes and the kinds of crimes they commit. The drugs of choice are now crack and powder cocaine, the users of which tend to be addicted to street crime since it takes less skill and planning than domestic burglary.

So what else will we witness in the future when it comes to crime? First of all there will be a rise in organized cybercrime, including cyberterrorism. The former will target hapless individuals, whereas the latter will increasingly focus on companies and critical infrastructure. In Washington, DC there is already something called Cyberspace Command (really!) to guard against precisely such infrastructure attacks. Meanwhile, according to some sources, China has been investigating US networks and has invested heavily in computer-based countermeasures in case someone attacks its own infrastructure. As always, the future is embedded in the present and Estonia has already had to deal with a cyberattack, which was variously blamed on the Russians and tech-savvy "hacktivists".

We will also see more and more failed states in the future, especially within Africa, the Middle East and Asia, which will become a major threat to civil order. In Sao Paulo, Brazil, for example, police recently stopped removing the *favelas* (street gangs) to concentrate on geographical containment of the problem. The city's rich have literally risen above all this by using helicopters to bypass no-go areas (there are now 240 helicopter landing pads in Sao Paulo, compared to just ten in New York).

Other cities with the potential to become "feral" include Johannesburg, Mexico City and Karachi, although much will depend on the success or otherwise of national and global economies. In short, if the economy is booming most places will remain relatively safe and secure; but if the economy crashes all hell could break loose, especially in areas where the very rich live in close proximity to the very poor (London, New York, Los Angeles and so on).

The doomsday scenario here, obviously, is criminal gangs aligning themselves with terrorist groups, resulting in the military replacing the police. This could ultimately lead to entire cities being walled off, much in the same way that Manhattan was fenced off in the film *Escape from New York*. While that possibility is very remote, private guards already outnumber the police by three to one in the US so to some extent it is already happening — rich individuals and households are isolating themselves from the outside world. In London there are even streets that have hired permanent private guards following street attacks.

Personality politics

The final aspect of politics to mention is voting. According to US political consultant Morris Reid, more people over the age of 18 voted on the TV program *American Idol* than in the US election the same year. In the UK, 50% of Britons are unsure whether they'll vote at the next general election, but the Royal Society for the Protection of Birds has more members than all three major political parties combined. As a result, politicians are now regularly elected by less than a majority of voters (Tony Blair was chosen by a mere 25% of the UK electorate back in 2001) and most people would probably vote for Bart Simpson if they had a chance. In other words, personalities are generally more important than policies.

The issue of voter apathy is a very real concern and is entirely the fault of opportunist politicians who believe that politics doesn't need big ideas and that politicians can be economical with the truth. To them, success is simply a matter of conducting research to find out what the majority of people want and then making them believe that you want the same. It's a bit like Kylie Minogue, really. She is successful because she doesn't stand for or say anything. She is therefore acceptable to vast swathes of any given population. This is not an attack on Kylie *per se*, it's simply that we don't want our personalities (or politicians) to have much of a persona because this polarizes opinion. Hence the less you say the more you sell.

It's also our own fault. The average voter is almost fully disengaged from the national agenda. They are up to their eyes in debt and are fully absorbed by their own material circumstances. They are selfish, self-absorbed and greedy, and will vote for any character who appears optimistic or nationalistic or both. And if your face is famous, so much the better. Clearly what's needed here is a commonsense revolution.

Historically politics has been about promising future riches. In contrast, recent studies suggest that it is not your personal level of income that matters but your income relative to other people you know and, even more critically, your level of income instability. In other words, while people still crave what they don't have, it's the fear of loss that ultimately influences elections.

Twenty-five years ago things were very different. There were two opposing worldviews (market capitalism versus state socialism) and this tended to reinforce class divisions and angst, certainly in the UK and Europe. As a result, people were engaged with a battle of ideas. Nowadays there is an increasingly convergent worldview; or at least there is in the West.

Am I optimistic about the future? Ultimately, yes. Nuclear war — involving the use of tactical nuclear weapons in a regional conflict, or a terrorist attack on a major city using a dirty bomb — is a serious possibility but still a remote threat.

Globally, serious poverty and inequality are starting to be addressed and while there is a growing polarization between the very wealthy and the very poor, most people are becoming better off. The ultimate question to my mind is therefore whether we will continue with a participatory and centrist system based on the individual and free markets, or whether we'll shift to a new idea, perhaps one based on the supremacy of the collective group where "freedom" is no longer simplistically defined as the right to choose. The other important issues are perhaps how and when the free market should be reined in for the public good, and to draw the line between the activities of government and the freedoms of the individual.

Events, as they say, will determine what happens next, although I'd venture to suggest that our newly found connectivity will also have a profound impact on how politics and political decision making operate in the future.

24 March 2047

Dear Sven

I've just come back from visiting a friend in a nursing home who has been complaining that some of the other elderly residents have been playing Pink Floyd and the Sex Pistols too loud again. Myself, I've just been on a walking trip in the Antarctic. The trees are lovely down there at this time of year.

Awful news about the floods in the Mekong delta though. The floods in the Yangtze delta were bad this time last year but this seems far worse. This is really going to increase tensions between Asia and the West and I doubt whether the US president will be re-elected, given the power of the Chinese and Vietnamese voting blocs. On the other hand, the US has invested a lot of money in biofuel refining in both of these regions, so the local warlords might act to restrain voter anger.

All I can say is that I'm glad I live in Paris. The city has taken on a fresh lease of life since the new French Queen took up residence in the city and everyone is so happy now that the European experiment is finally over. Mind you, they're still really upset about Hungary and the bomb.

Anyway, I must fly. Got to do my compulsory duty and vote on this week's referenda. Can you believe it? They want me to say whether we should bring back compulsory national service for urban D-graders and whether future voting should be weighted in favor of those with a 90%+ score in politics.

Best

Novac

5 trends that will transform media

Time-starved In the future, thanks to the acceleration of technology, we will be busier and have less spare time. We will also be stressed and sleep deprived, so if you want to connect with an audience you'd better make your offering quick and easy. This will lead to an increased demand for snack-sized formats and content available in a variety of sizes or lengths. Equally, the old model of edit first and publish second will be reversed, with content being published first and edited second (filtered by the audience). Long copy and rigorous analysis will become a specialist demand available on a pay-per-view basis, with journalists being compensated the same way. Conversely, people will seek out quality content (judged, increasingly, by external links) regardless of format, length or even language. All of this will also create a high demand for quality search, editing and "sifting" of information and entertainment.

Shifting Users will shift media to suit their particular requirements. For example, video on demand (or mobile video) will alter the way people watch television, much in the same way that podcasting has already changed the way people listen to radio. Both put the audience squarely in charge of programming. In the future, people will watch, read and listen to what they want, when they want, on any device they want, and content will be designed, edited and personalized for specific physical locations and situations.

Infinite content The supply of content will become effectively infinite. Media will continue to be created and distributed by traditional media companies, but also telcos, internet search firms and device manufacturers. Everything from walls and tabletops to cereal packets and soft drink cans will be transformed into screens and interactive media content. Meanwhile, the plummeting cost of content creation and distribution will tap into a new generation of talented (and talent-less) writers, commentators, photographers and filmmakers, while it will be increasingly challenging to attract an audience's attention and to build brand loyalty against this infinite noise. Consequences? A flight to quality, especially hard-copy media and physical experiences. Scarcity creates value in a million-channel universe.

User-generated content Is user-generated content the shape of things to come, or is it just that certain members of Generation Y have too much time and computing power on their hands? UGC will transform the entertainment industry, particularly gaming and other areas that tap into or rely on social networks. The Web 2.0 trend of cooperation and aggregation will also continue to affect the production of media content, although co-creation will largely be limited to local news and lifestyle and entertainment "news". Hard news, in contrast, will remain the domain of highly resourced professional media organizations, although amateur users will filter and sift content and occasionally rival their influence. Conversely, we will also see the emergence of technology refuseniks. In most cases these will be older people unplugging as a way of dealing with digital privacy concerns or escaping from information overload. However, some younger people will also move offline, because the peer pressure to be always online or to collect digital friends will create a form of Facebook fatigue or MySpace malaise.

Personalization and physicalization You will have paid under £25 (US$50) for this book. If you asked me to show up and read parts of it to you in person, I'd charge you several hundred times that amount. If you wanted me to personalize what I say, you'd be talking significantly more. On the other hand, if this book were online it would be free. In fact part of it is. So what's going on here? What are people paying for? The answer is scarcity. If the cost of creating and distributing digital content becomes practically zero, content will be ubiquitous and largely valueless as a result. Personalization and particularly physicalization (e.g. live events and experiences) will, on the other hand, be highly sought after. We will watch movies at home but we will pay more to experience them with other people in a cinema. Add to this a general flight to quality and media such as the best newspapers, magazines, television and radio could do very well in the future.

Chapter 4

Media and Entertainment: have it your way

In the future, everyone will be world-famous for fifteen minutes.
—Andy Warhol

I'm sitting reading a newspaper while waiting for a bus, having just bought the paper and a cup of coffee from a local petrol station. Out of nowhere a rather scruffy-looking man aged about 60 approaches me. He mutters something and points to a small white table-tennis ball on the ground that has rolled underneath the wire fence behind us. I get up to hear what he's saying and notice that his right arm is wrapped in a sling. He says that the ball is his and asks if I could get it for him. My initial reaction is that my bag, which contains my notes for this book, is about to be stolen by an invisible accomplice while my attention is focused on retrieving the tiny white ball. However, it turns out that there is no invisible man and that all he really wants is his ball back — because he uses it to exercise the hand he injured in a recent fall. I give him the ball, together with a rather limp smile, and bury my head in the newspaper so as to avoid any further eye contact. As usual, there is practically nothing of interest in the paper and I mutter something to myself about one day producing my own.

When I was growing up in Britain in the 1960s we used to get a newspaper delivered at home. We also had a black-and-white television with only three channels. What's more, the channels all closed down around midnight and didn't start again until lunchtime. I have a feeling they even played the National Anthem at the end of each day's programming, although this could have been a dream brought on by overdosing on Sherbet Spaceships and fizzy Tizer. In other words, it was a case of "you get what you get and you don't get upset". My media diet was force-fed and I had no control or input over the one-size-fits-all, any-color-you-like-as-long-as-it's-black-and-white media.

If I mention my early media experiences to teenagers today, they think I'm some kind of digital dinosaur who has lost his memory. In the last 40 years we've witnessed the birth of multichannel TV, digital TV, 24-hour programming, VHS, DVD, cable TV, satellite TV, all-news channels, MTV, color newspapers, weather channels, TiVo, Sony Walkmans, iPods, BBC iPlayer and the emergence of video on demand, or what's been described as Martini media — "any time, any place, anywhere". To anyone under the age of 25, this multichannel digital universe is just normal.

I don't say this to whinge about being born too soon, just that a lot has happened in the last 50 years and there is no reason to suppose that the next 50 are going to be any different. Indeed, as a general guide to what's going to happen to media over the next 10, 20 or even 50 years, just look at what's happened over the same period in the past and then at least double it to allow for the effects of technological innovation and globalization.

Having said this, many of the fundamentals won't change. Despite what doom merchants are saying, there will still be mass media and storytelling. It's just that the mass media will be different media and the stories will be more personal. People will still want to find out what's going on in the world and they will still want access to entertainment to escape from that knowledge. Will algorithms replace newspaper editors? Possibly, but a much more likely scenario is a trend toward quality and physicalization, both of which will be a reaction to the almost infinite amount of digital drivel that will be produced by the likes of you and me.

In the future we will still be viewing movies in film theaters and watching television at home. We will also still be reading newspapers, magazines and books made from dead trees and we will still be surfing the internet. If we want to, that is. If we don't, we'll be able to do any of the above anyhow we like or switch off completely.

Your own little youniverse

In the future, it will be easier than ever to turn on, tune in and drop out, because while mainstream media channels and events will continue to exist, so too will a plethora of micromedia appealing to every conceivable interest, belief, prejudice and opinion. The top-down model, whereby media owners hold the attention of millions and then sell that attention to other people such as advertisers, is being replaced by companies and individuals who attract the fleeting attention of large, promiscuous audiences and by niche operators who capture the hearts and minds of very tiny audiences.

In other words, the media universe is becoming polarized between very large and very small players. Moreover, the content produced by these totally different types of media organization will also be at two extremes, with the larger companies clustering around proven formulae and the smaller operators pushing the boundaries with original ideas. Both will obviously aim to appeal to as large an audience as possible, but only one will be able to survive when the audience is tiny. Equally, anyone stupid or unlucky enough to get caught in the middle will be history.

Newspapers are a good example. In the future most newspapers will be free — we will only pay for functionality, personalization and physicalization. A ridiculous suggestion? Perhaps not.

Fifty years ago 80% of Americans read a daily newspaper. Today the figure is close to 50% — and falling. Globally it's much the same story. Between 1995 and 2003 worldwide newspaper circulation fell by 5%. In 1892 London had 14 evening papers; now it has just one (or three, depending on your definition of a newspaper). Also in the UK, a staggering 19% of all copies of newspapers delivered to retailers in the first quarter of 2006 came back as returns, and three national newspaper titles had return (non-sale) rates approaching 50%. If these trends continue, the last physical copy of a newspaper will probably roll off a press sometime in the year 2040. Or will it?

As someone once pointed out, if newspapers were invented tomorrow they would be greeted as a miraculous innovation. They are dirt cheap, paper-thin, easy to annotate and don't use batteries. You can read them in the bath, outside in the sun (especially if they are stapled so the pages don't blow away) and when you've finished they can be recycled or thrown away. Unfortunately, they also go out of date the second they are printed, cost a fortune to distribute and their user-generated content is limited to the letters page and some classified advertising. And therein lies the problem.

Despite fearless predictions of paperless offices and a leisure society, we are all working longer and harder. As a result we are time starved and the family breakfast (along with the home-delivered newspaper) is being replaced by fly-by toast while we watch up-to-the-minute cable television. Either that or it's a drive-by milkshake from McDonald's while listening to the car radio, or drinking a cup of Starbucks' finest while reading an online newspaper in the office. Indeed, there is a direct causal relationship between media use and the speeding up of breakfast, longer working hours and the decline of public transport.

People don't even trust newspapers these days. Only 59% of Americans believe what they read in the papers, compared to 80%

who did so in 1985. (Amazingly, 36% of US high school students also believe that the press should get government approval of news articles prior to publication, but that's another story.)

We are becoming digital nomads. We read, listen and watch what we want when we want. We no longer have the time (during the working week at least) to read newspapers, and we are shifting our eyes and ears to online information sources delivered via everything from cellphones to iPods. Almost 1.5 billion of the world's population is now online and according to Zenith Optimedia, so is 8% of the world's advertising.

Online news is especially useful because the content can be controlled and personalized. If you're of the active (or exhibitionist) persuasion you can comment on the news through your own blog or send a homemade documentary or corporate video to YouTube, which is currently the eleventh-largest country on Earth in terms of population. In short, what used to be a passive, one-way conversation is turning into an active relationship. Content flows both ways and consumption has time shifted and place shifted.

According to research by ComScore, Six Apart and Gawker Media, 50 million people visited blog sites in the US in the first quarter of 2005 — about 30% of all US internet users or one-sixth of the entire US population. By the time you read this there will probably be 100 million blogs. What's more, they aren't all reading about "social-lights" like Ms Hilton; many of the most popular sites are about politics (sorry, Paris).

With this self-publishing or "citizen journalist" trend in full swing, are newspapers old news? Not quite, as they are already using innovation to improve their products. Some of the best new ideas include compact formats for commuters (in the UK, *The Times* and the *Independent* were available in a choice of two sizes for a while), kids' newspapers (four daily newspapers from Play Bac Presse in France) and newspapers written entirely by readers. *OhMyNews* in South Korea is created by over 40,000 "citizen reporters" and is read by 2 million South Koreans, while in the US the *Wisconsin State Journal* (the state's second-biggest-selling paper) asks its readers to go online every day between 11 a.m. and 4 p.m. to vote for the next day's lead story. Consequences include sports stories appearing on the front page.

We are entering what some exuberant commentators are calling the new participation age, where the traditional boundaries between creator and consumer are becoming eroded or are disappearing altogether. It's still unclear at this early stage what a fully blown reader-produced newspaper would look like, but it's certain that the amateur genie is already out of the bottle. Whether this is good or bad news depends on your point of view. Some claim that this democratization of the media is the best thing that's happened since Gutenberg, whereas others see nothing but hyperactive half-wits writing on water. For example, citizen journalism gives no weight to expertise. Wikipedia.com — the 17th-most-visited site on the internet — is written by millions of anonymous amateurs. In contrast, Britannica.com — ranked around 5,000 — is written by over 4,000 named experts, including 100 Nobel Prize winners.

One of the biggest questions arising from this type of innovation is: who owns openly created content? The answer to this question will drive new business models and radically transform the relationship between media owners and their audiences. The other big question is: how do newspapers (and other media owners) create revenue from content when readers expect it to be either free or sold at very low cost? At the moment we're not sure.

A second significant innovation is the growth of free newspapers. Most papers create revenue by double-dipping. Readers pay to buy the newspaper and then have to pay again if they want to place a classified advertisement in it. The theory is that this advertising (along with display advertising) supports subscriptions and newsstand sales — but it won't for much longer. One of the largest and fastest-growing newspapers in the world is the free *Metro*, currently published in 69 editions in 21 countries and 18 languages.

Another version of this idea is *Loot*, which costs money to buy but offers free classified advertisements.

Other interesting developments in the media have included a magazine created by Nokia and MTV produced almost entirely by their customers, who send in content via text and picture messages. Moving even further into the digital future, sites like Craig's List are giving traditional media owners something to think about. Classified revenues from accommodation, cars and jobs are moving online, as is time-sensitive information such as stock prices and weather forecasts. *The New York Times* recently announced that it was cutting back its stock market price tables because so many readers were accessing the information online, while the *Washington Post* has announced that it has hired the creator of Chicagocrime.org to create "mashups" (websites or internet applications that combine content from more than one source) for the online edition of its paper.

So who will be delivering tomorrow's newspaper? The answer, apart from the usual suspects, is you and me. Newspapers will still be published by mainstream media companies, but brand owners such as Wal-Mart or Tesco could also produce their own titles. Companies such as Nike and Procter & Gamble are already creating their own content and this trend will continue as content becomes effectively infinite and everything from walls and tabletops to cereal packets and clothes turns into video screens and interactive information displays.

I, for one, don't believe that newspapers will die, any more than I think that people will stop reading books. Part of the reason for this is historical (once established, habits and customs can take more than a generation to die), but it's also psychological. Newspapers are a ritualistic purchase and loyalties can run deep. If you ask people in focus groups why they read a particular newspaper, some can't tell you. "Because I've always read it" is a typical answer. I once did some work with United News and Media in the UK and found that quite a few people read the *Daily Express* and the *Daily Mail* because their parents and grandparents did.

Whether such loyalty extends to Generation Y remains to be seen, although early indications are that it doesn't — but perhaps this has as much to do with a lack of relevant Gen Y content as it does with delivery formats and platforms. Time will tell.

Sticking my neck out, I'd even go as far as to suggest that there could be a newspaper renaissance around the corner. Many local titles are thriving because they are personalized. The news is local and so too is the advertising — which is something that people are making a song and dance about in new-media circles. For example, in the US Fox Network is customizing its television ads so that local neighborhoods can receive tailored commercials. Newspapers know their readers extremely well and most also understand what's going on in their local town or city. For this reason alone, there are at least a few decades of revenue left in the old newspaper business model; over-caffeinated young journalists shouldn't start writing their own obituaries just yet.

The other reason that newspapers could make a comeback in the future is the ubiquity of online media. There is now so much digital content that it's becoming almost valueless and invisible. By contrast physical media — especially newspapers, magazines and books that are written, edited and designed by professionals — cut through this clutter.

In other words, the big news story is that although how media are created and consumed is changing, we will not totally abandon our old ways. Media content such as news or entertainment used to be created by professional media organizations and then distributed to a supposedly grateful audience who consumed it how, where and when they were told to. The news was on at 6 p.m. and 9 p.m. and if you missed it that was just too bad. These days prime-time is all the time and anyone and everyone can create their own media. Viewers, listeners and readers can choose what they want to see and hear, and decide how and when they want to access it.

But while there is a symbiotic relationship developing between mainstream media companies (for example newspapers, radio and television networks) and social media (for example bloggers, pod-casters, vloggers and online social networks), the relationship is unequal; so-called free content is rarely free. Indeed, much social media content that is not worthless is often stolen from a main-stream media company, which paid to produce it in the first place. Hence the real cost of citizen journalism could be the death of the very sources on which it depends. Who then will hold governments and corporations to account?

Famous for fifteen minutes

If the cost of creating and distributing digital media content is now very low, in the future it will be practically zero. This means that anyone with an idea (and, hopefully, a rudimentary grasp of spelling) can become a one-person pundit on any topic that inter-ests him or her. Of course, the trouble is that this is precisely what's happening. Most of this new-media content appeals to an audience of just one — the person who created it. For example, 99% of the blogosphere is composed of the illiterate rantings of wannabe Victoria Beckhams. Equally, the majority of content on sites such as MySpace and Facebook is produced by teenagers proving to them-selves and others that they exist. I'm sure video clips about how to eat a Jaffa Cake are of interest to somebody, but mostly the content is just exhibitionism that appeals to its maker and a handful of voyeurs or stoned college students with an interest in post-modernist irony.

YouTube and the current media revolution are significant, but in my view they are no more significant than the development of newspapers in the 1800s or the commercialization of television in the 1950s. Indeed, there are significant parallels.

It's the same story with a trend called life-caching. This is a fancy way of describing insecure kleptomaniacs who hoard things and won't throw them away. Examples of life-caching include websites where you can upload every detail of your daily existence: text messages, emails, voice messages, photographs, video clips and so on. This used to be called scrapbooking but, as you'd expect, it's gone high-tech. Why do people do this? Again, I think it's a cry from the subconscious saying "I was here". But perhaps this is not as silly as it sounds, given that people are genuinely worried about things such as terrorism and whether they'll live long enough to show their holiday photos to their friends in person.

There is an ironic twist here. When we do want to get rid of these digital files we often find we can't because they've been spread virally around various networks. Conversely, the stuff we do want to keep for ever gets lost because the technology to read the digital files goes out of production. Will we have a digital afterlife and digital funerals in the future? Probably.

Nevertheless, buried beneath this mountain of garbage is the occasional diamond. Some of the leading blogs have regular readerships that would put a national newspaper to shame; and if it's specialization that you're after, online conversations could be for you.

The Daily Me (or Me Media) has been talked about for years as a way of personalizing media content and the internet is finally making this a reality. So if all you want to read about is English football or Arab politics, you can do that. Anywhere. And it's not just print media or online discussion groups that can deliver this. One of the big trends on television is the fragmentation of digital channels to the point where, pretty soon, there will be a channel for everything. Is this a good thing? On the face of it, it would appear so. After all, under the previous command-and-control regime, user feedback and dialogue were almost non-existent. It was a one-way street, where audiences were consumers not creators. But ordinary individuals are now participants and they can contribute democratically and directly to the sourcing, analysis and ranking of stories. Nevertheless, having hundreds of channels doesn't necessarily mean that there's anything worth watching.

In the future we will see more and more people collaboratively creating and filtering content, although we shouldn't get carried away with the idea. The fact is that despite this technological and participatory utopia, most of us are lazy or tired or both. Putting aside young voyeurs and exhibitionists, most people have neither the time nor the skill to create anything even remotely worth reading or watching. Hence demand for quality content will increase, not decrease, in the future.

Moreover, we should guard against this participatory trend being taken too far, because originality has always gone against the grain of conventional thinking. Professional media and expert opinion have an important role to play and we would be extremely foolish to allow a benign regime of experts to be replaced by a dictatorship of fools.

I never tried it because I know I wouldn't like it

If the future of media is that it's all about you, the downside of such personalization is that if media is "narrowcasted" (created, filtered or targeted by or to small groups), this will have the effect of reinforcing existing prejudices. In other words, people won't get both sides of the story. This is bad news for individuals because we will learn more and more about less and less. Empathy and understanding won't be big in the future. Fewer and fewer of us will be able to see the broader picture. It's also bad for society, because media conglomerates will continually race toward the moral low ground in an attempt to reach what's left of the mass market.

Rupert Murdoch is exactly right when he says that media will become like food that we snack on, although I think that the correct analogy is junk food. Media will become so ubiquitous and so sliced and diced to capture our limited attention spans that it will be of almost no value beyond comfort eating to relieve boredom.

The ubiquity of media is a real challenge for media companies because the excess supply of digital content will put pressure on prices, in the sense that we will treat digital content as either a low-cost or no-cost product. This is a very real problem for businesses such as newspapers that invest heavily in journalists, editors and photographers, only to see their products copied and repackaged and given away for free by bloggers. One solution is to restrict supply, which is already happening in the sense that ownership of some of the key media properties is converging in the hands of a few very powerful organizations, but it is also simultaneously fragmenting in that there are more channels, so restricting access is almost impossible, at least online.

What's next at the movies?

Cinema is another good example of the fundamentals not changing. Back in the early 1980s, prophets of doom were predicting the death of cinema due to a new-fangled invention called the video recorder. This was an early example of time-shifting, in that the audience was now supposedly in control of what they watched and when they watched it. However, it didn't turn out quite like that. Sure, people recorded their favorite television shows and rented movies to watch at their convenience, but instead of replacing cinema the VCR enhanced it.

As life speeds up, people want to relax more. Crucially, as more and more of us start to work for ourselves or live alone, we will want more physical interaction with other people. While it's convenient and time efficient to rent a movie and watch it at home, it's not as much fun as going out to a cinema and talking to your friends about the experience afterwards. Live shows (one form of physicalization) will therefore become more popular than ever. We will even be able to buy social-network cinema tickets that tell us whether or not our friends are watching the same movie, or that introduce us to people with similar interests. Of course, we will also be able to watch feature-length movies on our phone; but most people won't, for the same reason that most don't cook their dinner in a washing machine.

What will change in movies is this: cinema audiences have been falling for more than 50 years. In 1946, 4.067 billion movie tickets were sold. By 2005, this figure had fallen to 1.4 billion. The primary reason was the emergence of new distribution formats such as the VHS and DVD. More recently, the emergence of alternative forms of entertainment has eaten into movie attendances too. One estimate suggests that the computer-gaming industry is now larger than Hollywood in revenue terms, while profits are being decimated as retailers such as supermarkets aggressively cut the price of DVDs. Hollywood is in trouble for other reasons too. India's Bollywood will produce around 800 films in 2008, compared with approximately 600 from Hollywood.

Moreover, production costs have skyrocketed. The average US movie now costs close to US$100 million to make and the window of opportunity for marketing and distributing it is limited to one or two critical holiday periods each year. The vice-president of a major film studio once told me that even the old idea of an opening weekend has now shifted to a matter of minutes. If an audience doesn't like the opening, they are immediately on their phones sending text messages to their friends: "Don't bother." Add to this stars' increasingly unrealistic wage demands and it's clear that Hollywood itself is looking more like a disaster movie with every year that passes. However, while things are going to get worse for a while, there is ultimately a light at the end of the projector, although maybe not one the big studios will welcome.

Digital projection will save the movie industry an estimated US$1 billion simply by removing the need to make and send physical prints of films to the theaters. But at the same time the co-creation and amateur production trend is hitting movie production, just as it's hitting television and other forms of media.

For example, young, tech-savvy computer gamers are creating machinimas, animated films made using off-the-shelf game software like The Movies from Lionhead.com. Add to this trend the availability of zero-cost distribution networks such as YouTube (or MySpace for amateur musicians) and you can see how low-cost movies could rewrite the book for Hollywood. Don't get me wrong: I'm not suggesting that blockbuster movies with expensive special effects and famous actors are history. It's just that, like everything else, the industry will polarize between the very big and the very small. The dilemma for the larger players will be how to recoup their multimillion-dollar investments when the movie is pirated or copied the day after its release.

Perhaps the answer is not just producing movies but creating ideas or properties that start in film and are then extended into other areas such as books, magazines, music, toys, games, theme parks and even food. Hollywood knows this, of course, but it needs to think about the implications more seriously. For example, it's not totally inconceivable that a film could be sold as a download for 99 cents — or given away completely free — to sell something else that cannot be copied. A good example of this is the BBC television series *Walking with Dinosaurs*. First, it illustrated the convergence between entertainment and education ("edutainment"). Second, the broadcast series became a DVD, which became a live show, which became a soundtrack and a book.

A new page for books?

The book hasn't changed much in 500 years, so will it be immune to technological innovation? The private library is largely a thing of the past and book retailing has undergone a revolution, but surely we won't be curling up in bed with a handheld device anytime soon. In fact we might, but that's another kind of device altogether.

The book-publishing industry is about to undergo a seismic shock. Books will still exist as we know them now, but in the future there will be a whole host of new alternatives in terms of what we read and how we read it. The revolution is already underway. For example, fewer and fewer people are reading fiction. What we are reading instead is non-fiction: primarily, other media content dressed up to look like a book. We have lifestyle magazines masquerading as books, television shows impersonating books and even movies playing the role of books. There is some good news as well. Popular science, current affairs and history are all becoming more widely read as some readers (not many, it must be said) struggle to understand the modern world and where we may all be heading.

However, it's not the content of books as such that will change most fundamentally but the way in which books are produced and distributed. The creation of a book already does not have to include an agent or a publisher. Authors can self-publish using software and online services such as Blurb. Blurb is in some ways like a PowerPoint template in that it offers writers a set list of layouts and typefaces, but at least the end result looks like a real book. Once you've added your pictures (cheap as chips these days) you simply send the completed document off to Blurb's contract publisher and hey presto, you're in print. What's really extraordinary is that if you just want a copy or two to send to your mum and dad you can do this, for about US$30 a copy.

There's clearly a pattern emerging here: the democratization of media. Whatever you want you can get it; and if you want to do it yourself, you can do that too. The downside is that this is yet another example of the explosion of media content. In 2004 1.2 million books were published in the US, but a mere 2% sold more than 5,000 copies. Traditionally this would have meant certain death for the other 98% of titles; thanks to technology and companies such as Amazon.com, this is no longer the case. Some 60% of Amazon's book sales now come from titles outside its top 120,000 titles. Allegedly.

So if you self-publish a book on vintage needlework from Kurdistan, there's sure to be a niche market somewhere for it and either you will find it or it will find you. At the moment this probably means listing with Amazon or Barnesandnoble.com, but in the future you'll be able to use an automated publishing machine (like an ATM but with a P). Via one of these vending machines you'll be able to search for any book ever written (including those that are out of print) and it will be designed and printed in front of your eyes (you choose your own cover design, typeface, font size and paper weight). Alternatively, you could simply download the soft-copy version onto your e-book reader or iPod.

You'll also be able to buy e-books in 99-cent installments, much in the way that Dickens produced serialized novels in the nineteenth century. Again, there could be a downside to this in that publishers are already being tempted to sell smaller, easier-to-read (dumbed-down) versions of classic texts. But is that really a problem if the original versions are still available?

The idea of downloading books onto a computer or handheld device has been around for ages and a handful of people regularly read books and comics this way. However, it has never really spread to the mainstream, largely because of the difficulties associated with reading large amounts of text on a relatively small screen.

In Japan this is changing fast as more and more young people are downloading e-books onto 3G phones. Not surprisingly, the most popular downloads are manga comic books, the animation "cell" format of which fits well with cellphone screens. Serialized fiction is proving popular, too. As you'd expect most readers are aged under 30, but women make up a surprisingly large segment of users (as much as 70% according to some reports). Pricing is generally bundled up into a monthly membership fee that allows users to download books from a digital library.

Will e-books take off elsewhere in the world? Companies such as Sony, Philips and Amazon clearly think so and have launched products that aim to mimic the look and feel of "real" books. The technology these devices use is E Ink, which mimics actual ink by using a series of tiny pixels. Interestingly, the technology does not need any power to display the type unless the "page" is turned, so up to 20 books can be read before the reader needs recharging. I'd expect Apple to launch something similar, not least because the iTunes music-store model could easily be adapted to e-books rather than the current audiobooks.

Prediction marketing

Given how much the advertising industry goes on about creativity and strategy, it's ironic that the big agencies have been so slow to embrace the brave new world of digital media. Perhaps this is because many prefer to kid themselves that they are in the movie business, or maybe many are still in denial about losing the strategic high ground to management consultancies.

Advertising has already started to shift away from traditional media such as television and newspapers to online and this migration will substantially increase. This is not to say that lavish 60-second commercials and full-page newspaper ads will disappear entirely, but most of the expenditure will eventually move online, where it will be significantly targeted and customized. It will also be highly accountable.

Thanks to the internet, everything can be tracked and the return on investment can be calculated precisely. Does this mean the end of brand advertising? Probably.

In the future advertising will become more short term and promotionally focused, while image will be created elsewhere, for example by the design of product and service experiences. However, even here there is a link between what goes on online and what happens in store or in the product-development department, because behavior and opinions can be tracked so easily.

As with other forms of media, customers will want to control advertising. This may mean filtering what they are exposed to. They may to turn it off entirely (70% of people in the US say that they like the idea of technologies that block advertising and almost 30% say they would accept a decline in their standard of living to live in an ad-free world). Conversely, I'm sure that other people would be willing to pay to have advertising target them personally. Both will be true and we'll probably see brands sponsoring ad-free spaces too, if that's not a complete contradiction.

People will also shift the timing and location of messages to suit themselves rather than the advertiser. Hence search marketing will continue to grow, but so too will location-based marketing, once the technology catches up with the concept. Implicit in location-based marketing is localization — so global ads will be tailored to local contexts and customs — but it also means reaching people at the "moment of truth" when they are alongside whatever it is you would like them to buy. So ads for soft drinks will "magically" appear on your cellphone as you walk past a vending machine on a hot day. Localization will also involve placing "real" car ads inside virtual street-racing games when your virtual car is off the road, or triggering a short animation on a washing-powder pack when you pass by the packs in the supermarket and they recognize you as a lapsed user. Call this "now marketing" or prediction marketing if you like.

However, it would be a mistake to assume that the internet will take over from old media entirely. The internet is primarily a place where people go to find information or entertainment, or other like-minded individuals. This means that advertising will be repackaged to look like information or entertainment and it will be used to facilitate conversations between the people who know about things (such as brands) and the people who don't. Therefore user reviews and rankings will become increasingly important.

Whisper who dares

But can the internet ever completely take over from the more traditional forms of media? Ads in magazines still have a future, because people are in a different headspace when they read a magazine and there is an opportunity to seduce them with photography that will never look the same on the web. Newspapers are often similarly superior in design and usability. Equally, radio ads won't disappear because radio, unlike the web, is truly mobile in that it can be consumed while you are doing other things. Given that attention will be in such short supply in the future, radio should therefore do very well. Radio also has a unique quality in that it holds something back. Television, and to an increasing extent the internet, are a full-frontal assault on the senses. They both shout at you. Radio whispers. To listen to radio you need to turn your imagination up.

But television will not disappear. It is undoubtedly true that it is suffering from a plethora of new competition, ranging from computer games to people just not being home as much as they used to. In 1995 there were 225 shows across British television that delivered audiences of more than 15 million. By 2005 there were none. But you can't blame everything on everyone else. You can't even argue persuasively that attention spans are so short that nobody will watch a one-hour television show or a two-hour movie. Sure, people won't watch an hour of rubbish — so if you want them to watch rubbish, you'd better make it short.

When a show is good people will watch television in their tens and hundreds of millions. The problem therefore is the lack of quality content. Make it and they will come.

Speed isn't everything

Media organizations have become obsessed with speed. This is partially to do with funding — there isn't any, so their aim is to get the raw news footage straight onto the screen as soon as possible without worrying about any analysis. This works, up to a point (it provides a certain level of realism), but accuracy and commentary are born of tireless fact checking, investigation and reflection — all of which cost money. This doesn't matter to some people. Indeed, there is anecdotal evidence to suggest that younger generations actually prefer speed to accuracy. But truth itself does matter. After all, journalism is founded on asking questions, not on reprinting press releases; there's not enough of the former and too much of the latter.

What are media companies for? What business are media companies in and what services do they provide? These are some of the critical questions that anyone involved with the media must ask themselves; and I can promise you that some of the answers they give today will not be those they will offer in the future.

One solution to monetizing digital content is to think about what people will pay for. The answer to this question is still far from clear, but it's likely that it will include time, space and the truth. What do I mean by this? Simply that if people are busy and stressed out, offering them even speedier products, even if they ultimately save time, will just make matters worse. What we will want are products that help us relax and find and interact with other people, including our friends and family.

This means that high-touch, not high-tech, will become increasingly important, so the opportunity for media companies is to become the starting point for journeys of exploration and self-discovery. A mundane example of this is Disney, which started off as a movie company but now embraces theme parks, hotels, cruise ships, publishing and even food.

If you are a trusted media company there is no reason why strands and brands cannot be extended and leveraged into other related fields ranging from television, movies, newspapers, magazines and books to cafés, holidays, cameras and cars. What would a car from Walt Disney look like? I've no idea, but it would be interesting.

Equally, how about a newspaper from the BBC, a digicam from CNN or greetings cards from the *New Yorker* magazine? That last one has already been done, but I'm sure you get my drift.

Let's get a little more specific. I read *The New York Times* every day, but I've never paid for it because I read it online. I'm also interested in the Middle East and I trust *The New York Times* to give me a fairly clear idea of what's going on. So what could the company sell me? Well for starters, how about a magazine containing its best coverage on the Middle East? Or a *New York Times* branded book? I'd also attend any talks it organized and might even go on holiday with the company if one of its Middle East correspondents was going along too, or it had special access to people or places.

One of the best descriptions of media companies is that they attract and retain people's attention — ideally on an industrial scale — by using some form of technology. In the past this was relatively easy. These days, thanks to various social and technological shifts, it's not. However, we are only at the very beginning of the second millennium and the media as we know it is still wearing short pants. There is no doubt that the technological revolution ahead will affect the media harder and faster than many other industries, although many of the fundamentals will remain unchanged.

For example, most of the change that is happening already has to do with content delivery. It's about how and when people receive information. It's about formats and devices. Content, although now co-created, co-filtered and partially disengaged from traditional networks of distribution, hasn't changed that much.

In the future, media companies will still be in the business of attracting attention, but it will be more about quality than quantity. Audience numbers will matter less to advertisers than information about where they are and when they're there. Equally readers,

listeners and viewers will pay for quality information and entertainment that's personalized or physicalized. Media companies also
need to attract people's imagination — not only in the sense of
attracting talent, but also in capturing their audience's imagination
through the interplay of words and pictures. The role of the media
will continue to be to tell us stories.

10 March 2047

Dear Wendy

I've just been sitting at the bus stop reading the ten-minute newszine I downloaded from my local Amazonbucks store while buying a coffee. A rather suspicious man approached me, but my newszine recognized him as a regular reader and we joked about the fact that we've both selected the same story to appear on the front page this morning. The story was about the demise of *The Globe*, a recently launched e-paper that was supposed to be written by and for the planet. Unfortunately it was plagued with technical difficulties and attacked by a plethora of local e-papers created by non-profit citizen journalists. The final straw, apparently, was a lawsuit brought by a 16-year-old phone-cam paparazzo who claimed that the newspaper had stolen one of his pictures. Bored, I clicked on the button underneath the story about a new restaurant and booked a table. Amazing what this new e-paper can do. After arriving at my office, I downloaded some vintage episodes of M*A*S*H to watch on my EyeView contact lenses over the weekend and refreshed my newspaper with a five-minute copy of *The New York Times* (Democrat viewpoint version with Republican argument overlays).

Cheers

Nicholas

5 trends that will transform financial services

Mobile, pre-pay and contactless payment Convenience is a mega-trend that will transform banking and insurance just like every other industry. Plastic is convenient, but once digital cash gets moved into electronic devices things really will be truly different. Objects holding digital cash will include cellphones and cars, but there's no reason for the list not to include clothing and even the human body. The pre-pay and embedded-value trend will also extend to private currencies and barter schemes.

Intermediaries If recent history has taught us anything it is that despite the need for convenience, people like to buy products and services from specialists experienced in a particular sector or able to provide an independent overview of the hundreds if not thousands of products available. Hence independent brokers will play an increasingly strong role, as will global monolines that specialize in just one area of the financial services market. In other words, independence, impartiality, transparency and specialist expertise will be big in the future.

Debt A few people still believe that we have entered an indefinite economic boom and that, with the exception of a few regions and industries, major cycles of boom and bust have ended. I don't agree. Moreover, the downturns we have seen recently are mere blips. Eventually there will be a major recession (probably global, because every economy is now hyperlinked and interdependent). And when it does come, the severity and hardship will be almost unprecedented because of the amount of debt built up by individuals, corporations and even entire countries. When will this happen?

Impossible to say, but we should all be planning for it. Businesses that will do well in such a situation include local lenders and banks with physical branches that have not been overly reliant on wholesale money markets to fund growth. Customers will seek security and familiarity, ideally with a human face attached, because the complexity and lack of transparency of wholesale money markets have hidden the true nature of risk.

Regulation   Banks and especially credit-card companies do not generally discriminate about whom they lend to and individuals are not very smart about the amount of debt they take on board. When money is very cheap, this doesn't really matter. If interest rates go up, it does. As society becomes more risk averse and litigious, governments will seek to protect their citizens (and their own financial liabilities) by tightly regulating the entire industry. Equally, regulation surrounding "securitization" will tighten. Big banks and credit-card companies in particular will come under increasing scrutiny about their lending practices; there will be calls for salary and profit caps in some extreme instances. Smaller operators will be deluged by a sea of red tape, regulation and compliance requirements and will find it increasingly difficult to operate profitably. Large companies will similarly see their margins eroded, especially since they will have to support an increasing number of channels.

Foreign and non-bank competition   Until recently banks, insurance companies and other financial services institutions had it easy. Innovations within retail banking were more or less limited to longer opening hours, telephone banking and, very recently, online banking. Beyond this, the internet has had very little impact on traditional business models within financial services, but this will change in the future; brands such as PayPal, Zopa and Prosper are very much the shape of things to come. Also expect to see hypercompetition in the sense that every major global player will attempt to enter every developed market, whether the local players — and local governments and unions — like it or not. This will include banks and other financial services organizations from China, India, Russia and the Middle East. For example, there could be a flow of between US$50 billion and $100 billion as Arab investors switch investments from New York to London, according to Peter Weinberg (formerly of Goldman Sachs). Indeed, the liquidity of countries like China and the Gulf States will have a profound impact on the ownership of financial services companies (and others) globally. Equally, Islamic Sharia-based investment is now a US$500 billion global market. Given that the percentage of Muslims in the world's population is expected to grow from 19% in 2000 to 30% in 2025, I'd expect this sector of investment to grow too.

Chapter 5

Money and Financial Services: everyone is a bank

The trouble with the future is that it usually arrives before we're ready for it.
—Arnold Glasgow

J on Merriman is the CEO of an investment bank and is one of
50 people in the US with a radio frequency ID (RFID) tag
inserted in his arm. Mr Merriman's firm is an adviser to
VeriChip, a maker of ID implants for pets and RFID-enabled medical bracelets. If Mr Merriman ("Chip" to his friends?) is ever
involved in a serious accident, doctors are just a scan away from all
the necessary data. The chip contains everything from bank
account and social security records to medical information. I'm
quite tempted to follow suit myself.

According to the research company ACNielsen, by the year 2020
only 10% of financial transactions will be in cash. The rest will be
digital, a mixture of micro-payments, contactless payments, stored-
value cards and plastic. This will be good news for governments,
because about 25% of all cash in circulation worldwide is used for

illegal purposes, so any restriction on its availability will be beneficial. Cash is anonymous and difficult to trace; e-payments are not. Equally, a cashless society will appeal to business because it will speed up transactions, saving banks and other organizations a bundle of money. Indeed, the only people who will be against the idea of a cash-free society will be some ordinary, law-abiding citizens who rather like the look and feel of paper money — much in the same way that many people prefer real newspapers and books to their online equivalents.

This, in a nutshell, is the future of money. We will see the emergence of countless new payment options and there will be a battle between the old and the new, with many of the latter foisted on people without their consent. Some of us will fully embrace digital transactions through the use of various devices ranging from computers to cellphones. At the extreme, some people will insert chips into their jaw or forearm. These chips will be used to gain access to safe-deposit boxes, to make payments, or to prove that you are indeed who you say you are. For this group of tech-savvy extroverts and security-conscious paranoids, banks and national currencies will become increasingly irrelevant.

The other side of the coin will be the traditionalists. These people will be keen to hang on to physical money and will fight to retain control of currencies that are symbolic of national identity and pride — a battle then between the global and the local and between high tech and high touch; no cash prizes for guessing who will win in the longer term. By 2050 there is every possibility that we will have one global digital currency, whether we like it or not.

To get an idea of just how strong the rejection of a single global currency might be, you only have to look at Morgan Stanley in the UK, which offers a credit card decorated with your national flag of choice (English, Welsh, Scottish or Irish). And if you think that's taking tribalism too far, American Express has launched the "IN" card which is only available to people who live in Los Angeles, New

York or Chicago. The cards link rewards and offers to local products and services.

In the future, even this will be surpassed as banks offer cards with designs downloaded by the individual customer, tied to even more localized products and services. Not only that but, rather than link things together geographically, banks and credit-card companies will start to realize that each generation and demographic actually consists of a series of "tribes". These tribes have very similar interests and beliefs, so we will start to see financial products and services aimed at, for instance, the computer geek community, the music crowd, petrol heads and bookworms.

Hot money

As usual, the early signs of change are here already if you take the trouble to look around. Anecdotally, I know of people in the UK who are so tired of carrying around coins that they are starting to give or throw them away. This is clearly a signal of prosperity, but it's also one of convenience. The average person now carries two to three times as much weight in their pockets and bags as they did two decades ago, so targeted personal fitness programs will soon have to appear unless someone invents a lightweight alternative or micro-payments become more widely accepted.

Coins and banknotes could also disappear almost overnight for another reason. In all the recent talk about the consequences of a global pandemic, it appears to me that one important implication has been missed: banknotes and coins tend to be dirty, so people will refuse to handle them if they think they could be a conduit for disease. In Japan, some ATMs already heat banknotes as a precautionary hygiene measure; in an age of anxiety, "hot money" could be a very cool idea.

Traveling to other countries like South Korea you get another glimpse of the future of money. Here, hundreds of thousands of phones are already fitted with devices that can turn a cellphone into a wallet simply by flashing the handset at a "dongle" located at a cashpoint or till. Small transactions, such as buying a drink or a train ticket, are instantaneous, whereas larger transactions require a four-digit security code. Why is this happening in South Korea? Simple: the country has the highest use of broadband and the second-largest mobile data-services network in the world.

Back in Japan, the use of electronic money is also growing rapidly, with over 43,000 retailers installing systems to accept payment by cellphone and 40 million "wallet phones" already in circulation. This means that you can shop for everyday items with your phone or send money to family and friends via a text message. This makes a certain amount of sense, because a cellphone (along with keys and a wallet or purse) is an item that people tend to carry wherever they go, so using the one to make the other two semi-redundant is quite sensible.

Phones can be charged with up to US$500 and, because the money is not connected to either a phone bill or credit card, security concerns are neatly sidestepped. Interestingly, the number of coins issued in Japan (around 91 billion) fell for the first time recently and it's much the same story elsewhere. In the US, electronic payments (including credit and debit cards) surpassed check payments for the first time in history at the end of 2005, while in the UK some retailers have actually banned checks. There are certain road tunnels and parking meters in some countries that you can only use if you have a vehicle equipped with a contact-less payment device (sometimes known as an e-tag) or have a cellphone. Asia is without a doubt the epicenter of cellphone payments and mobile retail, but Africa and the Middle East aren't far behind. In Kenya, for instance, there's a mobile payment system called M-PESA that allows people (typically low-income manual workers) to send money home by phone or download digital cash that can then be converted into physical money at the neighborhood store. The local banks rarely get a look in.

The idea of electronic micro-payments has been touted as the next big thing for years. Until very recently, though, there was a big problem with very small payments: there was nothing worth buying. But Apple changed all that. iTunes has doubled the percentage of web transactions under US$5, and while micro-payments still represent only 2.8% of all e-commerce, the percentage is growing rapidly. Online micro-payments for digital content are currently worth between US$15 billion and $30 billion in the US, and it's predicted that this will increase to US$60 billion by 2015, partly due to the convergence of online and mobile channels.

Another indication of change is McDonald's. Until quite recently the company only accepted cash worldwide. Now it takes credit cards in the US and is testing ideas such as the MasterCard PayPass system in some of its restaurants. Such e-payment schemes use the same technology as e-tags and mean that customers not only buy things without getting out of their car, they don't even need to find their wallet. The obvious beneficiaries of drive-through payment include other fast-food joints, but the technology could also spawn a new generation of drive-up and drive-through retail outlets, including petrol stations, convenience stores and perhaps even banks.

None of these ideas would appear in the least bit futuristic to a 23-year-old computer gamer (Deathifier to his friends) who once spent £13,700 on a Treasure Island that didn't exist. The island in question did exist in a role-playing game called Project Enthropia and as a result Deathifier made a real-life killing by selling virtual plots of land on his virtual island to other gamers to build virtual homes. He's not alone, either. In 2005, Jon Jacobs (Neverdie to his friends) paid £57,000 for a virtual space station — presumably so that he could sell virtual tickets to virtual space travelers in the future. According to one estimate, the value of this virtual economy in real terms is about US$800 million and the market shows no sign of slowing down. Indeed, we'll probably see virtual bankers, virtual insurance agents and virtual financial planners within the next couple of decades.

The serious point here is that life is blurring between the real and the virtual, and financial services are no exception. People are already exchanging real money for virtual goods and vice versa, so why not invent new products and services for this market? Several US-based retailers (including a real bank) have opened virtual branches inside virtual games, so why not open a bank-run virtual currency-trading exchange where gamers can exchange their World of Witchcraft EU gold or Second Life Linden dollars for real gold or US dollars?

If that's a bit too weird for you, how about a real credit card that earns the virtual currency of your choice when you buy a pair of real jeans or an iPod? It could work the other way around too: a real card personalized with a picture of your avatar that earns points every time you spend real money on virtual goods (like virtual clothes or real estate for your avatar). Such loyalty cards and points schemes are good examples of private currencies and we will see more of these in the future as the cost of running such currencies falls. The makers of Entropia Universe are planning to issue 400,000 players with ATM cards so that they can view their virtual cash; this is surely a sign of the shape of things to come.

What about when artificial intelligence really kicks in and you can speak to a fully automated, highly intelligent machine about the best loan or insurance policy? Would you trust it? The question is similar to whether or not you would allow a robot to perform surgery on you or whether you would climb aboard a plane flown entirely by computer with no human presence whatsoever. In a sense it's an academic question because, as usual, it's already happening — it's just that you and I don't come into contact with these machines, and even if we do they have not yet reached the stage where they can interact on a true human-to-human level.

Machines are already picking stocks and calculating risk–reward characteristics of share portfolios. In fact, they are probably buying and selling shares (or whole companies) for your pension fund as you read this. In theory, using a machine to assess which of 2,000 home loans is the best for you is no different. Algorithmic financial advisers will have several advantages over their human predecessors. First, they can work on your behalf 24 hours a day, 7 days a week, 365 days a year, and they don't get tired. Moreover, they are dispassionate, cannot be distracted and, most important of all, they don't fall in love with the things they buy. Of course, this also means that they only have the ethics they've been programmed with, but the thought of a totally automated process is quite attractive.

Of course, there's a downside to this increased automation and digitization of cash and that's identity theft. According to Forrester Research, over 60% of online shoppers are "very" or "extremely" concerned about the theft of credit-card numbers during online activity. ID theft is now a US$56 billion problem in the US and its incidence rose by 600% in the UK between 2000 and 2005. Electronic information is rarely totally secure and is often linked, so that anyone who penetrates a network can steal everything.

Ironically, the solution to this is more technology. Early ideas include verbal signatures, body double accounts (temporary bank accounts with fake IDs designed to expire after a single use), biometric ATMs, and two-way identity verification where both parties ask the other to prove who they are before revealing sensitive information. The banks are also getting into the game: Citibank has set up Identitytheft911.com.

It won't all be high tech, nevertheless. Some of the innovations will consist simply of adding new channels so that, for instance, you'll be able to take out a loan to pay for an expensive meal in the restaurant itself. There are already newsagents selling home loans and we'll soon have vending machines retailing stocks and shares. I've also seen a credit union (MECU) that sets the loan rate to buy a car on the basis of the vehicle's environmental impact, while in Japan one bank links the amount of interest paid to the level of waste produced by an individual, business or community group. This last idea is extremely interesting, because in the future we will see the growth of alternatives to individual loans. This means more bartering and exchange, but it also means using social networking to link people together to take out community loans or to club together to buy large quantities of the same product at a group discount.

Making friends with money

The future of money will not be entirely digital. People are happy to make small payments or to apply and receive loans digitally, but they are less happy transferring large amounts or making digital investments. This is human nature. When ATMs were first introduced there was a widespread feeling that you would be mugged attempting to take your money out. Even today, only around 5–10% of people feel confident about depositing money into ATMs because they are worried their electronic transactions will be snooped on and that banks will sell this information to others or flood them with junk mail. Given that over half of Americans say that a company has compromised the security of their data, this is not entirely fantasy either. Somehow, physical banks and human beings are just more reassuring, which is one reason neither will entirely disappear in the future. Indeed, in the US the number of physical banks is actually growing, from 82,300 in 1992 to 94,500 in 2006. So much for digitization.

As I've said before, the more life becomes digitized, virtual and remote, the more some people will crave emotional intimacy and human interaction. In banking terms, there has always been a need for trust and one of the best ways of developing such trust is through a human relationship. This isn't something that people need every day. Most of the time cost and convenience are the key drivers, but this changes when the stakes are raised.

For example, many people prefer to deal face to face for a large amount of money going out of their account or over a decision with long-term implications (such as a mortgage or a pension). This may be generational, but I'd suggest that even the youngest customers will rush into their nearest bank branch the moment the economy turns sour and they're worried about losing their jobs and missing their mortgage repayments. In other words, in the future people will use a variety of channels to do their banking and will visit physical branches less often, but the value of branch visits and the intensity of human interaction will actually increase. As a result, banks will invest heavily in new sites and refurbishments and particularly in ways of making the banking experience faster, friendlier and more convenient.

People in physical branches also have a bright future for another reason: banks are expensive to establish and even harder to get right. So done well, they are one of the best barriers to preventing competitors from entering the market.

What are banks for, anyway?

So what will the bank of the future look like? The standard futurist reply would be to paint a picture of a high-tech playground. Either that or people would argue that banks in the historical sense will cease to exist as we all move online.

For example, Zopa is a virtual bank. Essentially it's a peer-to-peer money-lending site putting individuals with money to lend in touch with people who want to borrow it. The company receives a 1% fee from the borrower for facilitating the introduction and takes a cut of the repayment insurance on each loan. Lenders set their own rate depending on the risk level they are happy with and borrowers are given a credit (trust) rating based on an Equifax rating and, over time, past behavior through the site. Actual risks are minimized because the loans are aggregated across groups of at least 50 similar lenders and borrowers (a spread bet, if you like) and also because each loan is subject to normal debt-recovery processes.

Interest rates are set by the individuals themselves and can be changed instantly, so niches like ethical or local lending can be tapped with great precision.

Prosper is the US equivalent of Zopa and similarly seeks to remove retail banks from the business of lending or borrowing money. Borrowers bid for how much interest they'll pay, while lenders bid on how much they'll lend and how low an interest rate they'll accept for a specific credit profile. However, unlike Zopa, Prosper allows an individual to front an entire loan and places borrowers into groups, with the group leader being made responsible for verifying the authenticity of each member. This is a very interesting idea and is similar in some ways to the community aspects of Grameen Bank in India.

At the moment Zopa and Prosper are novelties, but their existence raises the question of whether banking services need to be provided by banks. Banks make money by using our money and the really clever ones even charge us for it. They do a lot more besides, of course, like offering wealth-management and financial-planning services, but there is no logical reason that all of these services cannot be done by specialists. Indeed, intermediaries and monolines (specialist companies focused on one area of financial services) are taking an increasingly large share of bank business. Perhaps not in the future.

Ten years ago, applying to a supermarket for a credit card or loan would have been unheard of. Now Tesco Personal Finance has 5 million customers. A key argument in favor of supermarkets becoming banks is that they have a very high number of (theoretically) loyal customers visiting each week and they represent value, quality and convenience (for example, more branches and longer opening hours than banks provide) — precisely what people are looking for in financial services. Supermarkets are not a direct threat to retail banks because customers still turn to banks for more complex and higher-value products like mortgages. Or at least that's the theory. So far supermarkets have been content with selling credit cards, car loans and pet insurance alongside the baked beans, but this might be changing. A case in point is Asda (now part of Wal-Mart), which is testing the sale of houses on its online noticeboard, while Tesco has recently introduced health insurance alongside its fresh fruit and vegetables.

So the big question is: will supermarkets start selling mortgages and pensions as well? The industry says no, but I'd predict yes. There is obviously an issue with supermarkets selling (or mis-selling) complex financial products, but perhaps they won't be so complicated after the supermarkets have got their hands on them. One thing that supermarkets are very good at is looking outwards at the needs of customers. Retail banks, in contrast, still tend to struggle with the idea that they are shops and their product offerings remain far too complicated for the average bank customer (or employee) to understand. Simplicity is an opportunity in financial services and I doubt whether most customers care very much about who provides it.

So if everyone from supermarkets to car companies is offering financial services, where does this leave banks? One answer could be as low-margin suppliers of white-labeled or unbranded products and services for other companies, which is clearly a fast road to low margins, commodification and oblivion. Another answer could be for banks to remodel themselves as "wealthcare" companies: specialist independent advisers that help people to safeguard and grow their wealth. Or perhaps there's an opportunity in the convergence of healthcare planning?

One reason the game may soon be up for the banks is that ordinary people are finally working out how they play the game. After all, why should banks be charging us when they are sitting on all of our money? Surely it should be the other way around? Moreover, why in the age of instant communications does it still take four days to clear a payment through a bank?

Bankers' salaries are also starting to be seen by many people — and governments — as a sign of an inefficient system, running contrary to everything we are told about free-market enterprise and competition. A scenario where all banks are seen as greedy is a real possibility, so governments may be forced to tighten regulation and open up competition even further in the future.

Why, for example, can't I live in one country and use a bank based in another? To some extent PayPal (with 150 million accounts the last time I looked) is doing this already, although it is simply acting in the area of transactional fulfillment. But why can't I have a credit card from PayPal or a checkbook from a Chinese bank if that provider is offering a better deal than my one down the road? Monolines are also a threat to the banks, but the killer blow may eventually come from outside the industry altogether. Most radical innovation does not come from industry incumbents, and banking and financial services will be no exception.

For example, I firmly believe that Wal-Mart, Apple, Microsoft, Google and Vodafone will all eventually hold banking licenses. How would that feel in terms of competition? Wal-Mart has been processing money orders since 2001 and has been cashing pay checks since 2004. The world's largest retailer (allegedly responsible for 1% of Chinese GDP) also houses local bank branches in many of its stores. In the UK Asda, a Wal-Mart subsidiary, even sells insurance alongside the carrots and spaghetti. Will Wal-Mart go the whole hog and open up its own full-service banks in stores or in stand-alone locations? If it does — which I believe will happen within the next decade or two — it will not be the first. Sears Roebuck tried the idea back in the 1980s, although the experiment ended in tears.

Part of the problem is moving outside a store's core competencies, but another reason is the need for trust. Supermarkets are trusted — up to a point — and many people are happy to buy holiday insurance or perhaps get a small loan from a retailer, but they somehow lack credibility and expertise when it comes to much larger financial matters. However, this is simply a temporary branding problem. Eventually you will undoubtedly be able to buy a 50-year mortgage alongside your 30-second noodles.

If supermarkets are competitors to banks due to convenience, scale and the sheer volume of customers who pass through their stores, companies like Apple are a threat for another reason: style. The iPod is a classic example of business-model innovation meeting stylish industrial design, so what if the company created a fashionable gadget that securely contained all of your financial records along with instant access to 10,000 or so financial products from around the world? The device could be used to make phone calls, but it could also contain digital cash, which would make your wallet — and the need to carry coins — redundant. It would come in a choice of 60 colors and finishes and you could even customize aspects of its functionality and appearance. Want one? I certainly do. Would I still use a bank if I had one? Unlikely, although if the device was a joint venture between Apple and, say, GE Money, I'd have the option of talking to a real banker or visiting one of their physical branches if I so desired.

All of the information contained on the device would automatically be backed up by the company in case of loss; and since it would be equipped with GPS technology, it would also be able to assess risk for insurance purposes in real time because it would know where I go, at what time and for how long. It would also be intelligent, so it would learn about what I buy and this information — along with the locational information — could be used to send me highly personalized information or promotions. For example, the device would know that I like old cars because I've used it to pay for a subscription to *Classic Cars* magazine, so if I was walking past an old-car showroom it could send me a video message of what was inside alongside loan rates for investment vehicles.

Would a bank launch such a device? Unlikely. But a telco, a tech firm or a start-up working with one of these could. Realistically such a device won't appeal to everyone, but even if it captured half of Generation Y that would probably be enough to give the banks a headache that could last for a long time.

Mutually assured financial destruction

What else can we expect to see in the future? The answer will be shaped by various product, service and process innovations, although critically it will also largely hinge on external events, most notably the health of the global economy. In short, if globalization and prosperity remain generally intact (with a few exceptions and possibly due to financial support from China, India and the Middle East), this will drive interest in and supply of all manner of financial innovations, especially those delivered online. However, if the global economy slips into a serious or prolonged recession or if interest rates really climb or inflation takes hold, there is a likelihood that countries, companies and individuals will act defensively to protect what they have against loss.

Developed countries have traditionally been in favor of open markets for very selfish reasons: they want to sell more things to other countries. But as nations like China and India become the dominant economic superpowers, Western countries will move toward more nationalist and protectionist policies. This will, in turn, spawn a return to local community and a flight to trusted brands and institutions. In short, people will stick with what they know and trust; wherever possible, this will mean people rather than machines.

The biggest threat to the economies of countries such as the US and the UK will not come from external threats but from within (so-called endogenous threats). These include developments such as domestic housing bubbles or the EU slipping into deflation (or stagflation) caused by an ageing and unproductive workforce. In a fast-paced, globalized world, the love of the new dominates. But in a downturn, security will be paramount and new entrants and foreign banks will be rejected in favor of long-established local names.

Except, that is, if the name includes words like "Northern" and "Rock". I was in Australia in 2007 when the UK's fifth-largest mortgage lender became the first bank in Britain since 1866 to be the subject of a bank run. There were people queuing down high streets all over the country trying to get their cash out, until the government agreed to use taxpayers' money to guarantee their savings. It effectively said that it would bail out anyone who invested in a major UK financial institution that had forgotten that there should be some balance between borrowing and lending. The problem, of course, was that Northern Rock was too clever by half. Instead of using branch deposits to fund growth it used the global money market, which in turn relies on securitization to transfer risk. As a result the bank, which was essentially a local UK lender, became embroiled in the US subprime mortgage fiasco. Could such a situation happen again? Probably, although chances are it will be wearing different clothes next time.

Talking of debt, in the UK household debt will hit 150% of annual income by 2010, which means that it will increase from something in the order of £1 trillion to £1.6 trillion, give or take a few pounds.

At this rate, 50-year or intergenerational mortgages and loans will become commonplace and more than a quarter of home-owners will be paying off home loans after they retire. Likewise, if the US were a corporation it would have been declared bankrupt years ago, but it's in nobody's interest to upset the global status quo. The US borrows 75% of the world's savings and imports 50% more goods than it exports. As a result, US Treasury bonds to the value of around US$600 billion are issued every year. Most of this debt is financed by Asian countries such as China and Japan; if either country were to pull the plug, the US dollar and bond markets would crash. This would lead the US economy into recession and other countries like China would almost certainly be sucked in too. So, as Larry Summers (Treasury secretary under President Clinton) once put it, we are all benefiting from a "balance of financial terror" — a system of mutually assured financial destruction. That's assuming the US doesn't do something to antagonize China, so that it just pulls the plug regardless.

I want it and I want it now

Why is there so much debt around? In the US the figure for credit-card debt is close to US$800 billion — a 400% increase since 1990. People in the UK currently hold around 60% of all credit cards issued in Europe and have around 75% of total European credit-card debt — about £50 billion — or £1,140 for every adult, the last time I looked. Historically this would have been seen as a burden: something to feel ashamed of, and potentially even a threat to individual freedom. However, viewpoints have changed and will continue to do so for the foreseeable future. Over the past three or four decades we have shifted from a saving to a borrowing culture and these days people often talk about their level of personal debt in the same way that others brag about the size of their salaries, which is not surprising given that one tends to be indicative of the other these days.

The problem, of course, is that many of the people with gigantic loans are living right on the economic edge. When interest rates rise by a couple of percentage points they are in very serious trouble — or perhaps the banks and other financial institutions that lent them the money (or bought the debt) in the first place are. Personal bankruptcies in the UK are already at an all-time high, and even if there isn't a major crash these debts will last for a very long time. In the US the term NINJA refers to loans that are given to individuals who have No Income, No Job and No Assets. Little wonder, then, that the US subprime fallout fell so far so fast. At the time of writing further loan defaults look likely because many of the loans that were taken out at "teaser rates" in 2005 are starting to move to something approaching market rates, which could cause a second subprime tsunami.

More worrying, perhaps, is the attitude of Generation Y to debt. Under-25s are the fastest-growing group filing for bankruptcy in the US, partly because it's seen as "cool" and partly because of the bills caused by must-have technology such as cellphones and iPods.

Peer pressure to own these devices is strong, but so too are the marketing tactics of the banks and especially credit-card companies that are targeting teens with unmissable opportunities. And they are not discriminating between those who can afford debt and those who can't. As a result, the amount of debt owned by poor families has increased considerably.

People are also starting to use credit cards in different ways. My dad only used his credit cards for holidays and for other large purchases. These days I always seem to be stuck in a supermarket queue behind a 20-something trying to use a credit card to buy a loaf of bread and a bottle of milk. Maybe I should move to China. Believe it or not there are only 12 million people with credit cards in China out of a total population of 1,300 million.

To be fair, the younger generation has never seen a recession. What they have seen instead is their parents making a considerable amount of money by using debt to buy property, so you could argue that their attitude to debt is not their fault. But it is. It's also the fault of parents and schools that teach next to nothing about money and financial planning; and, ultimately, I suppose it's the fault of the government too.

One solution to this, especially for teens and tweens, will be the development of credit cards that lock off certain geographical locations or product groups. For instance, if your teenage daughter has a cellphone and iPod addiction, you'll be able to give her a credit card but she won't be able to use it to buy either. In the US the Allow Card is an early example of this.

The level of debt in American low-income households has soared by over 180% over the last decade, while the figure for older people was close to 150% over the same period. This is not a debt mountain, it's an avalanche waiting to descend, and the subprime fiasco was merely the first tremor. The UK government has already announced that it will pass legislation to apply "wealth warnings" to all literature and advertising about credit cards and loans; this will be just the beginning. In the future these warnings will appear on the credit cards and statements themselves and there will be tighter controls on lending and borrowing.

Transparency and regulation will increase across other areas of financial services too, which will significantly add to operating costs for financial institutions and will put many smaller players out of business. And don't expect customers — however stupid and short-sighted — to take responsibility for their actions. We will see a significant increase in litigation against banks, credit-card companies and insurance companies because "you made me have it" and "I didn't think that interest rates would go up that much".

This will make parts of the financial services industry akin to the tobacco industry today. Once upon a time it was used-car salesmen and politicians who were the least trusted people. In the future it will be bankers, financial planners and mortgage advisers whom people distrust the most.

One feature of national economies in the future will be that each country will exhibit differing degrees of prosperity and hardship depending on its geography, resources and population. For example, in some areas of London or New York real-estate prices will be up while in others they will be down. Why the discrepancy? The reason is globalization. There will continue to be a huge demand for resources while other areas of the economy will be flat. Equally, some skills will be in high demand while others will be unwanted. In other words, the high growth of certain sectors and cities will mask what is effectively a recession down the road.

Can the two opposites coexist? The answer is yes, although whether such coexistence will be peaceful is another matter. We haven't seen tax riots on the streets of London for several decades but there is no reason that they won't appear again. The economic middle class in particular is feeling aggrieved and could perhaps even become revolutionary. Ridiculous? I don't think so. And neither does the UK's Ministry of Defence, which has considered such a scenario in a report on future strategic shocks.

There will therefore be several futures, but trusted brands and genuinely independent advisers will prosper in all of these future worlds. Can the big banks pull this off? Possibly, although community banks, building societies, credit unions and local savings and loan companies are perhaps in a much better position to do so, given their scale, history and more personal relationships with customers.

Dad, can I borrow your salary?

Things really aren't looking that good for Gen Y. First they have inherited a planet that is becoming fuller, dirtier and more dangerous (or so we're told). Then they may have to tighten their belts because Gen X bankers have only done cursory checks before lending them money. Bummer.

The way lending operates will have to change. One option is 50-year or even 75-year mortgages. Another way forward will be the family loan. In the UK around 1 in 50 households is termed an extended financial family (EFF), more than one generation living together under one roof. By 2014 this is expected to have risen to 1 in 20. Typically, EFFs comprise grandparents, parents and children.

This is nothing new, of course. A few hundred years ago it was the typical household and is perhaps yet another example of how we will be going back to the future. Why is the number of EFFs growing? The most obvious reason is the high cost of real estate, but pension underfunding, increased healthcare expenditure (people are living longer, remember) and higher education costs are other factors. In the US, for example, it is forecast that 20% of GDP will be spent on healthcare by 2020, while in Japan it is predicted that there will be a 75% increase in those aged 75+ between 2005 and 2015, which will require a taxation increase of 175% to maintain the current levels of benefits for the next generation.

Another spin-off from the high cost of living will be that more and more parents will have to provide security, a deposit or even part of the monthly payment for their children's homes. Some lenders (e.g. Wizard, part of GE Money) have already responded to this need with products linking the assets and income of more than one generation. Another means to a similar end is giving money to your children in the form of regular payments instead of a single lump sum. Indeed, the very concept of inheriting money or property will become foreign to many young people, as parental assets are increasingly used up to help with loan payments. Another option is finding a complete stranger to stump up the money for a home deposit. This is precisely what sites like Home Equity Share are doing already in the US.

At the extreme, all this can mean having kids who simply refuse to move out of the family home because it is too expensive to rent or buy real estate, or because doing so would seriously dent their disposable income. In Japan these kids are known as "parasite singles" because they do not contribute financially to the running of the parental home, while in Australia the term "boomerang kids" describes those who leave home but keep coming back due to their accumulation of debt.

According to a survey by the University of Michigan, 34% of adults aged 18 to 34 receive money from their parents and 50% receive non-cash gifts in the form of time, which adds up to 367 hours of unpaid work per year. Cash payments are usually for housing, utility bills and expenses. Until 10 or 20 years ago, parents assumed that the financial obligation to their children (typically US$191,000 up to the age of 17) ended when they graduated from high school. Now the financial support can easily go on for another 17 years and can cost an additional US$42,000, because people are spending longer in education (which costs more than it used to), are getting married later and are entering the workforce later than before. However, as *New York Times* writer Anna Bahney has observed, the reason may also be that children these days are taking the "scenic route from adolescence to adulthood".

So what are some of the other consequences of these shifts? One fairly fundamental implication is that today's children will never enjoy the same standard of living their parents did. This is a generalization, but most things that used to be free now cost money and everything that costs money will be more expensive in the future, thanks to global market pricing and the increasing scarcity of resources (including skilled workers). Theoretically this could make for a very bitter and unhappy generation, but I don't think it will. If anything, material possessions will become less important and people will be judged by who they are and what they do for the rest of society rather than by what they earn or what they possess. Maybe we'll even see government-backed loans that lend money to people based on what they do rather than what they earn — the more useful you are to society the less you pay.

Some surveys claim that as many as 83% of people think that society (which presumably includes themselves) is obsessed with money and around 25% have recently sacrificed income to improve their quality of life. However, this figure really needs to increase to 51%, because individuals judge their happiness in relation to other people. Thus if the majority were to change their behavior the minority would follow suit, especially since most people fear loss much more than they crave gain.

At least, I hope this is what happens. Money is what most people worry about most often. According to yet another survey, financial worries come in way above relationships, employment, security, education and terrorism. And 30% of people think that they are overexposed to interest rate rises. In the UK over 20 million find it difficult to pay regular bills, according to the Post Office.

Maybe the way to remove these worries is to give everyone a lump sum at birth. People could have access to a certain amount every month until they die, which would be like living life in reverse — you have lots of money when you are born and when you are growing up, when you really need it, but receive less as you get much older and don't really need it. I know this is silly, but there's a sensible idea in there trying to get out.

Another reason it's not all doom and gloom lies in human ingenuity and technology. One of the biggest debates in countries like the UK, the US, Germany, France and Japan is how to fund an ageing citizenry. People are concerned by the fact that because we are living for much longer, healthcare and retirement costs are escalating and there are fewer in the younger generation to pay for all this. For example, in Germany and the US the level of public debt needed to finance old age is currently 65% of GDP, but this will rise to 200% by the year 2050 unless someone comes up with a clever solution or longevity starts to move in the opposite direction, which is quite possible.

One option is to extend the retirement age and this will happen — not once but several times in most countries. Some nations may even abolish the option of retirement altogether or refuse to use state funds to support asset-rich, income-poor citizens. Personally, I think that technology will eventually come to the rescue and productivity rates will soar as a result, thereby funding retirement requirements. I also think that people will simply adjust and learn to live on less with less. Real estate, for example, is not a god-given right and many more people may decide to live in government- or company-owned, rent-controlled apartments. We may lease or borrow more products too. Rather than lending to buy real estate outright, lenders may "give" people property free of charge or at a low monthly cost, then take some or all of the future capital gains. Indeed, perhaps we will see a return to a feudal model whereby property or land is owned by your employer and must be returned once your employment ceases. Of course, this could be a recipe for social unrest — as it was the last time it was tried — although maybe certain safeguards could be built in or tied to the length of your employment. One thing we will undoubtedly see is insurance against the possibility of living too long.

Back in 1840 you worked until you died (usually at age 40) or you relied on your children to support you. This was clearly unacceptable, so governments devised a system whereby the income generated by those working would pay for those who were not working. This intergenerational transfer of income worked fine while younger workers outnumbered older retirees, but a declining fertility rate coupled with increased longevity has led to an imbalance. The current idea is therefore that older people should save up and pay for their own retirement, but this is itself flawed because people have no idea how long they will live. Enter the financial markets. We have already seen the issue of so-called catastrophe (cat) bonds and cat derivatives that bet for and against events such as hurricanes, so the thought of mortality bonds betting on how long people will live is a natural extension.

In most developed countries the number of individuals aged over 65 is set to double over the next 20–30 years. In the UK there are currently just below 10 million people aged over 65; by the year 2025 this will have increased to 13 million. The beneficiaries of this trend will include healthcare companies and developers building residential care homes and retirement real estate, but other sectors will also gain.

For example, many older people will be both cashed up and time rich, so industries from gardening and DIY to caravans and exotic travel will enjoy boom times. Another area to benefit is what's been termed the dream-fulfillment industry. This includes garages selling classic cars to older people who drooled over them when they were younger but didn't have the money back then.

Would you like insurance with that?

Will the insurance industry change the same way as banks in the future? I think it will. The technology that's transforming banking is also capable of transforming insurance, in the sense that GPS-embedded devices and RFIDs will allow insurance companies to price risk in real time. They will know where we are and thus be able to cost insurance by the minute, opening up a whole new market of instant-cover insurance. For example, if you're worried about boarding a particular chairlift while on a skiing holiday, you could buy additional insurance to cover the five-minute trip instantly through your mobile phone. Equally, cars could be sold with insurance embedded in the vehicle. Payments would be made on a per-kilometer basis depending on time of day, location, speed and traffic conditions.

The annual cost of compensation in the UK stands at £10 billion, mostly billed straight back to you and me. Insurance claims have been rising at around 15% every year, largely due to an increase in litigious attitudes. But many of these claims are bogus and anything that can reduce the amount that insurance companies pay out or help them assess risk more accurately will be welcomed.

Insurance will also be personalized in the sense that it will be tied to our individual actions. Three insurance companies in the US, the UK and South Africa already do this, the idea being that the healthier you are, the smaller your insurance premiums become. PruHealth UK offers "vitality points" to customers who join a gym, give up smoking, improve their body mass index or read books about keeping fit. Discovery Health in South Africa and Destiny Health in the US offer similar "cash for health" policies. Given that auto insurance companies have been offering discounts to safer drivers for years, it's surprising that nobody has thought of this before.

Perhaps governments will link personal income-tax rates to an individual's health or lifestyle — if your waistline goes down, so too does your annual tax assessment. Somehow I think I preferred it back in the old days when I could go to the pub without my employer, the government, my doctor, social services or my health-insurance company knowing I was there.

In theory our modern world, with its anxieties and new risks, will be a bonanza for insurance companies, although too much risk could sink them too. For instance, the level of terrorism in Iraq means that insurance for foreign journalists is now so high that it's almost unaffordable, while global climate change and severe unpredicted weather could hit insurance companies very badly indeed.

Insurance isn't going away any time soon and neither are banks. Indeed, the insurance business will grow significantly in the future in response to new risks and fears, although quite what companies and individuals will be insuring themselves against is far from clear. Equally, while banks and credit-card companies will be damaged by the digitization of cash and the increase in mobile payments, micro-payments, pre-pay and contactless payments, I don't foresee banks being disintermediated entirely. They will hold on to larger transactions simply because big-ticket payments require risk management and default and dispute systems, which are generally too expensive and complicated from a compliance point of view for non-banks. Nevertheless, digital money will turn parts of the financial services industry on its head because the banks and credit-card companies will no longer be in sole charge of checkbooks, credit cards, ATMs and branches.

4 July 2036

Dear Li

Yesterday I walked into a branch of Wal-Mart bank and was waiting in the queue when someone I've never met pulled me out of the line, greeted me by name and offered me a decent mug of mint tea! (How did they know?) Somehow they guessed I needed a car loan and led me off to a rather groovy lime green sofa where they gave me all the essential information. I was also asked to talk into a voice recorder to make sure I filled out the form truthfully. This is now mandatory on all loans. There was no queue at the gold customer ATM so I verified my identity at the palm print verification panel and iris scanner. The machine recognized me and greeted me by name, so I withdraw about 500 GCUs (the new global currency unit). I usually wire this straight to my phone but this time I decided to play safe and hid the digital cash inside the tag in my shoe. I was then sent on my way clutching a leaflet about loans with my name on it, featuring a photo of the 246 GTS I'm thinking of buying. It also lists an interest rate and repayment table personally tailored to me. There was an advertisement playing on the wall for car loans as I was leaving the bank. It was interesting, but I was in a hurry, so I swiped the ad and took it home. I'm going to pop into the Industrial and Commercial Bank of China next week and see what they've got to offer. Having been the world's largest bank for almost 30 years I think they should be able to offer me something special.

See you next year.

Suzie

PS Have you seen those Secondwife credit cards?

5 trends that will transform transport

Embedded intelligence Cars can already be opened or started using fingerprint and iris recognition, so we'll see more technologies linking vehicle security to user identification. We will also see mood-sensitive vehicles that adjust their behavior according to the mood of the driver or occupants. Cars will also become mobile technology platforms linking data to other services such as healthcare. For example, if your car regularly detects an abnormal heartbeat or high levels of stress, this information could be sent wirelessly to your doctor. Obviously privacy issues abound, but cars could become useful data-collection and delivery points.

Remote monitoring Electronic data recorders are little black boxes that already sit covertly inside some cars and monitor your speed, acceleration and braking. When you have an accident the data contained within these boxes can be used by police or your insurance company to see who did what. Similarly, networkcar.com allows people to track remotely who's in their car, where it's going and at what speed. In the future all cars will be automatically tracked from space, making no journey entirely private. The good news in all this is that real-time data on where a car is and what it's doing will revolutionize the auto theft recovery and insurance industries and will foster various location-based services such as pay-as-you-go insurance.

Driverless cars Don't expect this any time soon, but by about 2040 we will see cars capable of driving themselves with minimal interference from the driver. Cars will also travel in social groups and correspond with other vehicles about conditions ahead or alternative routes. If drivers don't need to drive, this will open up a whole host of entertainment and information possibilities. Drivers (and passengers) will be able to turn sections of the car into mobile offices or part of their home, with video and music on demand and email services, food and drink all on tap.

The environment   Climate change, urbanization and resource shortages — most notably oil — will fuel a shift away from large petrol-engine cars to small electric and hybrid vehicles. There will also be a boom in cheap cars and bikes in emerging countries. Tax rates, license charges, car-loan rates and parking fees will increasingly be linked to vehicle type and we will see even more anti-car and anti-driver sentiment and regulation. This will be a catalyst for car-sharing schemes, green car rental, green car loans, green car insurance and bicycles. Conversely, though, there will also continue to be a demand for luxury and sports cars for at least the next decade, or until the global economic boom runs out of steam.

Reinvention of public transport   It would seem logical that, as urban roads and parking spaces fill up, there will be a growth in public transport. However, the car is so linked to ideas of individualism, freedom, private space and personal identity that we are unlikely to give up private car ownership in the short term. In theory high oil prices should stop people from driving private cars, but that's what we said during the last oil crisis almost 40 years ago. From a sustainability point of view the future must see the reinvention of mass public transport, but people won't embrace the idea until governments start thinking long term and build safe, clean, convenient and affordable networks. This means services that link supply and cost to real-time demand — and it also means politicians actually using these services themselves.

Chapter 6

Automotive and Transport: the end of the road as we know it

The future influences the present just as much as the past.
—Friedrich Nietzsche

In the future, we will all drive cars that fly. Fifty years ago that's what most people thought we'd all be doing today. Strangely, the idea persists. A cartoon entitled "Predictions for 2007" recently featured — you guessed it — dozens of flying cars, although what people were flying toward or from was far from clear.

The car is perhaps one of the top ten most significant inventions of all time, dating from roughly the beginning of the twentieth century. Will it survive another 100 years? The answer, I'd suggest, is yes, because it has to, although its form and precise purpose may change beyond all recognition. Last century the car was important because it stood for freedom and mobility. But ask a 12- or 18-year-old today what symbolizes these ideals and they'd probably name the internet and the cellphone. So perhaps what will happen in the future is that our freedom and mobility will become virtual.

Physical movement will be an optional extra. Open roads will be replaced by open source and our need for speed and convenience by virtual worlds and online delivery. But not quite yet. The combustion engine still has a few kilometers left in it.

The automotive industry, along with the oil industry, is a dinosaur roaming the Earth looking for what's left of its food supply. As with all large creatures, it is slow to move and adapt to changing environments and conditions; so I'd predict that while changes will be made (biofuels, hybrid vehicles, hydrogen power and ceramic batteries, for example), another industry will most probably reinvent the wheel in the twenty-first century: high-tech. As cars move away from the internal combustion engine and become mobile-technology platforms, auto companies will be vulnerable because their knowledge of computers, batteries and electronics is so far behind. Then again, perhaps we'll see a mega-merger between the old and the new, with a company like General Motors being acquired by Microsoft, or Toyota buying Apple, so as to deliver technologies to drivers via their dashboards.

Reinventing the wheel

From a technological perspective, the car you drive today is very far removed from the small and light vehicle you might have access to 40 or 50 years hence. The shape will be slightly familiar, although the materials the car will be made of will be as foreign to most people as a Lexus would have appeared to someone in the 1880s. First of all, most of the panels will be constructed from biodegradable plastic made from the starch found in potatoes and rice. (When you've finished with them, you could theoretically bury them in your garden to rot down into garden compost.) The panels will also be made using nanotechnology, meaning they will remember the shape they are supposed to be, so dents will fix themselves. The color will no longer be sprayed on in a separate and time-consuming batch process, but will be programmable by the owner, much in the same way that an iPod operates. In other words, you will be able to set the color of your car to change each week depending on your mood. The "paint" will be self-repairing, in that if it gets scratched or chipped the color will simply flow over the damaged area, making it look as good as new, and the exterior will wash and dry itself every time it rains.

There will be a safety override, so that if the weather turns nasty or there is an accident up ahead the car will sense this and automatically change itself from, say, silver to a safer, more visible color like white or yellow. Things will be pretty colorful on the inside, too. Given the amount of effort that automakers have traditionally put into color forecasting, it's surprising that the interior lighting of automobiles and other vehicles has received so little attention. Or perhaps not. Most people spend a lot of time and money discussing what color to paint the inside of their house but give virtually no thought to the lighting. In the future, cars' interior lighting will be fully programmable and, again, will automatically adjust according to the conditions inside and outside.

This means that if you select the sport gearbox option in a luxury saloon, the interior and exterior lighting may change to a safer and more visible intensity, but the car will override these selections if it feels you are a threat to other road users. In the future vehicles (and other machines, for that matter) will be mood sensitive and will adjust themselves to their owner's feelings. For example, if traffic conditions deteriorate (or you receive a phone call that makes you anxious or stressful) the vehicle will compensate with relaxing dashboard instrumentation, anti-stress lighting and chillout sounds. Either that or a spy in the sky will somehow recognize that you are a danger to yourself and other road users and you will receive a message through your radio stating: "Your speed has been reduced for your own safety. Thank you for your cooperation."

The opposite will be true, too, in the sense that military vehicles will use active camouflage systems to disguise themselves from the enemy by projecting video or still images of the surrounding area so as to appear invisible. More alarmingly, military vehicles and aircraft will probably change their interiors to combat mode when an attack is imminent to make their operatives more aggressive and focused.

Back in civvy street, safety will continue to compete with its nemesis, speed, with car manufacturers falling over themselves to offer the latest in high-tech safety features, including collision avoidance. Historically, car safety has generally focused on keeping the driver and his or her passengers alive in the event of a crash. This has meant higher and higher levels of crash and rollover protection, safety cells, airbags and improved seatbelt technology. However, drivers have become so cocooned from the world outside that they have started to become a real danger to both themselves and other road users. Indeed, as someone once remarked to me, the safest car in the world wouldn't feature any seatbelts at all but would simply have a sharp metal spike sticking out of the center of the steering wheel.

Thus there will be a shift toward protecting other road users, especially pedestrians, and preventing accidents, which will mean mainstreaming "sixth sense" technologies such as lane-departure warning systems (43% of all crashes are the result of vehicles straying into the wrong lane or off the road completely), skid avoidance, automatic speed adaptation and sleep-alert devices. Nevertheless, drivers are already so overloaded with information that unless these warnings are delivered by touch or smell, they're highly likely to be ignored.

Perchance to dream

Sleep is already becoming a major issue for the automotive industry worldwide as more and more drivers become tired, thanks to the relentless march of technologies that are always on, such as email and cellphones. In New Jersey, judges can jail drivers who fall asleep at the wheel and go on to injure or kill others; it looks as if sleepy driving will become the new drink driving in the years ahead.

The problem, obviously, isn't people who are knowingly sleepy when they step into a car, but rather those who are more tired than they realize jumping into the driver's seat after an extra long day at work, or perhaps after a weekend spent trying to recover from the week before. The danger is micro-sleeps rather than fully fledged naps. These often last for less than a few seconds but are nevertheless responsible for an estimated 30% of all road accidents. Solutions include infrared cameras to monitor eye movement, touch pads to check hand pressure on the steering wheel and chassis technologies to look for unusual directional movement. If a car thinks you are falling asleep, there are already various things it can do to wake you up. These include blasts of cold air from the dashboard into your face, audio alarms, vibrating seats and, our old friend, interior lighting. But don't hold your breath about any of this really working.

More low-tech solutions could include the mandatory requirement that all car journeys be shared. This is potentially a bit of a double whammy because car sharing has environmental benefits too, but it's been found that people drive more safely when they are traveling with a passenger — especially if the driver is male and the passenger is female. According to German research, 44% of men say that they adjust their driving style when a female passenger is sitting in the car compared to just 29% of women when a male passenger is close by. Taking a scenic route has a similar effect, so in the future perhaps we will see cars that sense whether the driver is tired and then automatically divert themselves to country roads rather than motorways.

Driven to distraction

Road accidents killed 43,443 people in the US in 2006 and it is estimated that by 2020 they will be the third-biggest global killer, second only to heart disease and depression and overtaking both HIV
and war. Unfortunately, this level of death and dismemberment is
likely to increase due to several reasons.

First, drivers will face more distractions. The use of cellphones
is a well-known risk: using a phone while driving increases your
chance of being involved in an accident by 400% (alcohol, by contrast, increases your risk by 200% at a level of 0.06%). This immediately begs the question of why talking to a passenger doesn't also
increase your chances of crashing. The answer is not completely
clear, but it's likely to be because when people are on the phone
they enter something that Dr David Strayer (a psychologist at the
University of Utah) calls the "phone zone", a virtual reality space
where they are momentarily transported to somewhere else outside their vehicle. Talking to a passenger, on the other hand, does
not involve emigration to cyberspace and both parties are fully
aware of each other's presence and the world outside. The passenger also provides a handy second pair of eyes to notice potential
hazards.

Phones and cars aren't going away for quite a while, so we can
fully expect accidents due to cellphone use to continue despite the
best efforts of police and law makers. Indeed, the feeling among the
general public is that using a handheld phone in a car is perfectly all
right so long as you don't get caught. This attitude is similar to
drink driving 20 or 30 years ago and it will probably take at least
this long to stop people talking or texting while driving.

I was recently traveling at night down a major arterial road when
ahead I saw a red sports car with a strange glow coming from the
driver's side. Being somewhat curious, I inched forward in the traffic to see what might be causing this. After five minutes — in the
rain, incidentally — I drew level and saw that the driver (the only

occupant) was a smartly dressed woman in her late 20s. She was on the phone and smoking. But the light wasn't coming from her cigarette; it was from the laptop she had balanced on her legs, which she was occasionally typing into. I kid you not. I know nothing about actuarial tables of risk, but I'd guess that she was what you might call an accident waiting to happen.

Thankfully she wasn't eating and drinking at the same time. In the US eating while driving causes 30% of all auto accidents, although only 57% of drivers will admit to doing it. Often the problem isn't actually eating or drinking but spilling your food or drink and trying to clean it up while still driving. Some 15% of American meals are eaten in cars and the big fast-food chains typically generate between 50 and 60% of sales from their drive-through windows, so this really is a big deal. Solutions, apart from obviously sitting down at a table for a meal, include the ubiquitous dashboard cup holder, and food and drink designed to be eaten or consumed on the move. Some automakers are even putting foldout tables into their vehicles, which are obviously not intended to be used by the driver — but there's nowt so stupid as folk, as my grandmother used to say. I've even seen a slow cooker that plugs into your cigarette lighter and cooks your evening meal while you drive home. And we call ourselves an intelligent species.

Of course, some of the best solutions to the growing problem of driver distraction and aggression will be very simple indeed. For example, 70% of pedestrian deaths happen after dark, so you'd think that a technology such as intelligent night vision would be a good idea. Two infrared cameras could be mounted at the front of a vehicle to sense warm objects in the dark and a computer could match these objects to a database of known shapes, such as humans. Distances would then be calculated almost instantly and an alarm sounded to alert the driver to the impending risk. This is a very good idea, but an even better one might be streets with absolutely no center markings, no curbs and no streetlights.

This probably sounds like a recipe for disaster, but it is actually a very serious experiment proposed by Kensington and Chelsea Council in London. The theory is that if you remove all signs, drivers will become disoriented and will slow down and start to think as a result. This obviously wouldn't work if the idea became common and expected, but in certain inner-city areas it could be a real winner. Add intelligent night vision, though, and it's back to removing the spike from the center of the steering wheel.

Death at the wheel

So what else can auto companies, councils and law makers do to cut road deaths and accidents? The question is both real and urgent, not least because of the rapid growth in car ownership in countries such as India and China. In 1990 there were 1 million cars in China; by 2004 this had risen to 12 million; and by 2020 it's predicted that there will be 140 million. Similarly, global car sales are expected to rise by 3% in 2008 but in China the growth will be 14%. Moreover, the country is also home to the world's third-largest road network, which wasn't even created until 1988. The result of all this is that there are millions of Chinese taking to the road for the first time, with low levels of safety awareness compared to other countries. The cost of road crashes in China is around US$12.5 billion annually, which is more than the national budget for public health services or compulsory rural education, and road accidents kill an estimated 100,000 people every year. And that's before car ownership has exploded there.

But don't be fooled into thinking that this is just a problem in emerging economies. In the UK road accidents are currently the largest single cause of death for young men aged 16 to 24 and the story is much the same in other countries. An idea that does seem to be working is that new drivers must be accompanied by a qualified driver; but of course this can simply have the effect of killing more people, not fewer.

One answer is the sale of speed-restricted cars to learners or recently qualified drivers, although perhaps an even better idea is the use of a smart key or "speed key", such as that developed by Volvo. The idea here is that the (theoretically) responsible adult owner of the vehicle can program the maximum speed using the special key. In the future, similar devices will limit the maximum power or acceleration of vehicles, or even lock off certain geographical districts or destinations. However, like the key drivers have to blow into to test for alcohol before the engine will start, the device is open to abuse, either by your average 12-year-old technical genius or by using another vehicle or key.

A better idea might be the use of a steering wheel that can judge a driver's mood and adjust the maximum speed or acceleration accordingly. Something similar to this already exists with a steering wheel that can test alcohol content merely by the driver touching it. Too much alcohol and the car simply won't start. But again there are problems: one can imagine two drivers trying to operate a car, one who's been drinking and one who hasn't, with one turning the steering wheel and one pressing the accelerator.

Other, slightly less daft solutions include night-time bans on young or learner drivers and not allowing newly qualified drivers to carry passengers. Or what about simply passing a law that those under the age of 25 can only drive a single type of car, power restricted with added safety features? This would be unpopular although possibly effective.

However, in the future the problem may not be young drivers at all. Quite the opposite, in fact. Populations are ageing all over the world and people are living longer and driving later than ever before. This will have a tremendous effect on how cars are designed and what laws are passed. For instance, older drivers have problems with mobility, slowed reaction times and poor vision. Hence better vehicular access (doors) and better forward, backward and side vision will become increasingly important engineering elements and testing of older drivers will eventually become commonplace globally.

Ultimately, though, the solution to both older and younger driver safety will be to take the necessity of driving away altogether. Along with flying cars, self-driving cars have been a feature of the sci-fi future for decades. They first appeared in the 1950s, although the idea never really progressed beyond the concept stage for a number of legal, social and technical reasons. Nevertheless, General Motors claims that it is building such a car and that it could be introduced as early as 2008. Fat chance — although if what GM is really talking about is adaptive cruise control, it's a possibility. This is essentially a system whereby the car recognizes that there is another car in front and sets a safe speed and distance using a clever mix of cameras and laser beams. If the car gets too close, the speed is reduced or the brakes are applied. Equally, if the car starts to stray out of its lane, the power steering corrects the mistake or else the driver is alerted using beeps, flashing lights or vibrations.

As with any early technical solution, there are problems. First, the technology won't work when there's no car in front (so it's not much use late at night or on country roads). More critically, there are serious legal implications to this type of technology. Last but by no means least, people actually like to drive their cars. Indeed, the car is probably the last private space available to ordinary people and it's highly unlikely that drivers will give up the freedom to get stuck in traffic unless they are forced to, legally or financially.

One way we might be persuaded to let go of the wheel is to allow us to do other things inside our car instead. Cars are already moving toward being mobile information platforms with iPod connectivity and video screens, although much of the latter is aimed at backseat drivers. There is clearly a strong latent demand for people to talk on their cellphones, read newspapers and check email while they are driving, so why not let them do it? Cars will increasingly shift from transportation devices to information platforms and anything we can currently do at work will ultimately be available inside a car — whether it's stationary, in a traffic jam or flying down the highway at 100 kph.

Gaming is another thing that we would undoubtedly do from the driver's seat if allowed. Once the strain of driving has been removed and most, if not all, of the control is handed over to the vehicle (think of the autopilot in planes), dashboard controls and windscreens could be used for other purposes. There are obviously numerous safety concerns with ideas such as these — not least the sense of letting someone play a racing game inside a stationary car and then allowing them to drive on a real highway moments later. Nevertheless, the technological invasion of the family saloon is well underway and we shouldn't forget the many possible benefits.

Goodbye freeways; hello payways

Once you start to think of cars, roads and even parking spaces as a network rather than as individual objects, you open up all sorts of possibilities. Satellite tracking will set safe distances between cars, tell vehicles about congested routes, identify passengers who wish to car share and also find parking spaces in real time, setting a daily or hourly price for their availability depending on demand. This could include private parking spaces in cities that could be released to the public if their owners could receive online bids for their use. Roads will obviously all be priced too, with charges varying from nothing to rather a lot, again depending on real-time demand. If you want to drive at peak hour or get somewhere really fast in a so-called "Lexus lane", then you'll pay. If, on the other hand, you are prepared to pick an unpopular time to travel, you won't pay nearly as much or perhaps nothing at all.

A more likely scenario is a mixture of public and private roads (economy and business class, if you like). The idea of private toll roads is nothing new — they have been around longer than the motorcar — and to some extent tolls have always been based on the idea that the use of such roads is not compulsory. There is usually a free road or route available, but if you wish to travel across private land or use a specially constructed route to save time, you pay. Governments love this idea because they are growing tired of publicly financing infrastructure projects such as roads, tunnels and bridges. So in the future if you want to wait — in a traffic jam, for instance — you will be free to do so, but if you hate to wait and want to use the faster route you'll pay through the nose.

There are obviously some meaty political issues here, not least because the public will increasingly be asked to pay to travel on roads they technically already own. However, where there's a whiff of revenue, central governments, local councils and investment banks won't be too far behind.

Embedding technology in vehicles — or using satellite spies to see where everyone is — will have some other benefits. The most interesting probably relates to insurance. Previously, risk was calculated and premiums set using fairly crude measures such as where the vehicle was kept and what type of person or persons drove it. In the future this information will also include real-time data on where the car is 24 hours a day, who exactly is driving it and what speed or driving style they are using. This is potentially bad news for privacy campaigners, but it does open up the possibility of pay-as-you-go insurance, bought by the day or even by the kilometer from your local petrol station. Norwich Union is already conducting trials of a similar idea in the UK, whereby risks are calculated in real time and payment is made monthly in arrears bundled up with other services such as route planning and emergency roadside assistance.

Another idea already taking off is the pay-as-you-go car. The notion that everyone needs their own vehicle is beginning to sound faintly ridiculous, especially in cities, where lack of parking spaces and congestion charging are making other forms of public or group transport more logical. A number of companies are springing up offering car-sharing services of one type or another. In the US companies like Zipcar are growing at breakneck speed, partly because small organizations and businesses are trying to cut costs, and car sharing makes more sense than traditional auto rental or taxis. In Switzerland 2% of drivers already use such schemes, while in the UK organizations like City Car Club are renting cars to people for as little as £4 ($8) an hour — including fuel. Better still, again because of remote-monitoring technology, there are companies that simply scatter share cars across a city. Users then find them via internet search (probably from their phone) and open the doors with either a membership card or a barcode contained within an SMS message. There's no paperwork, either, because the companies already know where you are and where you drive, so bills are sent automatically via email.

In the future, such services will be operated by retailers like McDonald's (the owner of one of the largest number of parking spaces in the world) and apartment blocks, where each apartment will come with a part share in a vehicle — or a range of vehicles — parked underneath the building. We could even see apartment blocks exclusively built for petrol heads or classic car buffs, with the above-ground architecture suitably in touch with the owners' sentiments and a range of machinery underground to suit the tenants' whims and passions.

In other words, usership will shift from the individual to the group and ownership will in many cases give way to rental or what some people call fractional ownership. Ten or fifteen years ago you couldn't rent a classic car for love nor money. The same was more or less true with exotica such as new Ferraris, Lamborghinis and Aston Martins. Now you're spoilt for choice. In the UK alone there are more than 20 companies renting classics like Jaguar E-types for the day or Porsche 911s for the week.

This is partly because people realize that actually owning something like this can be a headache (they break down and need constant care and attention) and therefore partial ownership or rental makes more sense. In effect, this is timeshare for classic cars. At the upper end of the market it can also make more financial sense to buy a share in a $500,000 car — which, to be honest, you'll hardly ever use because you're always at work trying to pay for it — than to buy outright what is generally a depreciating asset.

The future is the past

However, there is something much more interesting than dollars and cents going on here, especially with the boom in classic-car ownership and rental. Cars have now become so technologically advanced and packed with electronic features that they have lost their souls. They are an emotional purchase and customers are longing for the past when cars (and the world) were easy to understand. There is a simple element of nostalgia: people (especially men) in their 40s and 50s are longing for the cars they dreamt about and couldn't afford when they were growing up. But there's more to it than that.

In the US one of the latest trends is teens buying "grandpa" cars like Chevrolets, Buicks, Oldsmobiles and Cadillacs from the 1970s and 1980s, partly because they are cheap, partly because they are so "out" they're "in", and also because they are simple to understand and easy to fix. There are no on-board computers or sealed boxes of electronics; mechanically minded owners can work on (and, crucially, customize) them themselves. Another explanation for the trend is the influence of television shows such as MTV's *Pimp My Ride*, but I'm sure that the main reason is a combustible mixture of low cost, simplicity and nostalgia. There is even a magazine in the US dedicated to tricked-out old motors (*Donk, Box & Bubble*).

Manufacturers like Ford are all too aware of this trend, but it's very difficult for them to make something simple. It involves uninventing technologies, so the idea of recreating a perfect copy of a 1960s Mustang or Ford GT40 with remanufactured mechanicals will inevitably end up as a new twenty-first-century version packed with every gizmo and device under the sun.

Another good example of the power of nostalgia and simplicity is a small chain of fix-it-yourself garages in France. 'O' Garage is for people who own cars but don't have garages or tools. The garages are fully equipped professional workshops that can be rented for an hour, a day or a week; help is available on site if you don't know your wishbones from your brake discs. Given the boom in domestic outsourcing (that is, paying people to do things you are perfectly capable of doing yourself) this is a bit contrary, but I'm sure it's connected to a new need to get your hands dirty. As life becomes more and more technical and virtual, more of us will crave simple, physical tasks. So perhaps automakers should throttle back a bit on the computer-enhanced engine-management systems and design cars that owners can fiddle with themselves.

I suspect manufacturers are already on to this, in a sense. We've had retro car design for years (not quite the same as I've been talking about), but there is a new trend on the horizon. According to *Car* magazine, the next big thing is local design. Ever since car companies went global (a long time ago) and started using computers rather than pencils to design, cars have looked remarkably similar. Take the badge off a Hyundai and replace it with a Honda emblem and most people wouldn't notice the difference. Moreover, it's virtually impossible to tell where the car has come from, as they all look like the product of a world design studio. This wasn't always the case. Once upon a time a British car could only have been made in the UK and the same was true with cars from France, Germany, Italy and the US. Global markets, CAD design and worldwide focus groups changed all that. But not so in the future.

As with food and wine — and increasingly everything else — people want to know where what they buy has come from. Industrial provenance is important and localization is becoming a strong countertrend to globalization. Hence automakers are rediscovering their roots and in the future cars will once again look and feel like local products, even if they are made and sold internationally.

Suburban living

Another thing we'll see in the future — or, more precisely, won't —
is tunnels. Put simply, the cost of tunneling is going down. This
means that cross-city tunnels and, ultimately, underground cities
will become increasingly common. This would have delighted
futurists from the 1920s and 1930s who foresaw similar urban land-
scapes, and certainly gives new meaning to the phrase "suburban
living". By lowering the air pressure in long tunnels beneath the
streets, friction is reduced, which could also have significant benefits in terms of achievable fuel consumption and top speeds (the
latter more for trains than cars).

Future urban design will dramatically influence the way we
travel in other ways too. First and foremost, there will be a slow shift
back toward public or mass transport. This will partly be because of
urban congestion but also as a result of environmental pressure.
Private car owners will be edged out of cities due to a mixture of
social stigma and taxation. The British government recently
increased the level of road tax paid by owners of four-wheel drives,
resulting in a dramatic drop in these vehicles' secondhand value.
Superficially, this is because four-wheel drives are gas guzzlers that
pollute the environment. In the US, a direct-action group called the
Detroit Project has even accused four-wheel-drive owners of promoting terrorism on the basis that they consume more than their
fair share of oil reserves, thereby making the US more reliant on
foreign oil — which in turn provokes US military action in the
Middle East.

Meanwhile, the Alliance Against Urban 4x4s is hell-bent on
harassing drivers of such vehicles, while the New Economics
Foundation (a UK thinktank) has described them as "Satan's little
run-arounds". But is this so? A typical spin in a four-wheel drive
emits less than half the CO_2 produced by a dishwasher on an economy cycle, but we don't label dishwasher owners selfish or greedy.
Equally, the little electric cars that whiz around cities are not quite

as saintly as many people think. In most cases the electricity to power these "green" vehicles comes from — you've guessed it — giant coal-based, oil-burning or gas-burning power stations, so where's the logic in that? Better still, what about air conditioning? America has less than 5% of the global population but consumes 25% of the world's electricity; and the use of air conditioning is responsible for a third of that energy use, or 8% of global energy consumption. But nobody (yet) is proposing that air-conditioning users should pay additional carbon taxes.

In the future we can expect to see the vilification of direct-action groups intensify to include mass boycotts of car manufacturers because of the models they make. Indeed, companies may have to restrict access to particular vehicles or ensure that they are only used in certain places or specific ways. In the UK, another think-tank has seriously suggested that owners of sport-utility vehicles be forced to carry health-warning stickers, while Greenpeace activists have chained themselves to the gates of a Range Rover factory to demonstrate against "climate criminals".

What has been overlooked in this battle seems to be why people drive these cars in the first place. Generally speaking, I'd suggest that most urban four-wheel drive owners feel safe in their cars and like the sense of control that the driving position engenders. Taking a long-term view, neither of these desires is going to go away. As life becomes less safe and more uncertain, people will continue to want mobile fortresses. The downside, though, is that if people perceive themselves to be safer, they may be inclined to take more risks — which brings us back to the safety issue once again.

Two of the fastest-growing segments of the car market in recent years have been small cars and four-wheel drives. Both are relatively safe, especially if they crash into one of their own — but the problem is that they frequently don't. Large cars crashing into small ones and old cars crashing into new ones are becoming a serious problem, as older or smaller cars will generally come off much worse.

One future solution to this is a world car in one size only, but I don't seriously expect this ever to be acceptable. A more likely scenario is restricting car sizes or types to particular locations. So if you live in a city, perhaps you will be forced to buy an electric or hybrid vehicle with legally enforceable dimensions and safety features. If, on the other hand, you live out of town, your vehicle choice changes. Better still, perhaps drivers who repeatedly have accidents will be forced to drive certain types of car or be demoted to L-plates and small vehicles until they establish a safe driving record.

Can't see the road for the trees

Thirty years hence, one can imagine a situation where drivers of petrol- or gasoline-fueled cars will be forced to pay for the oxygen the engine uses as well as for the fuel. This is already happening, in a sense, with carbon credits being given to countries such as Brazil that own "oxygen reserves". The desire to be green has trickled down from countries through companies to the private car owner. There are now green car loans, green car hire companies, and even green car insurance. While most of this is gimmickry gone mad, biofuels and hybrid cars (and, ultimately, hydrogen-powered cars) are here already or are coming over the next few years or so. Alternative energy is certainly a hot topic and there is little or no indication that the bubble is about to burst. However, what's often forgotten is that the ideas are nothing new.

Rudolf Diesel, for example, displayed an engine at the Paris Exhibition of 1900 that ran on peanut oil and Henry Ford was a fan of ethanol fuels back in the 1920s. The point here is that, contrary to predictions of doom and gloom, the car is not about to be killed off due to a lack of fuel. There will be arguments in the future about what the fuels should be and many people will migrate from private to public transport or bicycles. There is already an increasingly vociferous debate about whether plants should be grown to fuel vehicles or to feed people. But a lack of oil alone will not kill off the internal combustion engine.

Whatever the detail (and whatever happens to the price of oil in the short to medium term), it's a very safe bet that the development of new fuels will be one of the largest breakthroughs in automotive innovation over the next 50 years. The reason for this is mainly political. The US, China, Japan and most of Europe have become too reliant on Middle Eastern and Russian oil and need to create some level of fuel security through the invention or discovery of other fuels or reserves.

Asia is expected to account for nearly 40% of global car sales and more than half of the world's auto production by 2020. Take this prediction with a pinch of salt because the figures are based on a linear extrapolation. Nevertheless, many car manufacturers are attempting to get into the Asian market — essentially China, but also India and Indonesia — by launching small, ultra-low-cost cars there. At the forefront of this competition is Tata Motors, whose five-seater Nano, priced at just US$2,500, was unveiled in 2008. Such a low-cost vehicle could have enormous appeal in India, a country where over 56 million citizens earn just $4,400 annually. But it's not just about selling cars.

Tata is interesting because it plans to involve local mechanics as franchisers for partially or fully knocked-down car kits, which can then be assembled and sold on site. However, the extra production of oil and carbon emissions will cause problems if countries like China and India do indeed turn into the giant car markets that many automakers and analysts predict.

Personally, I don't think that linear extrapolations of current demand can tell you very much about the distant future; it's quite likely that things will evolve in a way unseen by industry experts and analysts. China, for instance, may skip over the need for oil and develop hydrogen power instead, thereby decreasing its strategic dependence on unstable regions such as Russia, Africa and the

Middle East. Alternatively, China and/or India could falter economically, resulting in millions of new vehicles remaining unsold.

What we'll certainly see in the more immediate future is a boom in car sharing, fractional ownership, electric bicycles (especially in India and China) and the reinvention of the humble push-bike, especially in Europe.

We'll also see the emergence of some very clever new business models applied to transport, most likely using the internet and other forms of mobile communication to connect people wishing to travel to roughly the same place at roughly the same time. Pricing and routes will become increasingly variable, dependent on demand, but equally there will still be a certain level of status attached to using a private vehicle. In other words, it's not the death of driving as such but it's certainly the end of the road as we know it.

Being an optimist, I also think that it wouldn't be devastating if the oil ran out tomorrow and we were unable to find an alternative. According to the UK Department of Transport, over the period 1980–2004 people in all income groups became much more mobile. Road traffic increased by 81% over the period; rail trips by 43%; and air travel overseas from 18 million to 64 million trips. Walking and cycling both declined over the same time (walking by about 20%), which coincided with an increase in obesity among both adults and children. So perhaps the silver lining could be a stronger, fitter planet. In all probability this won't happen because innovation thrives on a crisis, so the end of oil will be a spur for all sorts of activity and imagination — but you never know.

14 April 2047

Dear Yofi

You won't believe this. I was at a garage in downtown Los Angeles at 2 a.m this morning with a group of eight men of all ages looking in awe at a 1949 Mercury Sedan. The vehicle's a museum piece but that's not why we were there. The owner (Steve G) was planning to do an illegal drive up the highway running the car on petrol. As you know, petrol is pretty rare these days but you can still buy it from various illegal sources. The petrol for last night's run came from a guy outside of San Francisco who discovered how to extract it from vintage plastic shopping bags and plastic bottles dug up from a Mexican landfill.

Man, that engine sounded unlike anything I've ever heard! You know how you can buy software to make those silent electric cars sound like old petrol-engine sports cars from the last century? Well, let me tell you, they're a pale imitation of the real thing! The exterior of the car is made of metal and isn't even glued together. Five of the guys jumped into the car and slowly inched it out onto the yellow road. The road was confused because it didn't recognize the vehicle. But since it was dark and the car doesn't have positioning or speed indicators it couldn't be tracked from above, so the only thing they had to worry about was an automated police vehicle. They had about 15 minutes before one of these would pass by.

Afterwards I went outside and sprinkled the contents of a small packet onto the roadway. Within seconds nanobots had assembled a fully functioning vehicle atom by atom. Just $999.95 from Tesco-Mart. What a night!

Regards

Alexei

5 trends that will transform food

Convenience, portability and speed Individuals will lead time-pressured lives in the future and families will be time-starved and in a constant hurry. This means a further decline of traditional mealtimes, especially those where families sit down together, and an increase in eating on the move and between home and work. The idea of three full meals a day will be replaced with four, five, six or more grazing opportunities. Food will become faster and more mobile. This means it will be easier to buy, easier to cook and easier to eat. In some cases this will mean designing ready-to-eat meals in packaging that goes straight from the shopping basket into the microwave. It will also mean pre-washed and pre-cut ingredients, clearer labeling, faster checkouts and restaurants that know what you want before you do. Nobody will peel potatoes in the future.

Seasonal, regional and slow While some people will crave food that's fast and cheap, others will pay large amounts of money to slow things down. This means locally grown food eaten in season. It also means animal rights and all kinds of information about where food is from and how it was produced. For some people provenance will mean buying directly from the producer, while for others technology will allow them to interrogate individual products or the companies that make them. The food-miles debate will move to center stage, as will fair-trade products and practices. For people with the luxuries of time and space, growing your own fruit and vegetables will make a comeback as the ultimate form of traceability.

Health versus indulgence We eat with our eyes. We also eat with our heads and our hearts, so while our logical side tells us to eat healthy foods, our emotional side tells us to eat things that we shouldn't — foods that are naughty but nice. Most people will therefore operate a kind of credit and debit system whereby feelgood foods and indulgences will be offset by healthy foods or exercise. Food will become polarized between what's good for you and what's not. Both are a reaction to anxiety in some form; and both, increasingly, will need to be within arm's reach, as convenience will generally trump both the desire for health and indulgence. Food will similarly become polarized between low cost and luxury. That's unless food inflation starts to bite, caused by resource shortages, in which case the tables may be turned.

Nostalgia   As we become more stressed, depressed and lonely we will try to comfort ourselves by eating "old food". In other words, we will use food to transport ourselves back to what we believe were simpler, safer, more certain times. This anxiety will fuel nostalgic eating habits, ranging from comfort foods and childhood favorites to baking bread and buying authentic jam.

Food science and technology   The food industry will merge with the pharmaceuticals industry to create a host of "farmaceuticals", "nutraceuticals" and functional foods. Products will range from apples that cure headaches to water that suppresses appetite. Equally, technology will deliver faster and more convenient food choices. Medical records will also blur into shopping lists, as common conditions are treated with food rather than drugs. This will mean that food packaging will become more tightly controlled and legislated.

Chapter 7

Food and Drink:
faster *and* slower

If enough people predict something it won't happen.
—J. G. Ballard

A little while ago I was sitting in on a research debrief concerning the attitudes and behavior of 20-somethings. The highlight, for me at least, was a video clip of a young man complaining about the time it took to get served in McDonald's: "I mean, you go in there and place your order and sometimes you have to wait, like, almost a minute... and they call it fast food."

In 1950 some people were predicting that the world was going to run out of food. The Earth's population was exploding and the result was going to be starvation on an unprecedented scale unless scientists could create synthetic alternatives to naturally farmed foods. Hence we would all be consuming techno-foods produced in laboratories and ingested in tablet form. Half a century or more later and most of us are living in a world characterized by abundance not scarcity; the major public-health issue for the developed world is too much food, not too little.

Part of the reason for this shift is technological. As a race we have learnt how to apply scientific knowledge to farming, with the result that agricultural yields have skyrocketed and the cost of food has declined. For example, while the world's population has indeed exploded, doubling since 1950, cereal yields have tripled while the total amount of land under cultivation has hardly changed.

There are currently 800 million undernourished people on the planet, but this is expected to fall to around 600 million by 2025. Moreover, by 2050 the global population will level off at around 9 billion, taking some of the pressure off natural habitats being turned into farmland. Having said this, there are still problems ahead. As countries develop and people become richer, their diets tend to change. Out go cereals like rice and in come protein-rich foods such as red meat, which are "hungry" in terms of land use and water. One solution is to switch to fish, but here the situation is even worse. According to the UN almost 50% of the oceans' fish are already close to the limits of sustainability, and another 28% are either overfished or nearing extinction. How will we meet the demand for fish, which is expected to increase by 50% between now and 2020?

Fish farming will go some of the way (30% of global demand is already met by this means), but land-based fish management is proving unpopular for a number of environmental and political reasons. What we'll start to see, therefore, is the farming of fish in open water — gigantic cages of fish floating around the world's ocean currents, feeding on natural prey until they are large enough to be hauled up onto similarly huge factory ships.

Is "fish ranching" a good thing? When compared with people not having enough to eat, probably yes; and while there are some very real concerns about semi-farmed fish mingling with the wild variety, people are ultimately more important than fish — or at least, human lives are more important than the genetic purity of plants or animals. It's progress; get over it.

Back on dry land we'll see some dramatic changes too. "Precision agriculture" is an idea whereby farmland is monitored and controlled meter by meter, with seeds sown at exactly the correct time and fertilizers and pesticides applied almost on a plant-by-plant basis.

Similar techniques exist for cattle, allowing individual herds to be monitored and controlled by satellite and the history of an individual animal to be tracked from paddock to plate. RFID chips are one way to do this, but an even better way is to test for DNA. However, in the future the dining tables will be turned. At present RFID chips are a logistical tool used by supermarkets and their suppliers. In the future customers will tap into these chips to monitor where their food is from and how it was produced.

There is already a DNA test available called FoodExpert ID that can check for the presence of 32 common animals (including humans) in foodstuffs. The test can be used to test for food contamination such as the presence of pork in kosher foods or to identify meat cheats who bulk out chicken with beef waste. In the future such tests will be available to ordinary individuals like you and me who just want to know what we're eating for dinner.

However, it's genetically modified (GM) crops that will really change the agricultural landscape. So far the reaction to GM crops has been quite hostile, especially in Europe; but many new technologies encounter resistance when first introduced and it's highly likely that the arguments against GM will fall away once the benefits are widely understood and the safety fears addressed.

Some of the products ultimately delivered by GM technology will be suitably futuristic. Apart from crops with built-in disease and drought resistance, it's likely that we will see foods stripped of "problematic" properties and foods with added health-related properties, such as memory-enhancing vegetables for older people. Some of these "nutraceuticals" and "farmaceuticals" will undoubtedly justify their existence, but one does wonder if the world really needs appetite-suppressing toothpaste and breakfast cereals that treat acne.

Food for thought

Why have we become so interested in food all of a sudden? One reason is our increasing interest in personal and environmental health. Food has become a consumer issue tied up with everything from politics and globalization to fashion, economics and national identity. And it is this last point that's often overlooked. Recent debates about immigration and ethnicity have thrown the spotlight onto culinary heritage and food has become mixed up with trends ranging from tribalism and wellbeing to nostalgia and nationalism. This means we'll see everything from food terrorism and the rise of food-related, single-issue action groups to backward-looking, nostalgic food products.

One development that's definitely coming is personalized food, which will come in two flavors, so to speak. At the serious end we'll see diets and foodstuffs tailored to our individual genetic makeup or medical history. If, like me, you have high blood pressure, it will be possible (perhaps compulsory) to eat a range of ordinary, even indulgent foods modified to treat this particular condition. Equally, nanotechnology will allow us to change the properties of an individual product at will, so you will be able to increase the vitamin E content of an orange-juice drink after you've bought it.

At the silly end of the spectrum we'll also see nanotechnology being used to store certain ingredients or additives inside food products to be called up at will. For instance, you may wish to change the color of your soft drink or dial up the spice level of your ready-to-eat curry by firing a command off your cellphone. None of this is going to happen next week but, sure as eggs are eggs, if you can dream it you'll be able to do it.

Back to now. What are we already seeing in food that we'll get more of in the immediate future? For a start we'll be eating fewer meals at home and more snacks between home and work. In the US 15% of meals are already eaten in cars and roughly 60% of fast-food breakfast sales are made at the drive-through window.

"Grazing", a buzzword in the 1980s and 1990s, is now being replaced by phrases like "portability", "eating on the hoof" and "drive-by dining". The reason for this is primarily that we're time-starved, but it's also linked to other societal shifts like the social acceptability of eating in the street while walking (unthinkable a generation ago).

As a result, food manufacturers are developing a host of new products in portable packs to be eaten on the go, although whether they are creating demand or responding to it is somewhat unclear. Chocolate bars and other snacks are now available in cup-holder packaging so you can eat while driving (if the fat-laden crisps don't kill you directly, the car in front probably will). Meanwhile, 50% of soup is now consumed outside the home, whereas a few years ago the figure was just 2%. By the way, if you're wondering about driving while consuming hot soup, don't worry: the trend is primarily for office-based consumption. Speed and convenience (together with anxiety about health) will also drive plain-language labeling over the next few years, together with small-plate meals and single-course restaurants.

A lack of time isn't just shifting consumption away from the home: it will also change how we shop for food and even what we eat in restaurants. We are already seeing growth in online super-market shopping and home-food delivery, and this will increase in the future. As a result there will be two types of food shopping: the regular weekly or monthly repeat buying of items consumed day-in, day-out (most of which will eventually go online with auto-mated ordering, shopping lists and delivery); and impulse buying, where we shop for premium foods and meals in highly sensory, high-touch environments.

How fast our food gets will, of course, depend on where we are and what we are willing to pay for convenience. Fast-food companies such as McDonald's, Burger King and Taco Bell are currently testing a product from Hyperactive Technologies that can predict what you eat based on the car you drive. A camera "reads" your car model as you enter the drive-in and it compares this data with what drivers of similar vehicles have ordered in the past. An order is then sent to the kitchen, which starts preparing your meal before you've ordered it, thus saving you vital minutes. Clearly the model isn't perfect, but it's good enough to interest the fast-food companies because wait times have dropped by at least 60 seconds. Interestingly, staff retention levels have also improved because kitchen stress levels have declined.

So how about a supermarket that "reads" its customers the moment they walk into a store? This is quite likely. Tesco in the UK has 13 million loyalty card holders, so asking customers to swipe their cards when they enter a store would provide vital information about what they are about to buy. If it could then predict a sudden rush on white-bread sales within the next two minutes, shelf facings and special offers could be adjusted accordingly. And that's before you start introducing RFID cards that can be read remotely (no need to swipe them) or software that compares customer body size and shape (and clothing) to what similar-looking customers have bought in the past.

A trend sweeping the US at the moment, and certain to appear elsewhere fairly soon, is the do-it-yourself dinner shop. Also known as fix-and-freeze companies, these are stores where time-hungry customers concerned about what they are eating purchase pre-prepared ingredients for assembly in the store. Leading the field is Dream Dinners, which has grown from around 50 stores in 2005 to over 200 in 2008. Competitors include Let's Dish, Super Suppers, Dinner by Design and Really Cool Foods. While the names and menus may differ from company to company, the setup is essentially the same: customers go online to choose a range of dishes and book an appointment to visit the store. Once there, they assemble their meals from pre-cut color-coded ingredients, customizing them to suit their particular taste or dietary requirements. If they need help it's available and meals are packaged and ready for the freezer, complete with full cooking instructions and use-by dates.

The idea behind these self-assembly food stores is that they allow time-starved people to provide their family and friends with a nutritious hot meal at a lower cost than takeaway or supermarket dinners. There's no time spent shopping; there's minimal cleaning up afterwards; and because you only buy what you use, there's minimal waste. If you want organic you can have it — and if you're really pressed for time you can cook up a whole month's worth of meals and have them delivered to your door.

There's another possible explanation for the success of these food stores. It could be argued that the social aspects of meal preparation (women usually visit the stores in small groups) are compensation for increasing loneliness or that the hands-on, participatory nature of this type of cooking alleviates some of the problems of increasingly virtual and remote lives.

A simple choice

Strangely, something else we'll see in the future is less choice. One problem with abundance is that there's just too much of it, a point well made by Barry Schwartz in *The Paradox of Choice*. He argues that having too many options is paralyzing our ability to make quick and meaningful decisions.

One solution to this in a supermarket is simply to throw out any product that doesn't offer a real point of difference or to replace the countless "me-too" brands with private-label alternatives. Another is to heavily edit or curate what's available. Replace complexity with simplicity.

Ranking Ranqueen in Tokyo is a small chain of stores in which everything is sold by lists. For example, the store only sells the top five pasta sauces, top five soups and so on. Taken to the extreme, this will mean stores that only sell one type of cheese, although perhaps the variety might rotate from week to week. This, too, is already happening and we are also starting to see restaurants that offer very little choice. Salt restaurant in New York gives diners the choice of just two main courses and Clarke's in London generally offers only a couple of fish, meat and vegetarian alternatives.

This is an excellent example of how some trends go in cycles. If someone opened a restaurant tomorrow on the basis that high-flying city types were stressed out from making decisions during the day so they needed a restaurant that makes all the decisions for them (no choice at all), I suspect that some would regard this as an innovation. The reality is, of course, that this is exactly how things used to be. The menu was made up each day according to what was available at the market, and there was next to no choice because holding stock or preparing ingredients that may or may not get used was expensive. So if there's anyone out there thinking of setting up a restaurant called Red or White, where the only choice is the color of the meat and the wine, I suggest you do it very soon before someone else does.

In the mood for food

In the future restaurants will become much more savvy in terms of getting people to spend money. It's reasonably well known, for example, that playing certain types of music can change a person's mood. Classical music makes diners feel rich and sophisticated and they tend to be happy to pay more for their meal as a result. Pop music, in contrast, makes people less willing to spend, although one suspects that everything depends on the age of the particular customer, the type of restaurant and which specific piece of music is being played.

This is all perfectly legal, although food retailers may be tempted to push the boundaries. Food itself, after all, is very good at influencing mood, but I'm not just talking about the difference between eating proteins or carbohydrates or the mystical properties of chocolate. Adding tryptophan and valerian acid to desserts and petit fours, for instance, would make customers more relaxed and therefore happier about paying a large bill.

The relationship between mood and food is well known in food-industry circles and is slowly making an impact at the customer level too. While we are now aware of the link between food colorings and hyperactivity in children, we have only started to scratch the surface in terms of which foods do what and how they are sold as a result. A good example comes from a supermarket in the UK that noticed a spike in sales of food such as broccoli at the same time every year. At first the company couldn't work out what was going on, until its managers realized that the sales spike coincided with school examination periods. Word had got out that broccoli was a brainfood and anxious mothers were force-feeding it to their youngsters as a study aid.

Future developments will include other brain-enhancing foods (initially using omega 3 oils), those that aid relaxation (such as chocolate with added amino acids), anti-ageing products, anti-tiredness foods, some that send you to sleep and others that wake you up. We could even see dream-enhancing foods and foods designed to trigger specific childhood memories. People will also tap into moods by treating themselves with sensual self-indulgences. This will drive an interest in luxury food products and foods that are good because they're bad for you, if that makes any sense at all.

We'll also see more foods targeted at older people. As I've said before, one of the biggest trends affecting developed nations is ageing, particularly the increase in numbers of people over 60, many of whom find it difficult to chew or swallow or have very specific dietary requirements. As a result, we'll see more foods such as ice cream specifically developed for seniors, or crossover foods such as easy-to-eat vegetables and fruit purées that can be eaten by babies and seniors alike.

For people over about 45, food will increasingly be linked to wellbeing and medicine, which means body repair and longevity.

The name of the game will be not dying too soon, so foods that promise increased longevity or greater brainpower or memory will appear on supermarket shelves. For those under 45, eating will be about the control of body shape and appearance. Thus we will see more products like Norelift (a French jam that contains anti-wrinkle compounds) and perhaps more faddish products like Bust-Up, a Japanese chewing gum that allegedly firms up and improves the appearance of your breasts (honestly, this exists).

The future of food will thus be polarized between a number of opposites: the local and the global; the healthy and the indulgent; the futuristic and the nostalgic; the low cost and the luxurious; and the fast and the slow. For most people, convenience will be everything and if that means never peeling a potato or washing a lettuce, so be it. If it means eating less healthily, then so be it. Eating will be replaced with a series of "meal problems" and "meal solutions"; the faster some people can shop, cook and eat, the better.

Sometimes what people eat will be healthy but for the most part it will be comfort food — something that helps you unwind, that gives olfactory and oral pleasure, and perhaps that reminds you of what you ate as a child before food got so complicated and dangerous. We will see people swinging from indulgence to health on a daily or weekly basis — sometimes even in the same meal. We will save up food credits from healthy eating or exercise and then "spend" these points on indulgent foods or physical inactivity.

And what is "healthy" anyway? Is it a slice of white bread made from GM wheat to reduce calorific absorption or is it a carrot freshly plucked from pesticide-free soil? I, for one, am confused. The answer, of course, depends on who is asking the question. For a 60-year-old man with high blood pressure, genetically enhanced foods could be future lifesavers; for a baby, Mother Nature does generally know best.

Fat chance

If you took all the overweight people in the world and crossed them with all the underfed people, what average-size person would result? I have no idea, but we can be fairly certain that the average global size is increasing. One thing I do know is that the total number of overweight people on the planet has now overtaken the number of underweight and malnourished for the first time in history. There are now over 1 billion overweight people compared to 800 million who do not have enough to eat. According to the UN, 60% of US adults (and 15% of children aged 6 to 19) and 30% of European adults are already obese. In the US deaths from obesity are second only to those from smoking.

For food companies the concern is that food will become akin to tobacco, attracting spiraling legislation and lawsuits. So far this is a long way off, although theoretically all it would take to open the floodgates would be a piece of academic research proving beyond reasonable doubt that certain foodstuffs, or ingredient combinations, were addictive, and that some food and soft drink companies have known this all along. Perhaps in the future there will be a department of soft drinks, confectionery, alcohol and tobacco to regulate such matters.

Assuming for a moment that obesity gets even worse in the future, what can we expect to see as a result? Fat taxes have been openly debated for a number of years. The idea here is that if you knowingly sell foods that make people ill or susceptible to illness, you should cover some of the costs associated with future treatment.

This is obviously tricky, because how do you define healthy and non-healthy foods and where do you draw the line in terms of normal and abusive use? Perhaps what is more likely is that certain foodstuffs will attract supplementary taxes or tax credits. Either that or healthcare will be restricted according to your food history. In other words, you will be free to eat anything you want in any quantity you like, but you cannot then have access to the same healthcare services as people who have been more restrained or responsible.

Why, for example, should a 40-year-old vegetarian woman on a long-term self-imposed low-calorie diet (which drastically reduces blood pressure and cholesterol) have exactly the same access to medical services as a 40-year-old woman who smokes, drinks to excess and lives on a diet of burgers and chips? In the future she won't — or at least, her insurance company will know all about her food-purchasing patterns and will increase her health premiums accordingly.

Particular types of eating will be blocked off in much the same way that insurance companies currently prevent high-risk drivers from driving certain types of vehicle. How will they do this? Easy. In the future most transactions will be digital using bankcards, credit cards or digital cash stored in your cellphone, so anonymity will be virtually impossible. Insurance companies will be able to buy (or be given) data on their customers' eating habits and behavior and adjust their risk profiles accordingly.

We could even see food influencing town planning and house building, with national governments and local councils teaming up with cartographers to produce food maps showing how local food availability influences consumption and health. These maps could then be used to zone certain residential areas as "non-food areas", although politically this could be a hot potato. When I was growing up there was a sweet shop immediately opposite my school gates. As a result I have a mouth full of fillings. Will this be allowed in the future; if so, could children sue the shop owner for the cost of the subsequent dental work?

Another non-governmental solution to the obesity problem will be at the retail level. We have already seen supermarket loyalty cards in the US linked to FDA daily allowances: your purchases are compared to the recommended level of calories and vitamins and any shortfalls result in a money-off voucher printed on the back of your till receipt. Whether supermarkets should be made responsible for the health of their customers is an interesting question. Perhaps a more likely scenario is a cellphone that uploads information about what you eat (from the RFID codes on packs or the barcodes on restaurant menus) and makes helpful suggestions about what you are consuming. Such devices could be quite useful because they would contain your food history. For example, your doctor may want to be aware of how much alcohol you really drink or what your annual calorific intake is, while you might want to know how many days it's been since you ate a Caesar salad and where you bought it.

Why is food so controversial? Why are extremely fat and extremely thin people so media friendly and what is it about food that we are so afraid of? Again, context is everything. In northern Europe, the US and Japan there have been a series of food safety scares ranging from CJD to BSE and people are naturally skeptical about the ability of government and big business to tell the truth. Add to this distrust the fact that most food is grown on an industrial scale in artificial conditions and it's no wonder that people are flocking to farmers' markets and organic butchers, as well as growing their own. It's about control of information and trust. As a result, we're likely to see celebrities becoming farmers and farmers becoming famous.

An appetite for information

People want to know where their food is from, who grew it and under what circumstances. They may even want to know what the producer believes. In the US you can currently buy "Christian chicken" produced in accordance with the teachings of Jesus. Admittedly this is a bit on the fringe, but it's simply an extrapolation of the same idea as kosher or halal foods.

Tribalism will also make itself felt in other areas. Food will become more regional in the sense that we will no longer simply pop out for a Chinese or Indian meal. By 2020 such generic terms will be as meaningless as having an English. We will be eating Oaxacan instead of Mexican, Szechwan rather than Chinese and Tuscan rather than Italian.

Provenance will become increasingly important, not just for the chattering classes buying organic Welsh lamb in Harrods but for soccer mums buying sliced white bread in Wal-Mart. In other words, the type of information provided to the public on a bottle of wine (who made it, when, where and how) will become the norm on all other foodstuffs. This will mean a return to the consumption of seasonal products because they will be local, which means cheaper and more environmentally sustainable. If a product involves too many food-miles we won't buy it and we may boycott the company that makes it or transports it.

You can see the early signs of this already. Back in the 1960s and 1970s the slogan of US student activists was "No War". These days, although they may be protesting about the wars raging in Afghanistan and Iraq, they're also proclaiming "Eat Local" as they boycott national and global brands in favor of locally grown produce that supports the livelihoods of local farmers and that (they think) stops global warming and pollution. Back in 2001 the University of Portland, which dishes up 22,000 meals a week, spent just 2% of its food budget on purchases from local suppliers. Now the figure is closer to 40% and 200 other US universities have jumped onto the local-supplier bandwagon (over half of them since 2001). Students are busy pushing organic, seasonal, slow food and food-miles agendas to catering giants such as Sodexho and Armamark Corporation.

However, while these students are full of idealism for eco-eating, they (and we) are finding out the hard way the practicalities of global economics. Sourcing local ingredients from a multitude of small suppliers is time-consuming and expensive compared to hiring a single company with a global supply chain. But, like they say, principles aren't principles until they cost time and money.

Buying an organic tomato in a supermarket is all very well, but if the tomato has been grown using child labor in Zimbabwe and then flown from Harare to London by a company owned by a corrupt politician it's not ethically produced, is it? Thus sustainable agriculture will move to center stage and people will become genuinely concerned about the CO_2 emissions created by their food.

Part of the problem here is not only globalized production and air transport, but also the logistical operations of big supermarket chains that centralize warehousing and distribution. Thus a lettuce grown down the road can end up traveling halfway around the country before it ends up in your local supermarket. Hence retailers will not just emphasize the country and region of origin of food products, they'll devise a way of displaying food-miles and other sustainability ratings too.

At the other extreme, we will witness the continued growth of luxury food products that cost well in excess of what we and the particular food category in question have historically been used to. This could conflict with the need for local sourcing, although perhaps a compromise will be a renewed interest in rare wild foods found locally.

This trend toward regionality and seasonality is great news for local food producers and retailers and you can be certain that the larger food companies will follow suit. Some of this might be effective, like developing a local-products aisle in the supermarket or stocking fair-trade products. However, authenticity is a complicated issue. For instance, when does a dish or ingredient gain or lose its "authentic" status? Is feta cheese made outside of Greece really feta? (The EU doesn't think so.) Is a pizza truly a pizza if it's eaten outside Naples? Equally, what does "fresh" or "natural" really mean and should there be legislation to prevent the abuse of these terms? These days "organic" is increasingly just another offshoot of global agribusiness. In some countries the term doesn't mean "no pesticides", only that they have been used sparingly. Animals are even suffering because organic rules prevent the continuing use of antibiotics.

The current debates about food-miles and fair-trade products will thus grow in stature and food retailers will be forced by customers and politicians alike to support local producers and Earth-friendly production whether they like it or not. In the US, Heritage Foods (a poultry company) already provides detailed information about how its products are produced and offers a web link so that customers can visit its farm online. It would be interesting to see what the reaction would be if you turned up in person and asked to see the conditions first hand.

Another spinoff from localization and sustainability is the movement to grow your own food. It's interesting to note that in the UK the four largest seed firms recently reported that sales of vegetable seeds exceeded those of flower seeds for the first time since 1945, when the entire nation was being encouraged to dig for victory as part of the war effort. Why is this happening? It's obviously connected to the need for traceability (control again), but it's also indirectly connected with technology and busyness. As technology moves further into our lives, we are feeling disconnected from the natural world. Growing our own food is one way to connect with nature. Meal preparation is also an outlet for creativity and relaxation, which is why we'll see a rise in activities like hobby baking too.

The other reason localization will happen is because of globalization and resource scarcity. In theory it makes a lot of sense for food giants such as Unilever and Nestlé to source ingredients globally and then sell the same food products the world over. Unfortunately, this is not what people want. The homogenized approach will come under increasing pressure due to a number of factors. Labor costs will eventually equalize globally and transport costs will skyrocket as oil and other natural resources like water become more scarce. Add to this a grassroots backlash against local jobs going abroad (eventually supported by government tariffs and protection) and we'll see food returning to where it came from a century ago. But not for everyone.

Instead of an innovation replacing an incumbent idea, often the new sits alongside the old. Thus you will have a choice about what you eat and where you buy it. If you want cheap, frozen, farmed fish or low-cost hamburgers made from rendered beef carcasses you'll be able to get them, probably in a supermarket, but you'll also be able to buy wild fish and organic beef, all within a 2km radius.

A taste of the technology to come

As in other industries, technology will fundamentally affect not only how food is produced and bought in the future but how and where we consume it. RFIDs, sensor motes, smart dust and tiny flat screens and computers will help producers, retailers and consumers alike keep a track on where things are from and where they are now.

Foodstuffs will be made safe — or at least appear safe — through the use of technology. In Japan you can already scan the barcodes of some fruit and vegetables with your cellphone to find out where they're from and precisely which pesticides and fertilizers have been used on them. In the future this will go much further. Identity verification will allow you to "interrogate" frozen mincemeat in supermarkets, or download information at home about which herd the beef came from, the name and location of the farm, the diet of the animals, the application of pesticides and fertilizers, and the method of killing. Such "tagging" is already commonplace with beef in countries such as Australia where "paddock to plate" information is captured, but currently data is not usually shared with the end-user or consumer.

Science will also help with food allergies. In most western societies about 25% of people claim that they have a food allergy, sensitivity or intolerance of some kind. According to one study, between 1997 and 2002 there was a doubling of the number suffering from a peanut allergy in the UK. Scientists are engineering safe copies of popular foodstuffs so that people with food intolerances and allergies can eat normally. The products are expected to be available in supermarkets by 2016.

One plausible explanation for the intolerance epidemic is to do with the high level of processed foods in the modern diet, while another lays the blame on our super-clean lifestyles that banish dirt — and resistance to illness along with it. We are not only becoming suspicious of food, we are becoming anxious and even paranoid about what it touches. Hence you can buy everything from knives and plates to workbenches and even garbage bags with anti-bacterial properties. I wouldn't be at all surprised if anti-bacterial ready-to-eat meals make an appearance at some point.

Another area where technology will be used is in speeding things up still further, although whether this is really good for us is another matter. People will want food that's easier to buy and to cook. This will mean designing ready-to-eat meals in packaging that goes straight from the shopping basket into the microwave. It will also mean pre-washed, pre-cut ingredients, clearer labeling, faster checkouts and restaurants that know what you want before you do. It will also mean kettles that boil water a few seconds faster, appliances that cool things down quicker and others that are net-worked and linked to devices such as cellphones and laptops so you can switch on your oven while you're still at work.

Wine bottles will have built-in thermometers that tell you exactly what their current temperature is, or will play a short film explaining where they come from. Milk cartons and eggs will flash danger symbols when they are past their use-by dates and cake mixes will speak to you explaining how to make them. Cereal pack-ets will play short animations to keep the kids amused at breakfast time and packaging "networks" will allow packs to speak to each other and interact with other household devices and appliances.

Does this mean that the internet fridge will finally take off? Probably not, because there is no real customer need and the com-puter usually gets old and out of date before the fridge does. Nevertheless, some way of reminding you of what food you've got in your house, what you can make with it and ordering what you need but don't have could be a winner.

In Japan, Mitsubishi sells a kitchen appliance with the snappy name of the Umasa Vitamin Zoryo Hikari Power Yasai Shitsu fridge. It's the first refrigerator in the world that increases the vitamin C content of the food stored in it through a process of photosynthesis. This is a good example of how technology will be used to increase the healthiness of what we eat.

Food slaves

They used to say that you are what you eat. If that's true, many of us will become paranoid schizophrenics in the future. Eating used to be a pleasure — it still is, for some — but many of us are becoming either frightened by or fanatical about food. Both are forms of food slavery. Food is getting to be either something you try to avoid because you think it will kill you or make you fat, or else something deeply inconvenient you'd rather do without altogether if only you could. We are either junk-food monkeys eating whatever is convenient and within reach, or food bores continually moaning about the water not being organic or that our boutique dark chocolate isn't made in accordance with Kenyan fair-trade principles and the wrapper isn't recyclable.

Not everyone thinks like this, of course. There are still people out there (large chunks of France and Italy, for example) who live to eat and continue to find the time to shop and eat properly too. Elsewhere we eat, but we seem to need to justify what we eat and the time we spend doing it.

Once people went home during their lunch break to eat. Others went to the works canteen. Work stopped for a brief moment and people sat and talked. Now we grab a bite on the run or sit at our desks alone and spill portable foods over our keyboards, like I've just done. And heaven forbid if you're tempted to have a drink at lunchtime if you're working. Don't get me wrong here: drinking eight pints of beer and then operating heavy machinery isn't a good idea. But a glass of wine over lunch isn't going to ruin your accountancy business.

Does any of this matter? Yes, because the dictates of global capitalism have overridden a natural human necessity. We are feeding our bodies but not our souls.

In the future, you will pay your money and take your choice. If you're feeling anxious about an increasingly uncertain and seemingly out-of-control world, you will escape into the supposed safety of your childhood by eating comfort foods like macaroni cheese or meatloaf, if you're a baby boomer. Your home will be a shrine to Aga nostalgia (at least in the UK) and you will dream of moving to Italy to grow your own organic lemons and bake your own rustic bread. If you're a microwave mum or a member of a hectic household, you'll eat a mixture of ready-to-eat meals and portable snacks suitably enhanced by science to offset their highly processed nature.

Most of us will live somewhere in the middle, juggling time and a need for speed with financial constraints and concerns about individual and environmental wellbeing: a crazy, mixed-up world where nobody is quite sure what we should be eating and suffering from feelings of anxiety, starvation and gluttony in equal measure.

12 September 2026

Dear Theodore

How's things? I'm in a rush as usual. This morning I checked my AiPhone to see what was in my fridge and a series of flashing icons told me all my milk and fruit was way past its use-by date. I sent a message to my cleaner to please remove it and ordered some more from myfridge.com. I grabbed one of the new WakeMeUp™ apples on the way downstairs and jumped into my Personal Electric Vehicle. It was still only 6.30 a.m. so I drove into my local MacBucks. Fortunately MacBucks' Intelligent Ordering System had already identified my PEV from my last visit and beamed my recent order history onto my windscreen. I scrolled down and decided on a free-range Ethiburger. "Do I want a happy drink with that?" You bet. Lunch, as usual, was a protein slice at 4 p.m., most of which ended up all over my Web gloves. Actually, that was quite lucky because one of the sensors in the right glove picked up traces of ZXD131 and I spat out the rest of the slice, adding the incident to my food history file and passing the matter on to my food lawyer.

The evening wasn't much better. It was my turn to cook, so I decided to pop past the 5-Eleven gourmet convenience store to see what tickled my tastebuds (sometimes it's fun to turn everything off, turn up unannounced and see what they do!). Eventually I tucked into a Yagga beefsteak from New Zealand. Drinks? I had a bottle of Irish Zinfandel. When I waved the bottle in front of the computer it played a film about how the 2024 harvest went. I could even press a button on the bottle and order another!

Cheers

Ronald

5 trends that will transform retail

Luxury versus low cost   Retail is polarizing between luxury and low-cost segments and this will continue well into the future — or at least until there is a major recession, at which point we will all become economy shoppers again. However, shoppers are contradictory and will happily buy standard $15 T-shirts one minute and custom-made $500 jeans the next. Because customers shop across all segments, we will expect high-quality service all of the time regardless of what we are paying.

Speed and simplicity   We are busy people and we want whatever we want right now. This is particularly true of Gen Y, which has grown up with high-speed internet connections and therefore suffers from what's been termed digital instant gratification syndrome. However, we are all running out of time and any retailer that can speed up or simplify a transaction will be rewarded. For example, queuing will become an even greater source of stress and aggravation. DIY customer-service kiosks, vending machines, contactless payment, drive-through, home delivery, city-center convenience stores and e-tail will therefore all do well in the future. So too will retailers that offer edited choice as a response to the avalanche of information and too much choice.

Changes in household composition   There will be many more old people in the future, so retailers will slowly respond by designing stores and products that appeal to the 55 and over crowd who have both time and money to spend. Thus promises of immortality, or at least longevity, will do well. The continued rise of single-person households (lived in by young and old alike) will also have profound implications for everything from store design to product formatting and packaging. Products will thus have to be available in ones as well as twos and fours. Similarly, old favorites and classics will enjoy a resurgence of popularity as older shoppers go all misty-eyed about the distant past.

Sustainability   Twentieth-century shoppers compared prices. In the twenty-first century they compare ethical standards. We've already had sweatshop-free clothing brands and the return of neighborhood retail, but we haven't really seen anything yet. In the future shoppers will be swayed by various green and ethical issues, some of which will be serious while others will be just plain silly. For example, there will be a crusade against retailers that sell lettuce on the basis that growing lettuces uses too much water; and a campaign to stop eating foreign food on the basis of its carbon footprint. Thus fair-trade products, food-miles, minimal and reusable packaging and products that benefit a local community or the wider world in some way will be in demand.

Storytelling, authenticity and trust   We are fed an endless diet of half-truths and manipulated statistics by companies (and governments) wanting us to buy something. The result is cynicism and a compensatory interest in authenticity or "realness". We want information. We want to know where things (and people) are coming from, physically and metaphorically. We also want to know what the story or narrative is so that we can make our own mind up about the "facts". This interest in information will only increase. Life-story labels will tell us how things are made and where they are from. This means real people with real stories to tell. This will be good news for brands with history and heritage, but it will also benefit retailers that can tell a story through a hands-on experience. Similarly, the issue of trust isn't going away any time soon.

Chapter 8

Retail and Shopping: what we'll buy when we've got it already

Predicting the future is easy. It's trying to figure out what's going on now that's hard.
—Fritz Dressler

Jump in a Volkswagen and take a quick trip to the town of Rheinberg, Germany. It's home to a 4,000-square-meter super-market created by Metro, the world's fifth-largest retailer. If you believe all the hype, you'll see the future of supermarket shopping right here.

In this store — and there are a few others like it scattered across the globe — you'll find the latest retail innovations, including "Veggie Vision" intelligent scales that can identify and price fruit and vegetables by sight, regardless of whether they're loose or wrapped in plastic. You'll also find computers that can be clipped to shopping trolleys and activated by inserting a customer loyalty card. Once signed in, you can download the shopping list you emailed to the store earlier, check your favorites, print out personalized special offers and get directions to the toothpaste aisle (which in theory could be any toothpaste aisle to compare products and prices if the store allowed customers to link to other shops via Google Maps, for instance). There are also information terminals scattered around the store to help you learn more about a particular product or to request a recipe for the fish you've just purchased. Needless to say, the supermarket also uses RFID technology to ensure that the shelves are never empty.

Looking a few decades further into the future, in-store ads will target you the moment you pick up a bottle of Heinz tomato sauce. You may be pegged as a frequent Heinz buyer and instantly offered a voucher rewarding your past loyalty. The ads — on individual sauce bottles — may even know how much sauce you have at home and remind you when to stock up, thanks to wireless links to cupboards and refrigerators. Indeed, everything you have ever bought will reside on a database somewhere, theoretically to help retailers track returns or model-buying habits and to adjust product availability in your local store.

But do you want Heinz, or for that matter the supermarket, to know that much about you? Some customers will, selling or giving away personal information in return for a fistful of discount vouchers. Others, like me, will guard their privacy jealously using cash — while it's still available — or fake loyalty cards to dupe the system and remain "off network".

Shops are already intelligent and they are getting more so. In the future, a store might greet you by name and direct you to a loyalty queue for a speedy checkout. Or you may not even have to check out: an RFID reader will scan your shopping bags as you walk out of the store and the bill will be sent automatically to your credit-card company or bank.

The Prada store in New York already shows footage of models wearing certain outfits if you hold the clothes up to a nearby screen. RFID technologies will scan your body from all angles and produce a 360-degree 3D model to help you find clothes that fit you precisely. Entering the data into a terminal will also instantly tell you whether certain items are in stock, or perhaps inform you of where products were made and under what conditions. Will customers really wear such high-tech innovations? Some will and some won't.

Retailers like Tesco have been collecting data on their customers for years using the euphemistically named loyalty card (surely the loyalty should be the other way around?). Indeed, one report has it that Tesco now knows more about every citizen in the UK than the British government does. The sheer amount of this data has created a bit of a problem for some retailers historically, but in the future data mining and prediction analysis will result in the personalization of everything from special offers and advertising to product design, revolutionizing how we shop. In the case of Tesco, this means listening to the needs and wants of very small subsets of the population whose voices are usually drowned out by statistically representative samples of the majority. Micro-segmentation and micro-trends are going to be big.

For the younger crowd technology will increasingly replace people, either through automated vending and robotic assistants or via smart kiosks and online commerce; not for all goods, but for anything that's a habitual or commodity purchase. Online stores will also blur the line between reality and cyberspace, with much of the brand experience and browsing being delivered by virtual stores built in virtual malls or other online communities.

E-tail is obviously a massive trend but in many ways online shopping is still divorced from the real world. Online supermarkets are usually just text-based lists of products — you can't walk through the store. Indeed, despite the convenience factor, online shopping has virtually nothing in common with its real-world equivalent and in some ways this is an opportunity. For example, online you generally have to know what you're looking for and most people shop alone. In the real world shopping doesn't happen like this: it's more of an event, an experience that is usually shared, and customers listen to the recommendations of friends and trusted experts. This obviously hasn't escaped the attention of some savvy internet retail entrepreneurs and we are therefore starting to see the emergence of social shopping sites. Examples include Crowdstorm, ThisNext, Kaboodle, Become and Stylehive. These are a mash-up between search engines and social networking sites and allow shoppers to browse and buy based on other customers' recommendations.

In the REI outdoor gear store in Seattle, smart kiosks supplement traditional customer service. Staff can only be familiar with a fraction of the around 30,000 different products that each REI store carries. Each kiosk, by contrast, carries information on 78,000 products and has flawless product knowledge. In a similar vein, American Apparel and a host of other retail brands are building stores inside games like Second Life to attract members of Gen Y. The American Apparel store is 180 meters of prime retail space. You can stroll upstairs and choose something you like, then touch a nearby information panel that triggers a web page displaying information about the garment — for example what sizes and colors it's available in, or perhaps information about where it was made. Of course the store only exists in cyberspace, but that's where Gen Y are found these days: they are becoming harder and harder to reach using conventional stores or physical marketing.

Becoming a virtual retailer has one profound implication: the reputation of products, services and individual retailers will be given a concrete value by customers. Retailers with a history of doing what they promise will be rewarded, while those who are new or have an indifferent history will be treated cynically or avoided altogether. You can see the shape of things to come on eBay with its vendor-rating system, but this concept will increasingly flood into other areas, making it more and more difficult to hide unpalatable truths or conceal poor products and experiences. This will be another example of the customer being in control.

By contrast, older people generally loathe new technology. Most seniors (over 65) like dealing with people face to face as they've always done; despite the emergence of "silver surfers", most will remain resolutely offline whenever and wherever they can.

Technology and ageing populations are two of the key drivers of retail change in the twenty-first century. While much has been written about the former, very little has been written about the latter or about other changes in the population structure, such as the breakdown of the nuclear family or the growth of single-person households in urban and suburban areas.

I'll come back to technology in a while, but let's first deal with some of the implications of ageing and the shift in attitudes and behavior among all age groups.

Old, free and single

Let's jump back into that Volkswagen and this time take a journey to the Austrian city of Salzburg. Here you'll find a store called the Adeg Aktiv 50+ food market, which is targeted squarely at the over-50s shopper. (The average age in Europe is 37.7, but this is expected to rise to 52.3 by 2050.) Here you'll see better-than-standard lighting, non-slip floors, lots of seats and large, easy-to-read prices. The store also features lower-than-average shelving (so it's easier to reach the top), shopping trolleys that easily attach to wheelchairs, and magnifying glasses on aisle ends so that people who have difficulty seeing can read the packaging. The only thing Adeg Aktiv 50+ don't seem to have is a defibrillator to revive older customers when they have a heart attack.

However, this retailer is clearly an exception; most stores are still firmly designed to attract younger shoppers. This is deliciously ironic, because baby boomers managed to get retailers (and manufacturers) to pay attention when they were young and had money to spend. Now that they're old and have even more money to spend, retailers (and manufacturers) generally aren't interested. Why? Because the companies are run by young people.

This is clearly another world compared to the virtual stores inside Second Life, but one thing older people increasingly have in common with younger people is that they often live alone. In Europe something like 20–25% of all households comprise one person, while in the US the figure is even higher. This has implications for everything from packet sizes to the type and frequency of shopping trips. Broadly speaking, singles tend to shop at the last minute, often on foot, whereas families tend to do weekly megashops using a car. Older singles tend to have more time and less money available than younger ones, whereas younger singles tend to have less time and more money.

Future migration back to cities also means that low-tech convenience stores, 24-hour kiosks and giant vending machines like the Tik Tok Easy Shop, Smartmart or Shop24 may be more in touch with future customer needs too.

You can already buy (or in some cases rent) iPods, shoes, movies, pizzas and cellphones from vending machines; and in Japan, the spiritual home of the vending machine and all things robotic, there's even a robot department store, although you'll have to wait a few years until the store is entirely staffed by robotic sales assistants. In the meantime, though, you can always get a robotic fix by visiting the Aqua City commercial complex on Tokyo's waterfront. Here you can find D1 security robots patrolling stores and entertaining the shoppers.

What vending machines and convenience stores clearly have in common is speed. Apart from browsing for luxuries, daily shopping takes too much time and any idea that speeds things up is welcomed with open arms; at least by certain sections of the population. Sometimes things can go a bit too far. US golf clubs are hiring service representatives to firmly assist seniors who take too long to finish a game, while some golf carts now feature GPS tracking so the club can monitor individual rounds and give slow people a "nudge". We don't have GPS in shopping trolleys just yet (apart from perhaps in Rheinberg), but I'm sure it's only a matter of time.

What we do already have are in-store nutritionists offering dietary advice to shoppers, "keep-fit trolleys" that help you burn calories as you shop, in-store massage to relax people waiting in queues, in-store poets and personal grocery shoppers. As for the massage, I'd seriously predict that along with other forms of instant stress relief like sleeping (at home, in-store and especially at work), it will become a fixture in the future as people's lives speed up even more and become more stressful.

The battle of the sexes

There are also male or female crèche areas inside various super-markets. If you think I'm kidding, just take a trip to British retailer Marks & Spencer, which recently tested the idea of male crèches in a number of its stores. Conventional wisdom says that men don't like shopping unless they are a "metrosexual" or "über-male" and therefore should be put inside playpens while someone else (a female) does the shopping. But this misses the point entirely. To most men shopping is either research or a game to be fought and won. Winning means getting the best deal and foraging is usually done alone; women, by contrast, tend to browse in groups, shopping being a social experience as much as anything else.

The differences between men and women have not been lost on retailers. As we find out more about how male and female brains work, we can expect to see more stores designed to appeal to one or the other — but very rarely both.

Women are well served when it comes to female-only spaces, while men are not. There are women-only floors in hotels (Switzerland), female-only department stores (Argentina), female-only health clubs, shopping centers aimed squarely at women (Venus Fort in Tokyo) and women-only banks. There's even a convenience store called Happily (owned by AM/PM) in the Toranomon district of Tokyo, especially designed for women. All staff are female (except late at night for security reasons) and products are designed and selected for women by women. One nice touch is a powder room featuring full-length mirrors, a dressing table and a stool for women to rest their legs on while they change their tights (this will obviously be seen as practical or patronizing depending on your point of view).

Nevertheless, designers and developers still seem to be getting the basics wrong by building the same number of toilets in shopping centers when it's well known that women need at least twice as many cubicles as men. But I'm going off at a tangent. Let's get back to some of the key drivers of change.

A day at the department store

In the 1980s and 1990s shopping malls seemed to appear everywhere and the Mall of America was supposed to attract more visitors each year than Disney World. Nowadays many gigantic enclosed shopping malls are starting to look like dinosaurs, because shoppers are too busy and too tired to fight their way through huge car parks and endless corridors just to buy a pair of shoes. In the last ten years the number of women who consider shopping a "pick-me-up" has fallen from 45% to 21% in the US, while in another survey 53% of shoppers "hate the experience". In a similar vein, in 2000 US shoppers spent an average of 4 hours per month inside malls, but by 2003 this had fallen to 2.9 hours.

Something is going on here. It could be that most shopping centers have no authentic identity or sense of self. I call them "anywhere places", because the look and feel are the same in Boston and Bangkok. But I'm sure the main reason is that while shoppers have more money to spend, they have less and less time to waste. There are several quite distinct types of shopping and to be honest I don't see malls disappearing altogether. Indeed, their number could grow significantly because of the need for everything from security and convenience (all under one secure roof) to a desire for entertainment (ski-slopes and water parks adjacent to the clothing and groceries). Nevertheless, the nature and focus of malls will have to change.

The first type of shopping is habitual shopping for commodity items or essentials, where price and location are critical. This is "unthinking" in the sense that the shopping list of products (but not necessarily brands) barely changes from one month to the next, although the definition of "essential" will differ from one shopper to the next. Time saving and convenience are critical, so much of this type of retail activity will move online, with substantial growth in home delivery and drop-off (at work, petrol stations or transport hubs, for example). Customer service for habitual shopping will be almost entirely irrelevant, as most shoppers will prefer to bypass physical interactions if it means saving time or money. However, it doesn't mean that customer "servicing" (getting things right and responding efficiently when they go wrong) won't be important. It's simply that going above and beyond the call of duty will not be expected.

City-center supermarkets (in many cases inside apartment buildings and offices), convenience stores (some inside vehicles) and outlets modeled on the sari-sari stores in countries such as the Philippines that sell small packaging sizes will, however, all be perfectly suited to the needs of the hectic habitual shopper, so we'll see more retailers adopting these formats and channels in the future.

The second type of shopping is purposeful (often referred to as laser shopping). Purchases are more infrequent than habitual shopping and often involve replacing an existing product such as a toaster or fridge. Again, much of this activity will move to the internet, although this will be mainly to find information before seeing the product in the flesh. Speed will once more be of the essence, so the use of cellphones to research and then purchase products will grow as fast as high-speed data networks allow. Indeed, by 2017 I'd expect as much as 80–90% of all e-commerce within the 15- to 19-

year-old demographic to be conducted by cellphone. Already 80% of Ford's customers use the internet to find out which car they want to buy and how much they want to pay before they even set foot inside a dealership. Similarly, around 75% of cellphone buyers in the US use the internet to research products. Customers are seizing power and are now better informed about everything from prices and specifications to reliability and ethical issues. Nevertheless, seeing products in the flesh will still be critical, even if the final sale is made online.

This has profound implications for certain kinds of retail because some physical stores will become places where people touch and feel but do not ultimately buy. In other words, we will see more brand showrooms where you cannot actually buy anything.

The mindset of customers is also shifting, in the sense that we are moving from a permanent acquisition culture — where people save up and then buy something that they keep for a long time — to one based on instant gratification, where people sell or throw away things the moment they become bored with them. Thus stores may have to adjust to a model where customers can sell as well as buy new and secondhand goods, which are increasingly sold alongside each other (something many car showrooms do already). That is, of course, unless the auction culture remains almost exclusively online.

The third type of shopping — slow shopping — is more aligned with wants rather than needs and is therefore far more emotive and experience based. It is also very sensory, so we will witness a growth in the use of sensual (five-dimensional) branding, with retailers using smell, taste and touch alongside the more usual elements of sight and sound. This is shopping as a leisure activity, with the fun part looking rather than buying. Customer service is critical in this area, but it's people not technology who can ultimately deliver great customer service.

This is shopping as an end in itself and it is unlikely that this type of retail activity will move online until virtual worlds are able to capture the theater of a French market or a 1,000-year-old Moroccan bazaar. In the meantime, retailers will continue to sell the sizzle as well as the steak by adding services to commodity products. For example, a barbeque will be available with a cooking class or even a barbeque holiday as an optional extra.

Selfridges department store in London is a good example of retail theater. It describes itself as a theme park where customers are encouraged to buy souvenirs of their visit. Recent footfall (business) generators have included a regional food festival and a conceptual art installation in which 600 naked people rode up and down on the escalators. As they say, sex sells. Selfridges attracts 21 million visitors each year — about the entire population of Australia. If it can persuade even a tiny number of its customers to buy something, this translates into significant revenue.

This could all be temporary. Generally speaking, department stores are in trouble because they have lost touch with younger shoppers, who generally prefer big-box discounters, category killers, specialist retailers and, of course, the internet. The result is that some department stores have started to add restaurants and hotels, while shopping centers have begun to approach discounters to become anchor tenants in new developments, whereas previously department stores would have been the automatic choice.

Moreover, outdoor lifestyle centers, a fast-growing sector in retail, are now regularly built without any department store. Is there a solution to what is generally a downward trend? Looking at Selfridges you'd think so, but pulling off an iconic destination experience isn't easy.

Department stores will therefore move their brands online, while in the physical world they will continue to become destinations — days out — in their own right, thanks to a mixture of high-energy, crowd-pleasing theater and hands-on personal pampering, cocooning and relaxation, although one suspects that much of this might be rearranging deckchairs on the *Titanic*.

Stealth retail and fast fashion

A recurring theme in this book is that the more life becomes virtual and high-tech, the more people will crave the opposite: low-tech, high-touch. This means that there will continue to be a need for physical shops. Some people will always want physical interaction with human sales assistants and physical products, so don't knock down the old store just yet.

However, shoppers are getting fed up with giant retailers bull-dozing local communities and turning streets into homogenized strips devoid of life after dark. For example, 75% of people in Britain think that supermarkets like Tesco, which takes £1 for every £8 spent in Britain, have become too powerful and would support stricter government controls. This has not escaped the attention of the world's largest retailer, which is testing smaller neighborhood stores dubbed "Small-Marts".

Maybe the future is stealth retail: shops that don't operate like shops and malls that don't look like malls. This is not a new idea. Back in the 1960s Victor Gruen, the architect of the modern mall, called for retailers to incorporate civic and educational aims, so that shopping malls and supermarkets would function more like old-fashioned town centers, with non-retail elements like schools, doctors, libraries, churches and sport facilities. For example, Swiss retailer Migros has created health and education centers. However, connecting with the local community doesn't just mean parents collecting tokens for school computers. It means placing the school alongside the supermarket (Sainsbury's) or using retail space for community purposes by putting a police station inside a store (Tesco). Going local also means utilizing local labor and selling local produce. Farmers' markets have been so successful in recent years that there's even been talk of allowing them to use super-market carparks after hours.

Another area where retail is changing is in the creation and development of stores and products themselves. Once upon a time, stores and the products displayed within them were fairly static, in the sense that store designs changed infrequently and once a product became a bestseller it wasn't messed with. But two trends have converged to create "pop-up" stores and limited-edition products, where an annual model change is considered far too slow.

The pop-up retail trend, blending business and conceptual art, has been around for a while. Shops like the Meow Mix cat-food café in New York (I kid you not) work because they generate a buzz and people have short attention spans. We are also increasingly fed up with everything always looking the same. Thus we get guerrilla stores like Comme des Garçons in Berlin or Target's pop-up store in the Rockefeller Center, which suddenly appear without warning and then disappear in a similar manner, regardless of their success.

The idea of pop-up recognizes that in retail you can only be hot for so long. It is also arguably a reaction to high-concept retail (that is, flagships like the Rem Koolhass-designed Prada store). So where will pop-up go in the future? The answer is pop-up products and brands.

One of the biggest recent retail hits in the UK is a website called Asos.com (formerly known as As Seen On Screen). This e-tailer is a combined personal stylist and shopping destination that allows people (mainly women aged 16–35) to copy the look of their favorite celebrity, right down to their toenails. So when Gwyneth Paltrow was seen wearing a "Golden Balls" T-shirt given to her by David Beckham, the website had a batch of identical T-shirts made within hours and up for sale the following day. Shoppers can search by celebrity (say, Lindsay Lohan) or by category (say, sunglasses). The site also features up-and-coming niche designers. Like.com is a similar site that allows shoppers to conduct a visual search for a fashion item they have seen on a celebrity.

Spanish fashion retailer Zara is another example of pop-up or fast fashion, where designs are on a catwalk one day and in a physical store the next, although it is even more interesting because of the feedback loops between what customers walk in wearing and what shop managers report back to head office. Zara also works on the basis of producing limited batches, so that popular items automatically become scarce and you never know entirely what will be available when you visit, thus encouraging additional trips to the store. In an average year Zara launches 11,000 new products, versus 2,000–3,000 from rivals such as H&M and Gap, and spends just 0.3% of sales on advertising. It also hires unknown designers and keeps its manufacturing local, thus tightening its distribution networks.

Everything from food products to electricals is playing the same game, with the creation of limited-edition specials or celebrity-endorsed (or designed) products. I predict an increase in the influence of celebrities over everything we consume from bathrobes to butter. Oh gawd.

We'll also see limited-edition materials, colors and packaging, many of which will converge with regional and seasonal variations of nationally available brands. These trends clearly can't last for ever, as the strength of pop-up retail and limited-edition products lies in their being an alternative to the mainstream. If they become too common they will lose their value and will have to be replaced by something else.

Nevertheless, we have at least five to ten years left in the trend and what we'll probably see next are stores questioning what they are for. Tchibo (with over 1,000 stores worldwide) is a chain of German coffee shops that sells other products along with the coffee. There's nothing new here — it's just another example of the blurring between retail sectors — but the company seems to have dispensed with the idea that you should focus on one core skill and align new products to the principal offer. Instead, Tchibo has adopted a philosophy of "a new experience every week", so one week it sells bikes and the next ski suits alongside the latte. It's certainly different.

I just can't choose

Too much choice is an important trend that will drive profound change in retail circles over the next few decades. Put simply, there are too many choices available and customers don't have either the time or the inclination to edit or assess those options themselves.

In the film *Moscow on the Hudson*, Robin Williams plays a Russian defector living with a family in New York. As a goodwill gesture he volunteers to do the shopping, but passes out alongside the coffee aisle because the choices are just too overwhelming. The average supermarket in the US now sells 30,000 items. Typically this will include 26 types of Colgate toothpaste — there were just two in 1970 — and 724 varieties of fruit and vegetables, including 93 organic items. But why? Who needs that degree of choice?

To some extent, the proliferation of choice is due to retailers responding to customer demand. However, while some level of choice can be liberating, too much can induce paralysis. For example, in one study people entering a supermarket were offered 6 jams to taste; on another occasion they were offered 24. Both groups were given a $1-off coupon to spend on the jam. The result was that 30% of those tasting 6 jams bought a jar, compared to only 3% of those tasting 24 — apparently the decision-making process was just too complex and time-consuming. Similarly, when people were asked to react to a discounted Sony product in a shop window, most reacted with enthusiasm. But when a second discounted product was put alongside it, their enthusiasm waned. Back to simplicity, folks.

Consequences? Given that time is a vanishing resource, I'd expect more shoppers to outsource choice to various editors, curators, sifters and filters. In the US a chain of wine shops called Vino 100 sells just 100 different wines, all for under $25 per bottle. This I can empathize with. It's currently 4.30 p.m. and within the next 30 minutes I'm going to receive a phone call or email asking what we should eat for dinner. I have no idea. We have about 60 cookbooks at home but only eat about 15 different dishes. Whatever we choose to eat we haven't bought yet and we may well end up eating out, in which case the very last thing I want to see is a 60-page menu offering every specialty under the sun. No surprise, then, that when a supermarket decreased the number of products it sold by 20%, it saw an 11% increase in sales.

According to Professors Gourville (of Harvard University) and Soman (of the University of Toronto) there are two types of choice: "alignable choice", a variety of offerings along a single dimension such as size or color, for instance Levi 501 jeans; and "non-alignable" choice, where companies add features that involve trade-offs across dimensions. For example, toothpaste and cold medicines come with an almost overwhelming number of choices of features and benefits. Of course, cynics will say that we've seen this all before and they'd be right: in 1879 Frank Woolworth opened a store that featured limited choice and fast access.

Saving the planet

Another important trend is everyday low pricing, which is not without its costs. For example, Wal-Mart is accused of offering prices that are too low due to a business model that's too efficient, and along the way allegedly exploiting cheap labor and materials. Tesco is suffering much the same fate, although its supposed crime is destroying local shops and communities.

However, customers are free to shop anywhere they want and in most cases there is an alternative — albeit one that may take extra effort. And that, in a nutshell, is the problem. We feel that we should be doing something to save the local high street, but when it comes to a $10 pair of jeans our principles go out the window. It's the same with the environment. We see nothing ironic about filling the car with petrol to drive out of our way to The Body Shop to refill a plastic bottle so that we don't waste packaging that uses oil and damages the environment. We are all becoming conflicted, contrary and confused.

So what would happen if the world's largest retailer — and arguably one of the most powerful companies on Earth — decided to save the planet? Well, we're about to find out. Wal-Mart (with revenues of more than US$300 billion per year) recently laid out a plan to turn itself, and by default its suppliers, staff and customers, green. Its aims include increasing the fuel and emissions efficiency of its vehicle fleet by 25% by 2009 and doubling this by 2016. The company also plans to lower solid waste (that is, packaging) in its US stores by 25% by 2009. Critics say this is obviously greenwash, but the company claims otherwise. It has already become the world's largest buyer of organic milk and organic cotton and is also starting to buy food locally to reduce food-miles and increase freshness.

Nevertheless, there's a dilemma. Wal-Mart set up its stall on the basis of low prices, which helped the little guy. This is fine if the little guy wants to save the planet, but what if she or he does not? What if, for instance, ordinary Americans still want to buy bottled water when most experts agree that the product harms the environment? The answer, in the short term, is that Wal-Mart will respond to existing customer needs, but there is a bigger game at stake. Through its sheer size, the company has the power to affect what people think and want and therefore to democratize the sustainability issue. Watch this green space.

If Wal-Mart's plans succeed we will start to see fringe products such as organic shoes and organic furniture move into the mainstream. This could gather some serious momentum if localization also takes hold, and pretty soon we'll have shops selling loose products without packaging — like a century ago — and these will mostly be made or grown locally. This will correspond with the rise in tribalism and economic protectionism mentioned in Chapter 1.

Realistically, though, both extremes will co-exist. There will be big-box retailers selling globally produced products at knock-down prices, while up the road the mom-and-pop store will be selling local apples and homemade cakes. The future will therefore be a heavily polarized and confusingly paradoxical place. The retail market will be split between austere low-cost and indulgent luxury sectors, and we will become passionate about single issues while simultaneously displaying contradictory shopping attitudes and retail behavior.

Low-cost goods exist as a historical and political accident. They are dependent on process innovations, which suffer from the law of diminishing returns, and on access to low-cost labor and materials brought about by globalization. Eventually labor rates will equalize and materials will start to run out, especially if the global population continues to increase. In the long term resources and labor problems will be solved through technology; but in the short term low-cost products could very well become a thing of the past.

This issue doesn't apply to virtual goods and services and it's possible that accelerated technological innovation would allow the low-cost model to last for longer, but it will end sooner or later. Until then, markets will continue to polarize between the luxury and economy segments and most retail areas will experience some level of premiumization or trading up (assuming that the global economy doesn't crash, in which case all bets are off). For example, we'll see the emergence of high-security "black card" malls and stores where customers will only be allowed in if the store owner or mall knows who you are (either personally or via electronic identity verification).

Why will this happen? There has been a steady growth in household and individual incomes over the past 10 or 20 years. In addition, more women are working and earning more and there are more single-person households (often without children), which tends to raise incomes even further. This means that what was once seen as a luxury is now increasingly seen as a necessity.

Add to this ageing populations with high levels of asset wealth and a billion new middle-class consumers in Asia, Africa and elsewhere, and you can start to see why there's now a market for Gucci toolkits and pet carriers.

Another more mundane example is coffee. In barely more than a decade real coffee has moved from a US east-coast boutique phenomenon to an everyday necessity across an increasingly large part of the world. If you add up what you now spend on coffee across a year you might be in for a shock — but you can afford it. Will this last? I think ultimately not. The luxury bubble will eventually burst, probably due to a global recession caused by the collapse of a major economy such as the US or China.

Maybe this is no bad thing. Perhaps we will witness a shift away from consumerism and physical consumption to the consumption of experiences. The current trend toward bigger and bigger global retailers may reverse and we'll see a resurgence in all things local. There is some evidence of this happening already.

Location, location, location

Ever since Henry Ford invented mass production, companies have pursued a strategy of standardization. Given globalization you'd think that standardization would be intensifying — but you'd be wrong. The problem is twofold. First, consumer markets are fragmenting. In the 1970s the US population was typically segmented into 40 lifestyle groups. Nowadays there are 66. This diversity comes in many forms — lifestyle, beliefs, values, income, ethnicity, family structures and so on — all with one thing in common: they dislike homogenization.

The second problem is that standardization stifles innovation. Making things the same reduces points of difference and leads to commoditization. Customization, on the other hand, encourages experimentation, which drives innovation. Local customization is also very difficult for competitors to track, let alone copy. As a result, retailers are starting to customize store formats, products and even service offers according to local tastes.

Equally, manufacturers are formulating specific products for specific regions or groups. For example, Coca-Cola has created four different canned coffee drinks for the Japanese market, each targeting a particular region. Wal-Mart varies its selections of canned chilli peppers according to store location. It carries about 60 varieties of chillies in total, but only three are stocked nationally, as the company tailors its stores to its local clientele. Too much localization or personalization can obviously breed logistical chaos and dilute the brand, so customization is usually carried out in clusters using local geographical or lifestyle data.

So what, apart from customer fragmentation, is driving this trend? The answer is information. Customer data can pinpoint not only who is buying what, but increasingly when and why. So data from Tesco can identify need states based on the time of day, allowing an inner-city store to stock sandwiches at lunchtime and ready-to-eat meals in the evening. This is hardly rocket science, but retailers like Best Buy in the US have found that localizing stores can result in a sales increase that is twice the company average. Websites like Nearbynow come at this localization trend from another angle by making the inventory of local malls searchable by local shoppers.

In other words, price and choice will no longer be as important to shoppers as they once were. Location will become the most important factor, both in the sense of being most convenient (closest) and the most local (made locally or in tune with local tastes and history). The idea of "local" will be an important factor in other ways too, with some enlightened retailers seeing it as their purpose to help build and support local communities. This is perhaps another example of going back to the future.

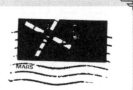

12 January 2010

Dear Alexandro

You asked me at Christmas how retail had changed since I was a kid and I've finally had a chance to sit down for more than five minutes to think about it. First of all, there was no internet. Letters and postcards like this were the only way we could order things from far away. Shops were also closed on Sundays (it was actually illegal to sell some things on a Sunday). Some were closed on Wednesday afternoons too. Shopping was more of a necessity, not a form of leisure activity, and some popular products used regularly to run out. Supermarkets had just been invented but shopping centers and malls were non-existent where I lived, as were superstores and factory outlets. Most shopping was still done by women, in the local high street or town center. Shops closed at about 5.30 p.m. — no late-night shopping or 24/7 convenience stores. Most of the local names have disappeared now, replaced by giant overseas retailers. Perhaps the most amazing thing though was how little choice there was. Products from abroad just didn't exist generally. There were no croissants, no fresh mangoes, no lemongrass and no pesto unless you knew a small shop run by a foreigner. Believe it or not, we also used cash to pay for things — nobody took credit cards — and most people cooked meals by themselves from scratch.

Hope this helps with your homework project.

Lots of love

Vasiliki

5 trends that will transform healthcare

Ageing Ageing is a trend that will have an enormous influence on healthcare as people not only live longer but expect to be well for longer too. In China 134 million people are aged over 60 — 10% of the entire population, and this is predicted to increase to 30% by 2050. Obvious impacts include higher expenditure on pharmaceuticals and care for the elderly, but the type of common diseases will also change. This will affect everything from memory recovery to the replacement of body parts. Also, expect to see more generations living together under one roof and more debate about subjects such as euthanasia and sex for the over-70s.

Telemedicine Increasing hospitalization and higher treatment costs, together with developments in remote monitoring and wireless communications, will create a boom in home-based monitoring, remote diagnosis and treatment, or "hospitals at home". Conversely, there will be a countertrend toward home visits and hands-on physical contact for those who can afford such things.

Sleep science In the future, people will feel increasingly burnt out all of the time, which will cause breakdowns, anxiety and depression. There will be a boom in research into the so-called architecture of sleep: the different sleep states and how they influence health and potentially even learning and intelligence. Indeed, sleep will become so sought after in the future that it's possible it will replace both money and sex as the status symbol *du jour*. Thus we'll see an increase in sleep retail (for example MetroNaps) and specialist sleep consulting. Also, expect a major boom in the sale of high-quality (expensive) sleep products such as beds, mattresses and pillows, some of which will become very high-tech indeed. There will be pills to provide the equivalent of up to eight-hour doses of quality slumber, freeing us from the need for genuine sleep, although it is uncertain quite what the longer-term consequences will be of this or for people who work or play for 22 hours non-stop and sleep for just 2.

Medical tourism   Healthcare will become globalized in the sense that patients who can afford it will travel anywhere in the world to receive high-quality treatment or to save money on what will become standardized procedures. We will therefore have the development of menu pricing for medicine, medical tourism agencies and luxury hospitals that resemble hotels, offering everything from intelligence implants to memory treatments. Meanwhile, at the other extreme there will be drop-in clinics in supermarkets. Both ends of the market will be owned by just a handful of global corporations that will outsource mundane tasks globally to low-cost suppliers.

Memory recovery and removal   To misquote Milan Kundera, the future will be a struggle of memory against forgetting. Our individual and collective forgetting will be driven by an ageing society and by the increasing pace of life, which will contain too much information. New technologies will also wash away our recent words and pictures because we can't be bothered to keep proper records or transfer files from one format to another. Whether it's a bad date, a corrupt politician or genocide, we also increasingly forgive and forget, which is a problem at both an individual and a societal level because we tend to repeat the mistakes we can't remember.

Chapter 9

Healthcare and Medicine: older and wiser

The future is already here; it's just unevenly distributed.
—William Gibson

D o you want to live for ever? How about to 130? That's not too far-fetched. Already half of those born today into a middle-class family anywhere in the world will almost certainly reach their 100th birthday. A century ago few people lived until they were 56, while today most of us make it to 80. A few decades of medical innovations could easily push this figure to 110 and then onwards to 130. If you really want to explore the boundaries of what's possible, the ultimate sci-fi future is one where humans have figured out a way to download consciousness into a machine, thereby effectively becoming immortal. But back to the more immediate future.

I'm sitting in Foot Heaven trying to have a massage. I'm still suffering from something I caught in economy class on a plane almost a month ago, so I thought a bit of relaxation might help. Unfortunately though, the person right next to me is on the phone

— and stays on it for an hour. I leave feeling even more stressed. Still a bit wobbly a few days later, I stagger into my local doctor's surgery and wait my turn. On the wall is a bank of leaflets and one in particular catches my eye: "Your Genetic Sports Advantage: ACTN3 Sports Gene Test™". The idea here is that a simple genetic test will identify whether you — or your child — are naturally oriented toward sprint/power sports or endurance events. Again, I'm not making any of this up. This exists right now.

A pill for every ill

Among a host of medical developments and discoveries in the next few decades, we'll be presented with techniques to grow artificial teeth, artificial bladders and new breasts. And if you are still feeling queasy about human face transplants, get ready for brain transplants. We'll also see artificial blood, brain food for babies, pills that remove the need for exercise, female Viagra, biodegradable scaffolding (for new organs such as breasts), memory pills, bionic eyes, human limb farms, brain-function tests, anti-suicide pills, artificial hearts, gene silencing, "cluster bomb" treatments for cancer and age-retarding pills. There will be vaccinations to help people resist food, alcohol, cigarettes and drugs such as cocaine, along with jabs to treat asthma, arthritis and high blood pressure. Developments in genomic medicine and molecular biology will drive the creation of a host of new compounds, some of which are likely to make it onto pharmacists' shelves in the very near future. For diabetics, daily injections of insulin could soon be a thing of the past and sufferers will inhale insulin instead. There will be various drugs to manipulate hunger and a plethora of new treatments to help people get to sleep or stay awake.

Indeed, we aren't that far away from a society where there's a pill for every conceivable ill. As society speeds up and becomes more competitive, many perfectly healthy people will also regularly use

pills to enhance their daily lives and performance. Drugs will therefore move from specialist areas into routine domestic and work use.
An example is Ritalin (methylphenidate), which is already taken by
some students to improve test results and by some business people
to improve performance in high-pressure situations such as key
presentations.

In the US, the military has used Modafinil to help soldiers stay
awake and improve concentration and planning skills. It is looking
increasingly likely that various Alzheimer's drugs will eventually be
used to improve the memory of otherwise perfectly healthy people.

There will also be a revolution in how medical professionals and
patients monitor health and work out whether or not they are ill.
There are already some interesting developments in this area.
Russian researchers say that they have found a way to detect
whether someone is about to become ill by looking into their eyes.
Apparently the eye is one of the very first parts of the body to reg-
ister a temperature increase, often a prelude to infection or a more
serious condition. Add a dose of technology to this idea and you
can come up with highly sensitive thermal-imaging devices that
individuals can use themselves. In theory such devices could also be
used on people without their consent — for example crowds of
people at airports during flu pandemics — which takes us into the
area of medical ethics. Maybe one day you'll be able use your cellphone to scan your eyes every morning and wirelessly transmit the
test results to your doctor. Any irregularities would result in an
instant appointment sent by SMS.

Sound is another way of telling whether you are ill. Back in 2001
James Gimzewski (a US nanotech expert) had an epiphany: if
human cells have tiny moving parts, then surely they must produce
tiny vibrations? This in turn would create tiny noises. Theoretically
the sound produced by cells would also vary according to levels and
types of sickness, so it might be possible literally to listen for cancer.

And then there's smell. Using dogs to smell whether someone is
sick is seen by some people as crank science. But Professor Michael

Philips at New York Medical College has created a machine that can analyze an organ-transplant patient's breath to see whether he or she is suffering from organ rejection. Future breath tests could sniff out breast cancer, lung cancer, eclampsia and angina. The theory here is that we all have two types of breath: "dead space" breath from the upper air passages and alveolar breath from well within the lungs. The latter can tell doctors what's going on deep inside your body.

I'd also predict that there will be a boom in regeneration research. The human body has a remarkable ability to regenerate itself (new skin, fingernails, hair and so on), but animals like the humble newt are on another planet. Newts can self-repair lost legs and even eyes, so the question is whether the human body can be assisted to do the same.

Killing me softly

It won't just be the healthcare industry that will be innovating in the future. There are now approximately 1,400 pathogens in the world that can kill people. According to researchers at Columbia University, new pathogens have emerged or re-emerged 409 times over the past 50 years and the trend is accelerating. Moreover, most of the new human pathogens are coming from animals. What's driving this increase? Nobody knows for sure, but somehow the way the world is changing is giving pathogens fresh opportunities to infect new species or get into different areas. The list of likely culprits includes rapid urbanization (more people living closer together) and intensification of agriculture (more animals living closer together and closer to people). However globalization, which means that everyone is increasingly connected to everyone else, is the most likely suspect.

First, it means that animals are moved from one place to another more frequently. Second, people are traveling more often and faster.

The illness SARS (which was of animal origin) was spread by international travel. As we become more connected through cheap travel, the globalization of jobs and mass migration, we are more susceptible to new and old diseases alike.

This brings us on to the issue of global pandemics. The 1918–19 flu pandemic killed somewhere in the region of 20 to 100 million people. Nobody knows for sure how many died, but the figure is almost certainly greater than the number killed during the First World War. Most (but not all) experts agree that another pandemic is overdue, possibly not on the same scale but devastating to our mental state nonetheless.

You could argue that we already have a pandemic — HIV/AIDS — but this seemingly doesn't count because it's largely confined to certain continents and minority groups. So what else is most likely to kill millions of people in the future? There's still the possibility that H5N1 bird flu will make it big, but perhaps the most likely future plague is something from our past. Smallpox and polio could experience a comeback due to a lack of immunization and of course there are the 1957 and 1968 variants of flu. There could even be a bug from outer space. However, none of these is very likely to my mind, for reasons I'll explain later.

Precision healthcare

Global warming will also influence sicknesses in the future. Currently 13 million people in the UK suffer from hayfever and 2006 saw record pollen counts across much of Europe. Part of the problem is that the hayfever season is starting earlier and running for longer, but the severity of the allergy is also increasing. This may be linked to higher temperatures putting plants under greater stress, which in turn causes them to produce more protein on pollen grains. It is this protein that is the allergen. CO_2 emissions related to the burning of fossil fuels (to run more air-conditioning units to compensate for the higher temperatures) could also be linked to an increase in asthma cases, according to some sources.

Even old diseases are becoming new again. Cases of gout have doubled in Britain over the past 50 years because people are eating and drinking too much (and arguably eating too fast as well). Rickets is back, possibly because children are spending too much time playing indoors and are not exposed to enough sunlight, a major source of vitamin D.

Osteoporosis is also enjoying a new moment in the sun. Traditional wisdom says that drinking more milk and eating more dairy products is the way to prevent it; but according to some experts this could be contributing to the problem. High-protein diets and foods such as meat that are highly acidic may cause a leaching effect that removes calcium from our bones. One study has even suggested that teenage girls are suffering from bone fractures because they are drinking too many soft drinks containing phosphoric acid, which again drains bones of calcium. In fact, the future isn't looking very good for young teens because another study claims that their teeth are being damaged because they have stopped drinking tap water, which often contains fluoride, in favor of bottled mineral waters that do not.

Other future "diseases" include a variety of conditions affecting people who are too busy. "Leisure sickness" is an affliction whereby seemingly healthy people get sick the second they go on holiday. The theory is that as soon as busy people relax, they start to recognize signals from their body that are ordinarily covered up when they are at work and busy. Or perhaps there is some positive relationship between stress and resistance, so when people become less stressed they are more susceptible to infections.

It's a similar story with kids. Back in the 1980s the idea was that the lack of childhood infections (caused by too much vaccination and too many antibiotics) was damaging children's wellbeing. As a result, their immune systems overreacted when exposed to otherwise harmless allergens and led to an increase in allergies. This hypothesis is slowly being replaced by a new theory that even though a lack of early-childhood infections may have an influence, the real culprit is the lack of exposure to common microbes. In other words, our houses and children are far too clean for our own and their own good.

Given the lower incidence of allergies among people who grow up on farms, perhaps in the future we will see "dirt holidays" where children are exposed to farmyard animals, mud and filthy water. Or perhaps next to the Microban in the supermarket you'll be able to buy aerosols of common bugs to spray on kitchen surfaces, baths and children.

Talking of supermarkets, for years retailers have used so-called precision marketing employing sophisticated social-segmentation techniques to help them decide where to build stores and to achieve maximum impact with their marketing budgets. In the future health planners and strategists will use similar techniques to target local communities and even individuals who are most in need of health intervention. The process can be employed to target specific streets, schools and workplaces. Recently a campaign in Slough in the UK targeted individuals in need of screening for type-2 diabetes. Of the 2,000 people identified using social categorization, 106 were discovered to be undiagnosed type-2 sufferers.

While precision healthcare can be highly effective, what are the costs in terms of privacy and even social stigmatization? What are the implications of health departments (and, in the future, private healthcare providers and insurance companies) targeting people who aren't actually ill yet but will be? Moreover, should governments then be allowed to restrict the sale of certain products such as alcohol in particular areas if they are found to be hotbeds of future illness? The mind, as they say, boggles.

So here's an idea. In the past, healthcare was about making sick people well. In the future, it will revolve around making well people even healthier for those who can afford it. We will see a shift from reactive to preventive healthcare (and from a wholesale to a retail market generally). This doesn't just mean curing an illness before it takes hold. We will increasingly delve into people's deep hereditary history to solve diseases they would otherwise suffer from perhaps 20, 30 or even 60 years hence. This will be a spur for a convergence between financial planning and healthcare planning, with people saving up for treatments they're going to need in 10, 20 or 50 years' time.

A future shortage of death

Let's turn to a few trends that will have an impact on healthcare and medicine in the future. The first, which is impossible to ignore, is ageing. As people not only live longer but expect to remain well for longer too it will have a tremendous effect on healthcare. Obvious impacts include higher expenditure on pharmaceuticals for the elderly, which is already at record levels in many countries. Healthcare spending will represent 10.6% of global GDP in 2008 and was a staggering $1.3 trillion in the US way back in 2003.

The West is facing a shortfall in the availability of younger doctors and nurses to treat the greater numbers of older people needing treatment. To some extent this will be addressed by importing healthcare professionals from other countries (especially Asia), but it will also be partially solved through technology and automation — shoes with GPS so that nurses can stop patients with Alzheimer's wandering off, or using robots to dispense drugs.

We'll see anti-ageing drugs on sale at the local Wal-Mart and anti-ageing surgery will develop into a multibillion-dollar industry, with people opting for voice-lifts so that they sound as young as they look. Older people will also receive transplants of young blood or, more likely, artificial blood or pills that mimic the fast-repair qualities of a young person's blood.

There will be convergence between the life expectancy of men and women, although women will still live longer on average than men. As a result, four- and even five-generational families will exist. This shift will make aged care yet more complicated and expensive, not least because young couples and individuals will have to devote more time and money to the care of older relatives. And because seniors will be around for longer, hospitals will become even more clogged up unless hospitals at home, telemedicine or robotics can take up the strain.

There has been an increase of over 150% in the number of Americans being treated for heart failure, not because of a higher disease or diagnosis rate but simply because people are living for longer. Also, very old people tend not to suffer from just one disease but five or six simultaneously. Add to this the cost of treatment, which often goes through the roof in the weeks and months before someone dies, and we have what is in many ways an unsustainable situation — or, as one commentator put it rather unsentimentally, there will be a future shortage of death.

People are supposed to grow old and die so that the next generation can take over. But what if they don't? What if older generations simply refuse to go away? The obvious implications are financial; but socially and attitudinally there are some interesting potential consequences too. For example, innovation and change are generally driven by the young, so an imbalance of older people could have seriously adverse effects.

People are already starting to question the need to live beyond a certain point (a point defined, one imagines, by some measure of quality of life for yourself or for others) and this debate will intensify in the future. Assisted suicide is an ethically charged issue the world over, but so-called suicide tourists are now traveling to places such as Belgium and the Netherlands where euthanasia is legal.

In theory, pharmaceutical firms could produce suitable drugs to be administered by doctors, thereby avoiding the rather shady "exit specialists". The problem here is that there's a slippery slope between voluntary and involuntary killing, and spurious arguments can easily be constructed to justify eugenics on the grounds of removing individuals considered dangerous to the rest of society.

In the past religion gave life and death meaning and provided a ritualized exit, but now that religion is receding in some Western (Christian) societies there is for many a feeling of hopelessness. The last thing society should do is give these people the proverbial push off the bridge, no matter how bad their suffering.

It's also interesting that there has been a kind of reversal since Victorian times, in that sex is now talked about while death has become taboo. There is a feeling in modern societies that medicine can cure everything. Death is something that most people (and the media) now avoid. However, as healthcare budgets get more stretched, dying at home will be more common and this will make death more visible.

According to UK charity Marie Curie Cancer Care, 64% of people would prefer to die at home if they were diagnosed with a terminal illness. Only 25% actually do, but this will change in the future, not least because more seniors will live with their children and grandchildren. Indeed, there is some evidence to suggest that seniors who are surrounded by young people are likely to live a longer and certainly happier life than those who aren't. At the moment most aged-care facilities are pretty dreadful places, but they won't stay that way. Old people's homes will be part of mixed-use developments and will be built alongside and even within schools, so that the different generations can interact and learn from each other.

Don't forget to remember

What are some of the other consequences of an ageing population? Growing numbers of people aged 60-plus mean that the science of memory recovery and preservation will become a major growth industry in the future, because people lose their capacity for recollection when they get older. Conversely, the removal of memories in younger people will receive an increasing amount of attention. For example, 49% of rape victims suffer from some kind of post-traumatic stress disorder (PTSD), as do 17% of people involved in serious car accidents and 14% of those who suddenly face the loss of a member of their immediate family. Add to this an increase in war and terrorism-related PTSD in both soldiers and civilians and you can perhaps see why venture capital is flowing into this area. The US government is even researching how combat experience can be downloaded into the heads of raw air-force recruits. So how long before you and I can download other people's experiences into our brain?

In the future we will be able to buy pills to remove unwanted memories or take memory pills to find recollections lost in the sands of time. That is if we remember to take the pills, of course, which brings me to another point — how to get an ageing population to remember not to forget to take their meds. There are already countless innovations aimed at achieving this goal and we will undoubtedly see more. In Japan a company called Menicon has developed a contact lens that can slowly release medication. A better idea might be an iPill. An intelligent pill has been developed in Canada that, once swallowed, will dispense the correct amount of drugs according to pre-programmed instructions. It is about the size of a five-cent coin and the "brains" of the device are no bigger than ten blood cells. Once the pill has done its job it simply disappears, along with your food waste.

Hospitals at home

The internet will revolutionize the future of medicine, aggregating demand for medical services and increasingly helping to commoditize the pricing of basic products and services. Patients will use information delivered by search engines to self-diagnose and self-medicate, much to the chagrin of governments and the medical establishment. Already 25% of Americans use the internet at least once a month to access medical information; you can imagine the doctor's reaction when he walks into a room only to find "his" patient surfing the net for a second opinion.

Digital plasters will continually monitor all the body's vital signs. If anything appears abnormal, the plaster will wirelessly send information to your doctor. Power consumption will be almost zero, allowing the device to operate off a printable battery. And if you prefer to wear your heart on your sleeve, you can — clothing will be embedded with computers that similarly monitor your heart rate. A few years ago scientists in Singapore even developed a shirt that calls for help if you fall over.

Our medical records will reside in cyberspace. In the short term e-records will be held by your doctor and will be accessible by any hospital in the world. But sooner or later the information will escape and will be accessible by you and me (medical iPods, anyone?). In the more distant future these records will reside in our own bodies, which is the most sensible place for them when you come to think about it.

And hospitals themselves will be vastly different. First off, information technology will utterly transform care. Nurses and doctors will have instant access to life histories, making mess-ups less likely. Currently around 7,000 patients in the US die every year simply due to poor information about drug interaction, while the same number die due to doctors' bad handwriting.

Even using PDAs to allow nurses to fill in information at a patient's bedside is said to reduce paperwork errors by as much as 50%. And we'll need to reduce those errors. The speed and sheer volume of information will be staggering. Not only will the availability of patient information increase, the amount of data on scientific discoveries and the latest developments will reach a point where no human can possibly keep up to date. Finding means to access and digest this information will thus be critical.

In addition, hospitals won't really be where the future action is. They cost money and, ironically, they are breeding grounds for bugs, so anything that can be done elsewhere will be. The very idea of a hospital will change from a physical space to a repository of information and expertise that can be accessed through a variety of channels. Developments in remote monitoring and wireless communications will at the same time create a boom in home-based monitoring, diagnosis and treatment.

The drive to reduce the cost of healthcare services will be a catalyst for a number of DIY medical procedures and services. Areas ripe for self-medication include wound treatment, mental health and the management of long-term chronic illnesses. Some of these treatments will be provided by the patient, perhaps with the help of remote cameras and the internet, while others will require temporary home visits by healthcare professionals. Although telemedicine has been around for a while in some countries, to date it has largely been confined to hospitals monitoring patients at home in terms of vital signs or drug delivery. Not so in the future.

An emerging area of care is e-therapy, where psychologists and psychiatrists treat patients remotely, either to jump long queues or because the patient lives far away. The technologies used include everything from email and cellphones to websites and streaming video and conditions as varied as PTSD, anxiety and addiction can be treated in this way. In Australia diabetes patients can send their blood-sugar readings to their doctor via a cellphone equipped with a blood glucose meter, while in South Africa patients are sent text messages if they fail to open their medications (the cap of the bottle is connected to the phone, which is in turn connected to the hospital's computer). In the US My-Food-Phone helps patients with high cholesterol monitor their diet. They take photographs of their meals (which is easier than writing a food diary) and send them to a nutritionist for a weekly critique of their choices.

Even some of the technology once found only in hospitals is now routinely available in ordinary homes. The idea that today's luxuries become tomorrow's mass-market necessities certainly applies in areas such as household goods and electronics, but in the future it will increasingly apply to medical equipment. Take the defibrillator. Once these were only found in city hospitals, but now you can buy one on eBay for US$1,495 or less, secondhand. So what's next? A combined ultrasound, MRI scanner and 3D computerized tomography machine to treat your own tumors?

But again, is all this technology what people really want or need? Sure, it saves hospitals time and money, but is our quality of life being improved or reduced? A significant part of medicine is the human element and physical interaction is surely vital in both diagnosis and treatment. Research conducted by the Mayo Clinic found that if a doctor sits down during a bedside visit it increases patient satisfaction. For the study doctors were asked either to stand or sit during their initial evaluation; when questioned later, patients whose doctor stood underestimated the length of the visit by an average of 4%, while those whose doctor sat down overestimated the time by 11%.

In a similar vein, US researchers have found that when people are anxious or in pain, holding hands has a soothing effect. If more people are going to live alone in the future, a simple service where a person having surgery could hire someone to hold their hand could make a remarkable difference to stress levels and recovery rates. When it comes to caring for people technology is only part of the answer; making things too remote or soulless may not make us ill, but it will make us less well.

This is yet another example of the dualistic future. On the one hand we will have nanotech and cellular-based medicine where science will be able to switch genes on and off, build nanomachines to repair severed nerves, or get inside tumor cells and change them. On the other hand, patients are already embracing all manner of alternative and natural treatments. In many ways "high-tech" and "alternative" are opposite and contradictory, but both will happily live side by side in our bathroom cabinet in the future.

If you think I'm kidding about alternative medicine, simply take a trip to the US and visit a pharmacy called Elephant or Pharmaca. Between 1984 and 1994 the number of independent American pharmacies declined by 28%, largely due to the power of Wal-Mart and giant drugstore chains such as Walgreens. So how can small chains flourish? The answer is by appealing to a niche that the big guys either haven't noticed or have chosen to ignore. In Pharmaca's case this means holding seminars on new-age treatments and placing kiosks in-store where customers can read up on alternative medicine.

Personal pain

Another future megatrend will be the personalization of medicine and the shift of power away from professionals to the end consumer of healthcare services (that is, patients). At the moment 90% of drugs don't work for 30–50% of people, so in the future we'll see treatment programs and drugs tailormade for specific groups and, ultimately, individuals. We'll also see diets customized to particular groups of people and genetically based treatments.

Personalization obviously works at a group and individual level, but it also exists at one of the most fundamental levels: men and women. Until 1990 two-thirds of all research on medical conditions that affect both men and women was done purely on men. Men and women are different when it comes to capacities such as memory, verbal abilities, spatial awareness and even facial recognition, so why wouldn't they be different when it comes to medicine?

For example, men and women experience heart attacks in different ways. Men tend to have crushing chest pains while women tend to feel upper abdominal pains. Men and women also process drugs differently, meaning that doses sometimes have to be increased to have the same effect. When it comes to severe pain men and women seem to prefer different painkillers, with men opting for morphine and women choosing nalbuphine. From an evolutionary point of view this makes perfect sense. Historically men and women have been subjected to different types of pain, so coping mechanisms may have developed accordingly. This provides a tremendous opportunity to develop gendered versions of all kinds of drugs. Male and female headache pills, anyone?

Personalization also means that different patients respond differently to treatment regimes, so gene chips will be developed that allow treatments to be personalized to the genetic makeup of an individual patient. This idea is revolutionary in that it will mark a seismic shift away from the blockbuster business model that is already at something of a watershed in pharmaceuticals.

In recent times fewer and fewer drugs have been launched, and more and more have been withdrawn. For example, in 2004 there were 113 submissions for approval in the US compared to 131 in 1996. Second, refocusing R&D toward individuals or, more accurately, subgroups of individuals means that pharmaceutical companies will be forced to address subpopulations in regions such as Africa and India. Moreover, there has been a historical tendency to treat regions such as Africa as cheap testing grounds rather than primary areas for development. If individualized treatments do take off, genetic diversity will be an integral part of the testing process and developing countries will be much sought after for both research and treatment.

Too tired to sleep

But back to future ills. Life is speeding up and more of us are living alone. Stick these two trends together and you'd expect to see a significant uplift in stress levels in the future.

Various studies, including those conducted by the University of Chicago, have shown that being alone can be bad for you. A Danish study has also found that older people who live alone have a greater risk of a sudden heart episode than those living with others. Moreover, pessimists are more likely to get depression and die from heart disease.

What will we get stressed about in the future? The answer will be pretty much the same as we worry about right now: debt, relationships, work, success, our appearance, terrorism, crime and so on. The difference is that work hours will be longer and job insecurity will be greater.

We will also be more stressed because of increased levels of change, which may well make us sick. Believe it or not, a study, again by the University of Chicago, found that animals that are frightened by new things are 60% more likely to die than animals that are open to new experiences. Could the same be true of people? Will we adapt to embrace our ever-accelerating societies, or will the speed of change and levels of uncertainty eventually kill us?

Apart from loneliness and depression, one of the biggest problems in future years will be getting enough sleep. Western societies are already sleep deprived and the result is that people are becoming clumsy, stupid, unhappy and dead, according to Dr Stanley Coren. Social observers have coined the term TATT syndrome to describe people who are Tired All The Time. Whether you buy into the phraseology or not, the condition seems real enough and sleep is set to become the new sex — one of the hottest medical and societal issues over the next few decades. The figures certainly speak for themselves. Back in 1900 Americans slept for an average of 9.0 hours per night; the figure is now 6.9 hours and 70 million people have trouble getting a proper night's sleep. The number of sleep clinics is increasing as a result: in Australia there were just 4 sleep clinics in 1985, but now there are over 70.

US$50 billion is lost every year due to sleeplessness. Add to this 100,000 road accidents caused by tiredness and you can start to see why getting a good night's sleep is keeping a lot of medical researchers wide awake. Conversely, the demands of our 24-hour society mean that people are also looking for ways to stay awake.

Sleep science is still a Cinderella area of medical research but this will change. There is already some evidence to suggest that a lack of sleep is partially behind everything from obesity and irritability to depression and low libido.

So expect to see pills that will provide the equivalent of two-, four-, six- or eight-hour doses of "super sleep". Eventually we could even medicate so we don't have to sleep at all. But what are the consequences of a society where people do that?

An international health service

Globalization is another key driver of change in the future of medicine. The movement of people and skills shortages in most Western nations have led to an influx of foreign doctors and nurses, with as many as 70% being born outside the country they are currently working in. Meanwhile, many patients are heading in the opposite direction.

Years ago if you were sick you had no real alternative to the local hospital. Perhaps you would travel a few hundred miles to a center of excellence, but that was about it. These days people are jumping on planes and traveling to countries as far apart as India, Costa Rica, Brazil, Thailand, Turkey and Hungary to have everything from their teeth and hips to their heart and nose fixed. Already 500,000 Americans travel to other countries for medical procedures every year, largely because costs are 30–80% cheaper than in the US. Medical tourism will enjoy enormous growth in the next few years and is expected to be worth US$40 billion by 2010. As a result, medical tourism agencies and intermediaries are springing up to advise on everything from hospitals and doctors to hotels and post-operative sightseeing trips.

Equally, since one-fifth of US GDP will be spent on healthcare by 2020, medical outsourcing is set to grow. This is where various services that used to be conducted by your local hospital (or at the very least in your own country) are now exported to low-cost countries such as India, much in the same way that banks are outsourcing their call centers. Hospitals in the US send X-rays to India overnight via the internet for initial screening. We will slowly see the globalization and ultimately the commoditization of all but the most specialist medical services.

Healthcare will therefore essentially become a retail market driven by brands (reputation), price and convenience and the patient will be firmly in control of most purchases. Countries such as China and India will become global centers for certain types of medicine and medical research, including the development of new drugs, at the expense of countries like the US.

However, diseases in countries such as China and India will also start to resemble those in the West and all countries will eventually experience the same illnesses and conditions. Obesity will be an issue everywhere in the future. Healthcare in all nations will also be split between health haves and have-nots due to the high cost of treatment, although this may be solved in the long term by technology. Computers will be everywhere, modeling biological systems and processes and testing drugs.

Computers have consequences for medical education too, and we'll see the increased use of hyper-realistic patient simulators for training purposes. In fact, in the distant future people will be amazed that testing and training were ever done on people, let alone animals. Advances in computer modeling and silicon simulations will mean that by 2050 there will be no need to test new drugs on animals or people, because software models of human organs and physiological processes will do it instead. Again, this type of activity will be centered in India and China due to the accessibility of relatively inexpensive, highly skilled labor.

The six-million dollar man

We cannot talk about the future of healthcare and medicine without at least a cursory nod in the direction of ethics, both personal and professional. Technology will continue to revolutionize medicine, but we are on the cusp of an era in which all sorts of choices will have to be made by society about what is and is not acceptable.

There is already a debate about human cloning and, sooner or later, an outlaw scientist will undoubtedly do what many people fear. There is also a debate about what it means to be human and at what point an artificially enhanced person ceases to be one of us. It is interesting to me that steroids are banned in professional sports but enhancement surgery is perfectly legal. While repairing damage to a ligament has been standard practice for more than a quarter of a century, new medical and surgical procedures are blurring the line between repair and enhancement. For example, wearing contact lenses is not regarded as cheating — but what if a major league cricket or baseball player had eye surgery or a partially robotized arm specifically to improve his or her (it is the future, remember) batting average? Surgical innovations will blur the line between human and machine; when millions of dollars of sponsorship are involved, this question gets very interesting indeed.

Another area sure to capture the imagination of the media is the use of robots, especially robosurgeons. Put simply, would you allow yourself to be anaesthetized and operated on by machines with no human involvement whatsoever? Add in some artificially grown body parts — possibly from a limb farm — and we really do start to enter the realm of science fiction for real. However, the area most likely to cause true consternation is medical privacy; specifically, who owns or controls the information held deep within our bodies? If, as is likely, medical science will be able to tell what a child will suffer from when he or she is 20 or 50 years old, should the child and the parents be told? If the answer is yes, what about their insurance company? Do insurance companies have a right to full disclosure once the hereditary Pandora's box has been opened?

And what if links were proven between a parent's current lifestyle and the health of their yet unborn children? What if governments decided to tax the parent on the basis of damage they are doing to the health of the offspring they haven't yet decided to have? Even better, if unborn children can be tested to determine future intelligence (read earning power, in some instances), would it be ethical for the parents to interfere in order to enhance these abilities through the use of drugs or brain surgery? Or what about the ethics of "cosmetic neurology" — essentially, cosmetic surgery for the mind? Finally, if we are all born with certain impulses such as aggression or selfishness, would it be ethically correct to modify these impulses at birth?

Someday, someone will have to put his or her mind to all of this.

12 December 2033

Dear Annie

What a day! I gave my doctor a sample of my blood a few days ago and today I got a premium email titled "Re: Nutritional Genomics" from my local supermarket telling me what I could and could not eat to extend my life by a guaranteed 20 years! The diet is not totally unique because I share certain characteristics with other people. But it turns out that I do have a problematic DNA profile, so the supermarket said that a personalized diet would be highly beneficial and recommended the weekly home delivery of certain foods and meals. If I agree to sign up to the program the supermarket-run health insurance scheme will instantly reduce my premiums by 20%. But if I do sign up someone, somewhere, will be watching what I eat and how I live for the rest of my life. All my food purchases, from anywhere in the world, will be automatically entered into their database and because cash no longer exists, all electronic and digital payments will automatically create a data trail. If I do this, certain foodstuffs will also be impossible to buy unless I can find an underground supply or a fake ID. My movements will be similarly tracked. If I walk less than 10km per week my weekly health insurance premiums are adjusted upwards.

What do I do???

Douglas

5 trends that will transform travel

Growth in tourist numbers According to the World Tourism Organization 1.5 billion airline trips will be made by the year 2020. In China there are currently 265 million couples aged between 40 and 64 with no dependent children and many of them are keen to travel abroad. Another September 11-style attack could change all that, but in the meantime the emerging middle classes in China, India, Russia and Brazil want to travel and their numbers will reshape the global tourism industry. Sheer numbers will eventually mean that the most popular attractions and countries will have to implement annual quotas and tourists will have to book months or years in advance. The vast number of people walking on or past certain attractions will also cause severe environmental damage and this will put pressure on their owners to limit numbers or to remove these famous sights from public view altogether.

Climate change In 50 years' time the climate will have had a dramatic impact on where people go on holiday. If the experts are even half right, some tourist destinations will be under water while others will be too hot to sustain large numbers of tourists without air-conditioning. Conversely, many ski resorts will simply vanish. On the upside, many destinations that were once too cold will be blessed with milder climates and many tourists will travel back to northern European resorts that were popular a century or more ago to enjoy a break from the sun. Such shifts could have devastating economic consequences for some regions. One solution might be sealed climate-proof holiday domes and other indoor areas that offer some of the benefits of the great outdoors without being at the mercy of volatile weather.

Resource shortages   You can run cars and coaches on batteries, trains on wood and ships on wind power; but apart from alcohol, there are no serious alternatives to jet fuel for aeroplanes. This problem will be solved once the issue reaches crisis proportions, but before that there will be a major switch to other forms of slower transport and a renaissance of local travel. Long-haul flight will again become an expensive luxury enjoyed only by the rich, who will have to withstand accusations of selfishness and eco-vandalism. Hotels will similarly come under pressure to reduce their carbon footprints and conserve vital resources such as water.

Staying at home   If flying from one city or country to another becomes too expensive, too time-consuming or too stressful, many people will simply choose to stay at home. This means that business and leisure travel alike will become more localized, making people both more insular and parochial. We will also holiday in virtual worlds on the internet or transform our homes and gardens into miniature resorts and entertainment complexes. Business teleconferencing, especially web-based virtual meetings and conferences, will become more popular, although the need for face-to-face meetings won't entirely disappear.

Time versus money   The tourism market will become increasingly polarized between the time-rich and the time-poor. In other words, it will be split between those individuals with lots of time but little or no money, and those with lots of money but no time. The former — usually individuals or groups of friends — will take long sabbaticals or holidays using low-cost options such as capsule hotels and pre-erected tents. At the other extreme, wealthy holiday-makers — usually couples — will scour the world to find micro-vacations offering instant luxury and relaxation. Thus we'll see backpacker and budget airlines sitting alongside private jets on the tarmac. We'll also see super-luxurious manifestations of every conceivable type of transport and holiday experience (e.g. luxury camping). Also expect to see more glamorous brands — especially fashion and "lifestyle" — entering the holiday market, along with value brands ranging from supermarkets to those aimed at young people.

Chapter 10

Travel and Tourism: "sorry, this country is full"

We should all be concerned about the future because we will have to spend the rest of our lives there.
—Charles Kettering

Why do we go on holiday to places that increasingly look like where we already live? Equally, why do we travel hundreds or thousands of kilometers to visit someone when we could make a phone call instead? These are a couple of the questions we will be asking with greater frequency in the future as the costs and consequences of physical human movement grow. This may strike some people as an odd thing to say, given that we are currently living in an age of low-cost airlines where distance is effectively dead, but we are on the cusp of a great shift caused by skyrocketing oil prices, increasing population, climate change and technology.

In the spirit of becoming at one with one's subject, I am writing this lying in bed (with a crisp white cotton pillow and duvet) onboard a Virgin Atlantic Airways flight from London to Sydney via Hong Kong. I have everything I could reasonably expect or need, although the start of the journey in London was far from comfortable. The journey by road to the airport took three-and-a-quarter hours to travel 107 miles, the last 19 of which took more than an hour. The traffic was bad, but it was a walk in the park compared to what greeted me at the airport. A few months earlier some lunatic had been arrested on suspicion of trying to blow up another plane. As a result, security was paranoid and queues were catastrophic. And that was in the Fast Track lane.

Once past passport and security control things got much better. I was wafted into a world of peace and serenity, otherwise known as the business-class lounge. I had a glass of champagne, a haircut and a massage.

This paradox, in a nutshell, is the future of travel. Holidays and journeys will become polarized between low cost and luxury, although even the top end will ultimately be reined in due to the sheer cost, complexity and environmental damage caused by billions of people moving from one place to another. The result is that we will all start traveling backwards. Foreign travel will once again become the preserve and privilege of the stressed-out, anxious rich, while the less fortunate, equally stressed-out and anxious poor will holiday at home or not at all. So enjoy your next cheap flight, because it may be your last for quite a while.

Sun, sand and making a difference

Currently 700 million people travel internationally each year "for fun" and it's estimated that this figure will reach 1.6 billion by the year 2020 — at which point tourism expenditure will reach US$2 trillion per year (US$5 billion per day). According to some experts this is already the single largest industry on Earth. However, tourism will come under increased ethical scrutiny in the future, being talked about in more and more negative terms by those who would like to regulate both travel and tourism on the basis of their environmental and cultural damage.

For some people tourism is neither innocent nor fun but an out-of-control industry wreaking havoc on the planet. Thus new concepts are being created such as "green tourism", "ethical tourism" and "responsible tourism". In the UK, Tourism Concern recently lobbied the government and industry to limit developments in some places due to environmental damage and to pull out of other areas altogether due to human rights abuses.

According to the World Tourism Organization, cultural holidays are the fastest-growing sector of the market. Part of this is what I call holidays that help (or reality tourism): vacations that combine interesting and sometimes exotic locations with assisting a local community or local landscape. Examples of travel firms offering such holidays include Earthwatch, which runs trips for volunteers to help scientists track endangered species; and Biosphere Expeditions, a non-profit organization through which you can study cheetahs in Namibia or Arabian leopards.

This "voluntourism" has been going on for many years but it's recently moved from a fringe, student or gap-year activity into the mainstream tourism market, with families, mid-lifers and disenchanted business people all swapping sea, sand and shopping for holidays that make a difference. Why? One reason is that it offers a temporary solution to our unease about the future. In other words, it says more about our need to find meaning and to de-stress in a pleasant peasant environment than about our desire to help others. This is borne out by anecdotal evidence from students I've met who have been asked to survey reefs that have been surveyed ten times before. Nevertheless, these forms of experiential travel seem to be what more and more people want. This means that companies expert in cultural activities — museums, for instance — will extend their products and services into travel and tourism.

On a related note, a North American company called Vocation Vacations offers its clients the opportunity to try out other jobs on holiday. There's even a theme park in Japan called Kidzania that does the same for children, merging education (the world of work) with entertainment. This may be stretching the idea of taking your work with you on holiday a little far, but it's certainly a good example of how the pursuit of work/life balance (how should I live my life and what's it all about anyway?) and happiness is affecting travel.

Another spinoff from this cultural travel trend is the growth of religious tourism. As societies become more secular, people are becoming more interested in where their ancestors came from and want to visit places relating to their history or "tribe".

However, while there is undoubtedly a growing need for holidays that make a difference, one suspects that many of these "new tourists" are more concerned about escaping the hell that is other people than with saving the planet. Moreover, while tourism has undoubtedly destroyed many places in the eyes of privileged tourists from developed nations, it has also contributed greatly to local economic prosperity and wellbeing.

A slow boat to China

What else is on the horizon when it comes to travel? According to a report by Deloitte and New York University, the answer — for the year 2010 at least — comes in four parts. First, we will see a growth in the market for travel into and out of China, India and the Gulf States. I would concur with this, especially with parts of the Gulf replacing the Mediterranean as a source of cheap (and not so cheap) sand, sea and sun, although some of these new tourism states are quite literally built on foundations of sand.

The second prediction is that the luxury end of the US travel market will continue to grow, along with spending on tourism in general, which is expected to double between 2006 and 2015. This increase is partly a result of growth in disposable incomes, but is also due to a third factor: the increase in the number of older people with both time and money to spend.

The growing number of people aged 65 and over will have profound implications for the way people holiday, with more opting for event-based and cultural activities.

The fourth and final factor shaping the future of the travel industry is technology: more people will rely on the internet when researching holidays and more will go online to book. The internet has already shaken things up in the travel industry by connecting people to low-cost operators and aggregating demand for various products and services. Crucially, it has also had the effect of removing intermediaries such as travel agents, as customers can use the internet to find out information and access special deals direct. However, this doesn't mean that travel agents will disappear because there is still a need for specialist knowledge; and as people get busier and information becomes more overwhelming, many will continue to delegate their relaxation and entertainment requirements to others.

Nevertheless, the influence of technology on travel and tourism will only accelerate in the future and eventually many of us will be taking virtual vacations in virtual worlds, aided and abetted by a 5D interface and experience-enhancing drugs. Fasten your seatbelts.

This is a while off, of course, so in the meantime we'll have to content ourselves with virtual tours of hotels, checking out which is the best airline seat online (via blogs and user groups) and buying social-network airline tickets and hotel rooms that tell us who else is traveling with similar interests or who knows someone we know. If you think any of this is pure fantasy, forget it. In Germany you can already use the internet to book hotel sunbeds and towels in advance; touch-screen kiosks in airports dispense information about the relative safety of countries and the latest security alerts.

Social-network airline tickets may still be a couple of years away, but we already have seat-to-seat texting on board Virgin Atlantic and most of the airlines are rushing to replicate other communications such as email, internet access and cellphone connections. Indeed, it won't be that long before you can download an e-paper airline ticket at home that contains both a flat screen and GPS so that the airline can send information to the ticket about boarding times and delays. It could even flash at you when the gate is closing and help you to find it.

In the US, an airline called DayJet allows business travelers to fly direct to regional airports, thus avoiding time-consuming connections and delays at big airports as well as unwanted overnight stays in small towns and cities. This is a good idea, but what's really exciting is how the company does this. It operates a small fleet of six-seater micro-jets at a cost of US$1.3 million each, offering airliner-style performance and luxury at a fraction of the cost. But the company has no set routes and no fixed prices. Instead, DayJet aggregates demand "on the fly", linking small groups of people who want to go to roughly the same place at roughly the same time. Routes and pricing therefore fluctuate in real time depending on demand and passengers are offered a series of prices depending on how flexible they are willing to be. Give a little and save a lot. What's really fascinating about this idea is how the business model of the airline combines a couple of the hottest current trends, both of which will affect everyone in some shape or another in the future. First there's mass customization, where customers order a personalized version of an otherwise standard product or service. Second there's dynamic pricing, where the cost of a product or service changes according to daily or even hourly demand and supply.

While we're on the subject of technology, it's worth a quick detour to mention tribal tourism, which is emerging as something of a cross between reality television and computer gaming. The idea is that holidaymakers can join a virtual tribe on the internet that will eventually exist on a real island in Fiji. For £120 ($240), "Nomads" can join for 12 months and are allowed to visit the real island — once it exists — for seven nights; "Hunters" join for 24 months for £240 ($480) and receive 14 nights' accommodation;

and "Warriors" subscribe for 36 months and get 21 nights for £350 ($700). Once the five thousandth member has joined the virtual community, a real island will be leased and the group will start to make real decisions about what to build there.

This is all slightly spooky and reminds me of people who go on holiday with the same friends to the same place every single year. Sure, it's comfortable and removes any form of risk and uncertainty — but isn't the whole point of travel to get to see people and places you wouldn't normally be exposed to?

Hedging your holiday bets

But will it still be worth traveling in the future if everywhere looks, smells and tastes the same as everywhere else? One of the upsides of trends such as globalization and connectivity is that you can get just about anything you want, anywhere. Tastes, ideas, brands and businesses have all traveled the world, to the point where most airports, shopping centers and hotels look pretty much alike. So why bother going anywhere? The answer, of course, is that people and places are only similar on the surface; and while humankind is indeed intent on standardization and homogenization, history and nature tend to behave otherwise.

Moreover, countries, like companies, are starting to wake up to their points of difference or unique selling points, and it's these USPs that create "country brands" to attract tourists. Some nations such as Britain seem to be intent on removing many of the USPs — double-decker buses and red phone boxes, for instance — but other, more future-oriented states like Dubai are still building them.

It occurs to me that what most people really want to see when they go on holiday is great architecture. In some cases this is man-made: the Eiffel Tower, the pyramids, the Tower of Pisa, Stonehenge, the Great Wall of China, the Taj Mahal, the Empire State Building and so on. In other cases it's natural architecture that stirs the soul: Uluru (Ayers Rock), the Grand Canyon, Niagara Falls, Mount Everest, Iguaçu Falls or a truly great beach. And therein lies both a problem and an opportunity. It's a problem because in the case of natural wonders they aren't really making them any longer, so an expanding global population (that is, at least a billion new tourists in the immediately foreseeable future) will mean that attractions and even whole countries will have to be booked months or years in advance. "Sorry, this country is full until 2015 — please call again." Manmade attractions are a slightly better proposition because at least you can rebuild them when they get worn out.

Perhaps a more immediate and less iconic architectural opportunity lies in the area of safe, climate-controlled buildings that house things ordinarily found outside. Let me explain. The world is becoming more uncertain and less safe, both in terms of climate and violence. There is already a booming industry in weather hedging and insurance; it's not too far-fetched to imagine whole countries taking out weather insurance to protect their domestic tourism industries, much in the same way that companies like Coca-Cola or the Oktoberfest already hedge against particularly bad weather. A better bet might simply be to build enclosures where the weather — and, up to a point, terrorists — can't dampen an otherwise sunny day. This may seem like a rather frivolous reaction to global climate change and worldwide terrorism, but it's already happening. In the future, more and more of us will be taking our holidays indoors.

Early examples of the trend toward climate-controlled artificial environments include Phoenix World in Seagaia, Japan, where you can ride 3-meter waves in a giant 300 x 100 meter pool, or lie on a manmade beach and enjoy the warm temperature regardless of what's happening outside. At the other end of the temperature spectrum there's the 405-meter ski mountain in the middle of Dubai, where the snow and the skiing are always perfect, even if it's 48 degrees Celsius on the outside (no worries about climate change and sustainability there, then). Of course, all we're really talking about here is Disneyland crossed with Center Parcs, so there's no need to get too excited. Or is there?

All this is happening right now, so imagine what might happen in another 20 or 30 years if you added some technology along with a few trends like the desire for fantasy or escape. What you could very well end up with are worlds like the one portrayed in the film *Westworld,* where guests can visit three different zones of a high-tech amusement park called Delos to indulge in their fantasies or behaviors outlawed in the real world.

Or how about sealed faith resorts where entry is only available to verified members of a particular religion? To some extent this happens already on a small scale, but what if the idea were pushed even further and incorporated into an enclosed environment free from terrorism or the threat caused by non-believers? We're back to a familiar theme here: the impact of anxiety and, to a lesser extent, climate change, although of course the two are somewhat entwined and interrelated.

R&R

As I've said before, life is speeding up in the sense that we are sleeping less and doing more. In the case of work, we are expected to do more than we used to and do it faster every year. This means that people are becoming more stressed and in some cases sick, so travel is becoming an antidote to anxiety. If you've got the money, this means ever more luxurious vacations, flying on planes that resemble hotels and staying in hotels that resemble palaces. Of course, going away makes you even busier when you get back, so people tend to take more work with them, which eventually turns these resorts into the very places they are trying to escape from. Durh! Will we see hotels and airlines banning cellphones and computers in the future? Quite possibly, although they will probably sit on the fence and design tech-free zones rather than applying the principle to entire planes or resorts.

Something we will definitely get is "sleep hotels", where guests check in just to check out for a while. We'll also witness a blurring between hotels and hospitals, with a return to the spa resorts and convalescence homes of yesteryear. For very busy people there is a growing problem with "sleep debt" (accumulated tiredness), so in the future we'll have hybrid hospitals. These will not be health farms but luxury hotels fully equipped with the latest medical technology and expertise.

This need for a respite will also drive a trend for sabbatical vacations, although in most cases what will really take off is the short relaxation break. Indeed, the idea of the annual family holiday will largely disappear due to time pressures. Instead, it will be replaced by a series of short, selfish mini-breaks, with children taking separate vacations. Couples building "parent retreats" at home are an early sign of this.

The need for structured environments to help people relax and unwind will also create opportunities for other sealed environments such as cruise ships and trains, where guests relax simply because they cannot get off. This will lead to the further development of long-haul luxury train journeys and cruises, many of which will be fully retro in an attempt to recapture the glamor and innocence of pre-September 11 travel. In some cases these ships, trains and resorts will be owned by or operated exclusively for individual companies, on the basis that the company will have control over the security of its employees; although ironically, this may make them more of a target.

At home away

The desire to escape from reality will also drive a few other changes. Remote real estate will become highly sought after as holiday homeowners flee the crowded and polluted beaches of the Mediterranean, seeking refuge from imaginary threats closer to home. So if you own land somewhere in New Zealand or Tasmania, hang onto it because the isolation that once made it cheap will soon make it very valuable. At the extreme, this means that inaccessible islands will become the ultimate holiday resorts and retreats.

You may be thinking that holiday-home ownership is a bit of a niche market, but you'd be wrong. There are 250,000 holiday homes in England and Wales (somewhat ironically, roughly the same number as there are homeless people) and this figure is growing at a rate of 3% a year, turning some areas of Britain into ghost towns. For instance, there's a village called Worth Matravers in Dorset where 60% of the homes are owned by people who don't live there. It's also been estimated that 15% of houses in northwestern Europe are now second homes. This is obviously causing great resentment among locals who can't afford to buy even a first home in these areas, so expect to see terrorists targeting tourists with second homes in the future too.

Of course, you don't need to own a second home to get away from the stress and strain of modern living, so hotels will do everything they can think of to make guests feel at home. At present this includes video-monitoring systems to enable you to see who's outside your room (at the Burj Al Arab Hotel in Dubai), motion-detecting lights, biometric safes (at the Langham Palace Hotel in Kowloon) and personalized lighting that can be set to "business", "romantic" and "relaxing" (at the Sofitel Arc de Triomphe in Paris). I've also seen sleep-tight anti-jetlag lighting, iPod mini-bars, mini-bars for kids (no alcohol), personal oxygen bottles and — my own favorite — a borrow-a-goldfish scheme for lonely travelers at the Monaro Hotel in Chicago.

Other innovations include women-only hotel floors, entire business-class (premium) floors, elevators with wi-fi access (why?), hotel rooms sold by weight (seriously: the more you weigh the more you pay at the Ostfriesland Hotel in Norden, Germany), hotels where you can purchase most of the contents of your room, including the bed, by mail order, and others where you can buy your room if you like it.

Over in Los Angeles (where else?) you can check into a hotel with a psychiatrist on call, while in New York if you're fed up with religious reading, you can book into a room with a copy of the *Kama Sutra* and a box of condoms where the Gideon's bible used to be. There are also rooms that resemble offices, with printers, faxes and business centers with personal assistants you can rent by the hour. These will presumably make their way on board aircraft sooner or later too (the personal assistants, that is, not the bible alternative).

That's if you have the money, of course. If you don't, you can check yourself and your bags in by yourself and even clean your own room in some budget hotels. At the easyHotel in London, the rooms are smaller than the average prison cell and there's no phone, wardrobe, shelving, chair or toiletries, apart from a rather lonely small bar of soap. There's no television and no window either — unless you want to pay extra — and the bed linen is fresh when you arrive, but after that it's up to you to keep it clean or pay extra for some more. On the plus side, the room is dirt cheap — around £20 per night, depending on demand — and you get good security and relative peace and quiet, as long as the bright orange floor doesn't keep you awake.

Is this the future? It is certainly another example of polarization. Hotels of the future will be either very cheap or very expensive. And people will live for long periods, and occasionally indefinitely, in both. Technology will not be applied equally, either. At the budget end it will be used to bring costs down; at the other end guests will demand and receive the human touch, suitably enhanced by technology.

Some of the other things we will definitely see inside hotels include robotic concierges, soundproof rooms (for stress relief), premium-quality air (the more you pay, the cleaner it gets), "soft" baths that mold to your exact body shape, and rooms that can be personalized through the use of sound and smell.

The same will be broadly true at 39,000 feet. For those who can pay the whole experience will be personalized, allowing passengers to recreate a series of environments resembling their office, their home or a favorite hotel. You will even be able to customize the window so that you can look down in real time on the African plains, even if you're flying from New York to Los Angeles. There will be seats with ergonomic memory foam that can remember your shape from your last flight, live television, pillow menus (you can get them in hotels, so why not planes?), private fridges, private cabins (with private mist showers), double beds, mini-bars and private chefs. Some of these ideas exist already if you fly in business or first class and new ideas will continue to occur here, simply because business and first class tend to create high margins that can be reinvested in product and service innovation. However, some of these ideas will slowly trickle down from the pointy end to cattle class, since economy is one of the fastest-growing segments of the market.

One point that should be emphasized here is that one of the reasons planes are starting to resemble hotels is that they are one of the last sacred spaces. By this I mean that if you lead a busy and stressful existence, planes offer one of the last places where "they" can't get you. An aircraft is peaceful and private (in business and first class, at least). You can sleep, watch a movie or feast like a king. But most of all, a plane is one of the few remaining thinking spaces where your mind can drift and dream. Airlines will sooner or later figure this out and design the environment accordingly. Trains and ships will cater to this need too.

The death of distance — for a while

So much for how we'll get to where we're going, but where will we actually go? One answer is nowhere. If flying from one city or country to another becomes too expensive, time-consuming or stressful, many people will simply choose to stay at home. This means that both business and travel will become more localized. People will holiday in virtual worlds on the internet, or they may transform their homes and gardens into miniature resorts and entertainment complexes with products and services like swimming pools and room service, all available for purchase or rent. This will create a boom in household outsourcing, although many people will still crave going somewhere different.

In the short term, overcrowding and the unpredictable nature of the weather will mean a move away from the annual mass migration to the southern Mediterranean and holidaymakers will be spread out more evenly across northern and eastern Europe. "Hot" regions will include the Gulf States of the Middle East (especially Oman), Latin America (particularly Brazil) and Africa. Equally, Australia and New Zealand will both become popular holiday destinations due to cultural familiarity, space and perceived safety.

However, while all of these destinations will be big in the future, one of the largest trends influencing the global tourism market is who will be traveling there. Traditionally the bulk of globetrotters have been relatively wealthy individuals from Europe and the US, with their less-wealthy counterparts booking two weeks of sun slightly closer to home. According to the World Tourism Organization, 1.5 billion airline trips will be made annually by the year 2020. Another September 11-style attack could rapidly move these numbers in the opposite direction, but the emerging middle classes in countries such as China, India, Russia and Brazil are starting to travel abroad and their numbers will radically reshape the nature of tourism — or at least they will until the oil price escalates even further, putting long-haul travel out of their grasp once again.

By 2020, for example, online travel bookings will be worth $2 billion in India alone. This is a country with a rapidly emerging middle class who want to spend their money on seeing the rest of the world. In 2003 4.5 million Indians traveled abroad. This may not sound like much, but it was enough to cause the country to lose millions in foreign currency due to the imbalance between out-bound and inbound tourism.

Some more figures: whereas it took 30 years for Japan to reach 17 million outbound trips, China got to this figure in just 5 years. According to the Pacific Asia Travel Association, the Chinese took roughly 800 million internal trips during 2003. That's about the same number as taken by the rest of the planet in that year, so imag-ine what will happen if even just a third of this number decided to come to Europe?

As I've said, sheer numbers will eventually mean that the most popular attractions and countries will have to implement annual quotas and tourists will have to book months or even years in advance. The vast number of people walking on or past certain attractions will also cause severe environmental damage, which will put pressure on owners to limit visitor numbers or even to remove certain famous sights from public view.

More extreme destinations will include the Arctic and the Antarctic, underwater travel and space travel. The wider universe has long fascinated Earth dwellers and the idea of space tourism has caught the collective imagination in recent years. Will it happen? The answer is, it already has; although whether blasting off into Earth orbit will ever feature in a mass-market tour brochure is open to debate. I personally think that space flights will appeal to a very niche demographic — namely, rich old men. But the US Federal Aviation Authority has published a set of proposed regulations for space-tourism operators, including everything from flight-crew qualifications to medical requirements and permits.

While outer space is certainly a fascinating, once-in-a-lifetime experience, many other future destinations will be a little more down to earth. For example, if everyone is rushing about and doing everything at the last minute, why not switch off and start a retro tourism trend of going from point A to point B using the slowest means of transport possible? Or using old and quite possibly out-of-date maps to get from one location to another in full anticipation of something awkward or difficult happening along the way?

Getting lost in order to find yourself has always appealed to a certain type of traveler, but doing so will become increasingly difficult in the future. Nevertheless, people will continue to strive for both. As life becomes less private and peaceful, we will desire time and space as never before.

11 February 2038

Dear all

Having a great time here at Holiday World. We're staying in "America", which is in biosphere two. So far we've seen rattlesnakes, eagles and some buffalo. There's also a whole tribe of native Americans that were brought here in 2021 after the first big North American pandemic. We're not allowed to get up close because of ongoing quarantine restrictions, but it's great to see some of the actual people who were responsible for the new enlightenment movement. However, the best bit so far has been seeing the recreation of the first Disneyland resort. Granddad says he can remember the real thing before it was blown up by terrorists, but I think that's just the memory pills talking again. By the way, I can't email or call from inside here because it's an enforced-relaxation zone, but if you do somehow get this please don't forget to water the plants and bring the herbs in during the day so they aren't exposed to too much UV.

By the way, we're all off to "Russia" to hunt virtual terrorists tomorrow. Can't wait.

Love to all

Pam and Reg

PS Tell Sean there was a virtual recession in Seventhlife yesterday so he should sell his virtual apartment before prices collapse any further.

5 trends that will transform work

Globalization and connectivity Globalization cuts both ways. On the one hand, millions of low-skill jobs will be lost to low-cost areas such as China, India and Africa, while at the same time geography will become irrelevant as highly skilled workers become more mobile. This means that companies will hire globally and workers will move internationally to follow opportunities. It also means that jobs can exist in one location while the worker is in another. Want to work for an investment bank in New York but live in London? No problem in the future, because companies will be far more open and decentralized. However, loyalty to corporations will dwindle and it will be very much a case of promiscuous workers moving to wherever the best opportunities lie. The trend of reverse migration will also intensify, with people in countries such as the US moving back to those such as India because the opportunities are better "at home". However, the biggest future shock will be the lack of workers due to declining fertility rates in almost every nation. Hence the war for talent — attracting and retaining the best people — will become even more critical until robotics and AI solve the problem.

Accelerating technological change We will see more employee tagging and surveillance in the future. Resumés will live online or perhaps inside tamper-proof ID chips implanted in our bodies (which could also provide secure office entry and computer login). Online job auctions and ID checks will also be commonplace. There will be technological solutions to work-related stress and virtual meetings (sometimes downloaded onto iPods) will increasingly replace the physical variety. People will work from home, on the road and on the move, but the office will continue to be vital as the central hub, not least because people will still need to interact physically with other people. Having said this, wireless technology and high-speed connectivity will mean that the office will be anywhere, so we will increasingly work on holiday and in remote locations around the world. Previously work-neutral spaces such as planes, trains and cars will also resemble offices and nowhere will we be entirely free from work.

Corporate social responsibility and governance   Companies will have to work harder to attract and retain workers and issues such as ethical behavior and corporate social responsibility will be uppermost in the minds of potential recruits and customers alike. Indeed, marketing will be turned inwards as organizations fight to create company brands that appeal to potential and existing recruits. Trust and transparency will become more important and customers will also be driven more by values then by prices. As a result, the boundaries between internal and external communications will erode and organizations will increasingly be forced to tell the truth, the whole truth and nothing but the truth.

Demographic shifts   There is a lot of hype surrounding Gen Y, but when it comes to work the next generation will change the rules of the game for themselves and everyone else. First, if the economy continues to grow, Gen Y will call the shots simply because there will be far more jobs than people. Employers will therefore have to become more flexible about how and where people work and how they are rewarded. Gen Y is also hyper-connected, so virtual and collaborative networks will grow in importance as a way of getting things done. Workforces will also become more balanced. There will be a greater spread of ages, more ethnic diversity and more women in the workforce, the latter significantly contributing to a shift away from the white middle-aged alpha male culture that has been dominant for so long. Decisions will be made using prediction markets and innovation will be run using open or distributed innovation principles.

Work/life balance   Instead of working less and enjoying a leisure society, we are working more. We are also commuting for longer periods. Being busy is a modern mark of prestige. This will all change. The open-all-hours work culture will be challenged by parents seeking more time with their kids and there will be law suits and regulation concerning the social costs of long work hours. Companies will be forced to pay for ruined marriages, stress-related illnesses and dysfunctional children caused by a culture of endless work, unrealistic targets and disappearing evenings and weekends. On a positive note, pressure from employees will create more flexible contracts and ways of working.

Chapter 11

Work and Business:
the new right-brain economy

What a business needs the most for its decisions, especially strategic ones, is data about what goes on outside it.
—Peter Drucker

The *Observer* newspaper has claimed that the majority of Britons would rather have a cut in working hours than receive a salary increase. If this is true, what does it imply? There are various explanations and one is that people are doing the wrong kind of work. But what is the wrong kind of work? While the answer is highly personal, in my experience it means working with people you dislike or doing something that's too easy or repetitive. It can also mean having a job that lacks meaning or doesn't make a difference. So perhaps the question we should be asking is whether the nature of work will change in the future and if so, how and to what?

According to the management thinker and philosopher Charles Handy, there are three key forces driving change at work. The first is our old friend globalization. As Thomas Friedman argues in *The*

World Is Flat, a single global market is emerging for everything from products to people. In theory, this means that you will soon be competing against everyone else on the planet for your job, although in practice there will be a limit to what gets outsourced. Nevertheless, if your current job can be done cheaper somewhere else, it might be worth looking at other employment opportunities. For example, if you are training to be a film editor you might want to bear in mind that editing can be done in India, and more cheaply. The same is true of tax returns, X-ray analysis and dealing with parking-fine disputes, all of which are currently being worked on in cities across Asia.

However, there's some good news too. The flip side of the global village is that if you're really good at what you do, companies will compete globally for your skills as jobs become more mobile.

X or Y?

The second key driver of change is demographics. Most countries face a demographic double-whammy where an ageing workforce collides with a declining birth rate. According to the Herman Group, this will mean a shortage of 10 million workers in the US by 2010. There is even a labor shortage in China right now. Employers will therefore have to get smarter about how they attract and retain good people. The war for talent will mean companies keeping workers on the payroll for longer, recruiting older people (especially those aged over 50) and starting a dialogue earlier with potential recruits. Crucially, we will also start to see more flexible working practices and the development of initiatives to attract older workers.

For example, DIY products retailer B&Q in the UK offers jobs to retired tradespeople. The results are improved customer service and lower employee turnover. Similarly, BMW in Germany has designed a factory to attract older workers, while Mitsubishi in Japan has already started to rehire its own retirees. Ford expected the percentage of its employees aged over 50 to have risen by 100% in Europe between 2006 and 2008.

A global labor shortage will mean that there will be a push to recruit more immigrants into domestic labor forces and in some cases we may even see the return of paid immigration. There will also be more women in the workforce. In the US 25% of employees already work for a female-owned company; this percentage is certain to increase, not least because women possess skills that will be highly sought after in the future. Women make somewhere in the region of 50–90% of all purchasing decisions, so in theory putting more of them in charge of corporations would seem to make sense. This is something that management writers such as Tom Peters have been pointing out for years.

Recently, *The Economist* magazine suggested that the appearance of women in the paid labor market has contributed more to the growth of global GDP than either China or new technologies. Moreover, at the risk of generalizing, I'd also suggest that women will be preferred over men in the job market of the future because of their empathy and intuition, both of which will be in demand. Furthermore, emotional intelligence translates into a higher level of concern for the wellbeing of others, whether they're other employees or customers. Incidentally, one clever idea implemented by consumer products group Procter & Gamble is reverse mentoring to help older workers (especially men) understand the problems faced by newly recruited staff (especially women).

Education and training will become even more important. In the case of adults, this means lifelong learning. The idea here is that education needs to be a continuous process due to the rapid change brought about by science, technology and globalization. However, for most people, if they think they need it, it will already be too late. A study by Harvard Medical School found that after the age of 40 around 400 genes become lazy, which affects learning, memory and communication skills. Another study found that workplace coordination and dexterity start to fall after the age of 25 and decline dramatically after 35. This more or less fits with the theory put forward by Thomas Kuhn in *The Structure of Scientific Revolutions* that radical breakthroughs tend to come from just three sources: young people, accidents and the cross-fertilization of disciplines. In other words, it's younger people who tend to create value. This is obviously problematic from one standpoint — that workplace remuneration tends to be based on age and experience — so maybe in the future we'll see employers putting more time and effort into keeping older minds young and also linking pay to results rather than just age.

However, the real solution to the shortage of workers will be to offer people a job with real meaning. This will be especially important for members of Generation Y, many of whom are now entering the workforce for the first time. The importance of Gen Y is, in my opinion, overstated, but there are a few things that mark this generation apart when it comes to work. First, they have never witnessed a real recession, so they tend to be confident (arguably overconfident) about the future. Second, they have grown up with connectivity and speed of change, which has two important implications for employers: they exchange information and they have very little patience. Add to this their interest in ethics and sustainability and you have a very explosive cocktail of young people who care passionately about how companies operate and interact with the wider environment.

A while back I overheard a conversation between two Gen X employers. One was complaining to the other that he had offered a very bright female Gen Y graduate a position at his accountancy firm, but before she accepted the job the graduate said she had been offered a similar position at a firm of rival accountants. Therefore she had a few questions. The Gen Xer was obviously expecting a debate about salary or holiday entitlements, but what transpired was a discussion about the ethical principles behind the firm and what it was doing in various areas ranging from poverty relief to recycling.

Whether or not companies engage with these issues remains to be seen, although there is anecdotal evidence to suggest that corporate social responsibility (CSR) is moving to center stage. The international standard for CSR (ISO 2600) will undoubtedly turn the heat up on firms when it comes to transparency and ethics. However, if past quality standards are anything to go by, this will be more a case of bureaucratic box ticking than a paradigm shift in the capitalist economy. The search by employees for more meaningful work lives and spirituality in their private lives does not necessarily equate with the moral transformation of work. As the late economist Milton Friedman said, the social purpose of a business is to make money for its shareholders.

Nevertheless, ethical investing has become a very hot sector and people are getting interested in the ethical dimensions surrounding the products and services they consume as well as the social responsibility of the company they work for. In Australia, The St James's Ethics Centre runs a telephone helpline to assist workers whose personal values clash with those of their employers, while in the US Wal-Mart is erecting wind turbines on the roofs of its stores in order to put something back into the environment.

The tension here is twofold. First, there is a mismatch between companies, which are run for profit, and the planet, which is not. If putting windmills on supermarket roofs saves money, companies will do it. Otherwise they won't, unless governments make it mandatory or customers move their business elsewhere. As German sociologist Max Weber once observed, when people pursue a collective goal there is a "parceling out of the soul", meaning that the bigger an organization gets, the less easy it becomes to keep it honest.

Another important element in staff retention is trust. If you believe surveys, something between 50% and 80% of people don't trust their boss and the feeling seems to be mutual. Some 75% of US companies regularly monitor employees' email and around 30% track keystrokes and the amount of time employees spend on their computers. Monitoring employee activity is nothing new — Henry Ford created a sociological department to assess whether his employees gambled or drank at home — but it is becoming more common and more pervasive, thanks to technology that makes it easier to find out where people are and what they are doing.

For example, at most call centers the length of all conversations is monitored, as are lunch and toilet breaks. There is even software such as NetIntelligence that, by snooping on internet usage, shows bosses exactly what their staff are up to all day. This makes micro-management relatively easy, but it also makes employees sick. People who are monitored too much or too closely tend to be more prone to conditions such as stress, depression, anxiety and exhaustion. Moreover, high levels of monitoring tend to reduce trust even more, which itself is a negative influence on productivity.

Of course, not all workplace monitoring is bad. Drug testing in the US is widely endorsed by employees because it makes the workplace safer, and capturing emails for posterity can be useful if you want to defend yourself against a future lawsuit. No wonder paper use in our supposedly paperless offices has actually gone up.

Digital nomads

The third key driver of change at work is technology. Thanks to mobile phones, laptops and the internet, work is becoming less tied to a physical location. Instead we are becoming a tribe of digital nomads, working whenever and wherever we choose.

This means that future employment contracts will have to change. Companies will need to realize that they are buying people for their ideas, not their time or physical presence, so annual contracts will be related to objectives met, not hours worked. This will mean an increase in sabbaticals and a further blurring between what's done at home and what happens "at work".

But technology is not all good news. According to psychologists we get stressed and angry because we have been sold the idea that technology will save us time. So when our computer crashes or develops a mind of its own, it takes our hopes, expectations and fragile perception of control with it. As a result, we snap.

In the UK there were 6.5 million workdays lost to stress back in 1995. By 2001 that figure had jumped to 13.4 million, and there is no reason to suppose that this trend won't accelerate into the future. However, taking a very long-term view, average hours worked have been declining for a century. So what's causing the stress?

One possible explanation is the increased pace of modern life caused by technology, but this doesn't really stack up either. The term "neurasthenia" was created as long ago as the 1870s to describe the nerve-racking effects of modern inventions such as the railway and the telegraph. However, what has changed is people's willingness to admit they are suffering from stress — now a badge of honor in many work environments. There is also the argument that as societies become richer there is more time for introspection and people begin to feel a sense of entitlement, which fuels anxiety when expectations are not met.

Whatever the reason, the problem is going to get worse. In the US 40% of workers say they have experienced verbal abuse at work, and murder recently emerged as one of the most common causes of death in the workplace. Allegedly.

One specific consequence of this is an increase in stress-related compensation claims. Email is partly the culprit here, but so too are open-plan offices, which reduce privacy and increase distractions and disturbances. In the US depression is currently costing companies $31–$44 billion every year.

An antidote to depression is medication, but in the future workers will regularly dose themselves up with drugs to improve their performance, in the same way that athletes pop steroids. Back in 1993 Peter Kramer, author of *Listening to Prozac,* discovered that medicated people were more assertive and better at bargaining —

precisely the traits most employers love. Those who are already well, with no mood or personality disorders, will therefore take drugs to improve their workplace performance and monetary reward. What if companies actually start prescribing drugs to employees to improve their personality, compliance or financial results?

Another probable cause of workplace stress is cost cutting, or delayering, which increases the workloads of those individuals who still have a job or three. Information overload? It's going to get much worse before it gets much better.

But this is all just the beginning. In another 20 or 30 years, artificial intelligence and robotics will have displaced yet another layer of workers. So if your job can be reduced to a set of formal rules that an intelligent and emotionally aware machine can learn, it may be worth looking at a career change — because your current profession may disappear.

We are facing a third industrial revolution. The first swapped fields for factories, while the second — the information revolution — replaced brawn with brains. The third revolution will be the shift from left-brain to right-brain economic production. During the twentieth century people were paid to accumulate and apply information. The acquisition and analysis of data are logical left-brain activities, but, as Daniel Pink points out in his book *A Whole New Mind*, they are activities that are fast disappearing thanks to developments in areas such as computing. For instance, speech recognition and GPS systems are replacing people for taxi bookings, while sites like completemycase.com are giving mediocre lawyers a run for their money. So dump that MBA and get an arts education instead. Better still, do both.

One fascinating statistic I came across recently is that 12 years ago 61% of McKinsey's new US recruits had MBAs. Now it's around 40%. This may be partly because of an oversupply of MBAs in the domestic market or the outsourcing of data analysis to cheaper countries. But it's also probably because arts graduates are in demand. In a globalized world, products and services become homogenized and commoditized. One of the best ways to create differentiation (and thereby growth) is through innovation, which means lateral thinking. It can also mean an appreciation of aesthetics, which bring us back to right-brain thinkers.

There are some future-proof jobs that cannot be done by a machine or outsourced to Asia. These include what I'd call high-touch jobs such as nursing and teaching, which involve a high level of emotional intelligence. They also include occupations that involve the application of creativity and imagination. But, as Richard Florida points out in *The Rise of the Creative Class*, these types of jobs don't work just anywhere. Cities become attractive to right-brained entrepreneurs and innovators when they score highly on the Three Ts: technology, talent and tolerance. Technology refers to the proximity of world-class research facilities; talent is the clustering of bright, like-minded people from varied backgrounds; and tolerance is an open, progressive culture that embraces "outsiders" and difference.

Overall, then, the workplace will become more decentralized and there will be a need for workers to become more adaptable in the face of changing technologies such as real-time speech recognition and translation, AI, robotics and nanotechnology, all of which will accelerate over the next couple of decades. The result will be a demand for a highly educated, highly skilled workforce that is mobile and able to work in multiple locations and on multiple projects simultaneously. In other words, the old factory model of every worker being in the same place at the same time is dead. Instead, individuals will work in small collaborative teams and once these teams have outlived their usefulness they will be disbanded. People will often work for more than one team and some will have more than one job.

Indeed, the barriers between companies and individuals will start to blur as separations between working inside and outside an organization fall away. Individuals will also have to look after themselves more, even if they work full-time inside an organization, because everything from pensions to healthcare and safety will become the responsibility and liability of the individual rather than the corporation. Organizations will adopt flexible structures and strategies, because the sheer rate of technological change will make products and even entire industries obsolete almost overnight. Companies will also start to look more like academic institutions, because this model is based on a fluid, decentralized and relatively non-hierarchical structure. In other words, there will be a shift away from a "command-and-control" management style to one based on employee coordination and cultivation.

Bonfire of the certainties

Not that this will necessarily help companies survive. Of the Forbes list of the 100 largest companies in the US in 1917, only 13 exist today in an independent form. The rest have either been swallowed up or have gone out of business. The same is true of many so-called world-class companies identified in books such as *In Search of Excellence* and *Built to Last*.

According to McKinsey only 0.5% of all companies perform well over several decades, so there is every reason to believe that the majority of companies around today won't exist in the future. The primary reason seems to be the need for them to perform two seemingly contradictory tasks to survive. First, they must execute flawlessly in the present. This requires strict control and tight hierarchies that reward individuals with extensive skills and experience. However, this experience and expertise can create barriers that prevent an organization from adapting to changed circumstances in the future. Organizations are disabled by their own experience and success. In addition, senior executives develop mental models about what is and what works based on historical experience. Moreover, successful organizations tend to evolve into large networks that become gridlocked; innovation and change are resisted because they inevitably have a negative effect on someone, somewhere. This in-built corporate immune system partly explains why most radical innovations don't come from industry incumbents and why turn-arounds usually involve fresh blood.

Is this the foundation of the next big management idea? According to business writer Jim Collins, one of these comes along every few decades; if true, this means we are overdue for another. In 1900 the corporation was invented, while 1920 saw the development of the idea that management was a science. We had continuous improvement in the 1960s, and the idea that entrepreneurship and innovation are repeatable processes in the 1980s. So what's next? Perhaps it's the thought that corporations are no longer the best structures to create value and that it is finally the individual who will wield the power.

Barriers to market entry are now falling. Scale is less important than it was last century and physical control is becoming increasingly difficult. Even the idea of short-term value is now under threat from longer-term considerations such as energy and sustainability, so perhaps it really is time for a new model of management thinking to emerge based on the idea of open innovation and networks. Companies are starting to move away from the concept that they are money machines reacting to the market and are embracing a more proactive model in which shareholders, employees, customers, society and the environment are all deemed equally important. And in this new environment, values and purpose are key.

Currently the vast majority of jobs still reside inside organizations, even though articles abound on free agents, homeworkers and telecommuting. Most of us feel happiest working alongside other people. In the UK over the last decade employee jobs have increased by 2 million while self-employed jobs have fallen by 250,000, a trend that is predicted to continue. Furthermore, approximately 60% of the new jobs will go to women, while a similar number will be casual or part-time.

To some extent this is good news. Employees are seeking more work/life balance and as a result there is a demand for greater flexibility in terms of hours. However, this casualization is also bad news in relation to emotional security. Work already seeps into our evenings and weekends and this will continue into the future, particularly as collaboration spreads across countries. As a result, fixed 8-hour days will start to disappear, replaced instead by 14-hour work windows into which people will dip in and out.

But will companies continue to exist at all? Corporations, like schools, were largely invented to suit the needs of the day. Things have changed and people are no longer as dependent on a single employer for life as they once were. In the future individuals could be directly responsible for much of the value created in an economy.

A good example of this is the trend toward consumer- or user-generated content. This term technically refers to online content produced by users as opposed to professional media companies, but the idea is applicable to other areas. The key point here is that once only large corporations could create value on a large scale, but in the internet era, size is becoming increasingly irrelevant. Moreover, key resources like computer storage and processing power are so cheap that it sometimes makes commercial sense to give them away. The result is that making things available for free is now a recognized business model on the internet. In the future it may be the *only* business model on the internet.

A good example is Mozilla Corp. This is the company that's part of the non-profit foundation behind Firefox, which is a suite of internet applications including a browser. The company has 70 employees and almost 200,000 volunteer helpers. Firefox itself has a 15% share of the global browser market and has been downloaded around 200 million times — or about 250,000 times every day. In other words this is a corporation whose main mass-market consumer product is free, which relies largely on unpaid workers and which might just be the model for a new type of corporation.

Along the way it could also remodel the not-for-profit sector and perhaps even capitalism itself.

As you'd expect, Mozilla raises a whole host of questions about everything from the definition of a corporation to the interplay between a company and its community. It has also, along the way, had to reinvent many of the ideas and assumptions about how companies operate. You might think that leadership within such an organization is easy, but it appears that it's actually more difficult than within for-profit organizations. For example, if workers are unpaid, bullying or incompetent managers are not tolerated. Nether are unfair conditions. Instead, workers simply walk away. A clearly articulated vision, clear communication and meaningful work are therefore essential. The rules of the game include the fact that the "best" decisions are those that gain the most buy-in from the people involved. Respect, accomplishment and camaraderie are also more important than salary, titles or holiday entitlements — all of which are in fact non-existent.

This model is widely applicable, not only to internet-based companies. Critically, such structures carry very little in the way of fixed overheads and can be dismantled and reassembled quickly to respond to changed conditions. Thus open networks will increasingly replace organizational pyramids and informal collaboration will replace direct competition.

Where in the world

What's going to happen next? First, the pool of low-cost labor will shift to include regions such as Africa, Eastern Europe, Vietnam and the Philippines. Developing nations, particularly those in Asia, have a vast surplus of younger people who, by most historical measures, are the most likely future innovators. One reason it's now fashionable to outsource R&D to Thailand, Brazil and Eastern Europe is because it's cheaper, but low cost is only half the story. Young brains drive innovation. They are hungry and, in certain circumstances, adversity drives invention too. So these regions will become the new global powerhouses of innovation and change.

Second, outsourced innovation will move upstream in terms of strategic content and ultimately there will be a reverse brain-drain, with innovators returning to work in their home countries.

This situation could potentially threaten the productivity and innovativeness of nations such as the US, Germany and Japan unless large numbers of young innovators can be persuaded to migrate to these countries. Therefore we may see companies adopting a military or sporting model, whereby young people are identified by talent scouts as early as the age of 8, 9 or 10 and then offered scholarships right through school and university. Organizations would also bid on pay and conditions, with the top children being fought over globally in multimillion-dollar contract deals. We might also see companies bypassing the traditional education system by setting up their own training establishments to keep a tight reign over their "investments".

Another possibility is that the young may affect the old in a very positive way. In the future, we will see three and eventually four generations working alongside each other, because people will be working well past the age of 65 or 70. This may have the effect of cross-fertilizing experience to produce a melting pot of new ideas.

On the other hand, it might not work at all. Perhaps we will see generational conflicts rising to the surface, with employers hiring generational consultants to sort out the mess. If people stay in the workforce for longer, in theory the final transition from work to retirement will also be more complex and traumatic, which could drive the need for further counseling and consulting.

Whatever happens, the world of work will not be the same in the future.

8 December 2026

Dear Tom

First of all, apologies for using snail mail but I know it will reach Georgie and she'll pass it on to you. Anyway, I just wanted to say thank you for offering me the job at AmazonBay, but I've decided to take the job with Ratamobile instead. The reason probably isn't what you expect. Rata have offered me a starting salary of $296,000, which is the same as AB, but they allow six weeks' annual leave rather than the standard four and they have also recently adopted a no Sunday work policy. They also have in-house childcare, a works canteen (how retro) and they sponsor an insurgency group in Myanmar. However, what really clinched it for me was their ethical standards policy. Maybe it's just an age thing but at 21 I'm really into issues like sustainability and ethical investments and Rata's policy of non-investment in Russia is way ahead of its time.

I really enjoyed hanging out with you guys at the retreat last weekend and please pass my regards on to Bob. I must say that the brain scan was quite revealing. I never knew I had a subconscious bias against women, but I guess that's some kind of inherited trait. The DNA tests were also fascinating, as it turns out I'm more suited to working on pattern recognition in visually based teams than projects that are purely logic driven. Anyway, I'm having it checked out and I'll beep the money for the retreat next week.

Cheers

Matt

Chapter 12

Conclusions:
where to next?

Change is one thing, progress is another. Change is scientific, progress is ethical. Change is indubitable, whereas progress is a matter of controversy.
—Bertrand Russell

Is doom and gloom a new growth industry? The evidence seems to be everywhere. Just scan the shelves of your local bookstore and you'll be assaulted by titles such as *The Long Emergency: Surviving the Converging Catastrophes of the Twenty-First Century, Is It Just Me Or Is Everything Shit?* and my own particular favorite, *How to Survive a Robot Uprising.*

Is life really getting worse and will we be anxious and miserable in the future? There are indeed many things to worry about: melting ice caps, flu pandemics, the erosion of privacy, living too long, terrorism and global economic collapse. According to some great minds we should add running out of oil, being overrun by organized crime, loss of biodiversity, space weather, counterfeiting, electromagnetic fields, earthquakes, hurricanes, TB, malaria, HIV/AIDS, Russia and China to that list.

We're all agreed then, right? Wrong. Some time ago, a lawyer in his late 70s accused me — in the nicest possible way — of living on another planet. Where was the anxiety of which I speak? Where was the evidence of life speeding up? And how could anyone compare a fear of terrorism with the threat of total nuclear annihilation that he had lived with in the 1950s and 1960s? Fair point, especially if you don't fly, own a cellphone or use email.

The future will not be a singular experience and neither is it a foregone conclusion. People of the same age, with the same job, living in the same street will experience the future in different ways and that future will be heavily influenced by local and highly personal events. The future is also something that we alone create. Some of us will embrace technology and globalization while others will endeavor to escape them. Indeed, to some extent the future will be a battle between those rushing toward it and those wanting to travel backwards in time to a sanitized and convenient version of the past.

Crucially, we are already becoming paralyzed by future possibilities. The future ought to be a place where anything is possible. Unfortunately, this is exactly what's happening. Worst-case scenarios are increasingly being thought of as most-likely scenarios and we have all but forgotten about present realities, especially the opportunities and threats on our own doorsteps. So let's all worry about influenza pandemics that haven't happened yet and totally ignore the fact that in 2006 2.6 million adults actually died of AIDS; or that, of the 4.9 million new infections the previous year, 700,000 were in children aged under 15.

The air we now breathe is in many instances far cleaner than it was 100 years ago, but we refuse to recognize this inconvenient truth. Serious acts of crime, especially those aimed at young children, are at the lowest level for years in many places; but again, we choose not to see it. So what is this new "miserablism" all about? It seems to me that when it comes to the future, it is safer — and lazier — to be a pessimist. Optimism takes work. It requires commitment, energy and ideas.

But enough. You probably want to know what you should be thinking about in terms of emerging threats and opportunities. Indeed, if you're the busy type, you've probably not even read the rest of the book but just want a quick summary.

OK, the first thing to think about is technology. While it will be possible to sidestep some of the consequences of individual technologies, I for one cannot see anything on the horizon remotely capable of stopping the overall rise of the machines. In the long term this means robotics and, ultimately, artificial intelligence, although the short term will be pretty interesting too.

Whatever you do will be touched by technology in some way in the future, and in many cases your world will be turned upside down by it. For example, all businesses will to a greater or lesser extent be e-businesses, whether they like it or not. Whether you view this as an opportunity or a risk will ultimately fit with whether your view of the future is positive or negative. Whatever you believe, it will probably come true.

Having said this, there will undoubtedly be a reaction against too much technology (and speed) at some point. Evidence of this will sometimes be obvious — as in people switching things off — but mostly our reactions will be subtle and the societal consequences will not be recognized for decades.

In the more immediate term, a key question for many organizations will be to what extent people (customers, staff and suppliers) will accept high tech over high touch. Will we embrace machines for reasons of convenience and speed, or reject further mechanization in favor of slower, more meaningful relationships with people? Another key question is how accelerating connectivity will affect what we do and how and where we do it.

The next key area is demographics and specifically the ageing of many developed nations. Demographics is still destiny; short of a global pandemic or a nuclear war, it's a very safe bet that there will be a lot more older people in the future. Again, you can view this as either a problem or an opportunity, so the question is to what extent you will thrive or merely survive in a world where older people hold the balance of power in terms of voting and spending.

Of course, it's not simply that there will be more oldies in the future. People will be living longer and feeling younger for longer too. Personally I think that living longer will on the whole be a good thing, although we should be wary of always equating quantity with quality.

If any demographic shift does worry me it's not ageing but the "singularization" of society, in the sense that more and more of us will be living alone. This has some very immediate impacts such as the need for more housing, but it also means that more of us will be spending the future in bubbles protected from the views and needs of other people. The power of two is important not just in terms of fertility rates but also because of the sex life of ideas. New ideas are inherently social and need conversation, serendipity and the rubbing together of two or more human brains if they are to grow.

Again, ageing populations and the increase in single-person households present an opportunity, in that both groups will demand products and services tailored to their own particular circumstances and needs. However, these shifts could also put a strain on the provision of everything from healthcare and housing to education and employment. Then again, perhaps it's the other way around. Maybe you can see it as ageing creating vast opportunities in everything from healthcare and wellbeing to transport, leisure, retail and even education.

Finally there's the area of sustainability. I have read various predictions and forecasts claiming that ethics, corporate social responsibility, corporate governance and even spirituality will be key business trends in the future. While I accept that these ideas are becoming more important, I cannot see them competing with sustainability in the broadest sense in terms of being a global driver of change across all industries, sectors and countries. Taking a very long-term view, it is the beginning of the end for non-renewable resources; while climate change grabs the headlines, we should also be thinking in terms of everything from topsoil erosion and groundwater to packaging use and transport. Resource shortages will be everywhere in the future and finding alternatives to low-cost inputs and making better use of natural resources through materials minimalization, reuse and recycling will be hugely important and tightly regulated issues. Any organization that thinks otherwise not only has its head buried in the sand but is building on it as well.

Sustainability also means acting in an ethical and socially responsible manner, both for the benefit of the planet and for communities closer to home. In the future connectivity will drive radical transparency and all companies will be forced to act ethically, either through regulation or by their network of customers. All brands will have an ethical component and all companies will seek further redemption by taking care of the wider welfare of their employees, customers and community.

As for key risks, there are many to choose from. The tension between globalization and localization is one contender. On the one hand global connectivity and interdependence may herald the dawning of a new age of cooperation. However, things could play the other way too. People may grow tired of belonging to a global village and strive instead to communicate their regional and national differences. This would be a world where the individual still reigned supreme and patriotism and nationalism flourished along with economic protectionism. In a sense this is going backwards, but there may be no stopping it. As resources such as oil start to run out, countries will strive to protect what they have and global trade could easily become local trade as the cost of moving resources, workers and finished goods no longer adds up.

I have avoided talking in too much detail about economic trends and factors so far because there are people far more qualified than I am to do that. However, money is undoubtedly a critical factor in terms of future risks and it is perhaps worth exploring this very briefly.

Money has been affordable — cheap by recent historical standards — and this has fueled economic growth and consumer spending globally. The combination of liquidity and innovation has made it easier than ever to borrow money. This is good because capital has been invested in physical assets (such as new factories) and people have started new companies. But because money has been so cheap, people — both individuals and corporations — have made riskier investments. In some cases this has meant paying what appears to be too much for something, but it has also resulted in lenders becoming less discriminating about who they lend to and under what circumstances. This in turn has allowed poorly run corporations — and badly run households — to stay afloat and avoid ruin.

If the cost of money stays reasonably low for the next 5, 10 or 20 years, this situation is sustainable. But if interest rates start to increase substantially, it could all end in some very big tears.

However, the biggest uncertainty or risk factor is technology. As I mentioned earlier, the history of human existence has largely been that of science and technology, invention and discovery. Our ideas and innovations have shaped who we are, how we act and what we believe.

Science and technology will continue to influence the future, although it may not be immediately obvious to us that this is occurring and very few of us will stop to think about the long-term consequences. What will probably happen is that we will silently wait until there is a disaster — a major nanotech, biotech or AI accident, for example — and only then fully appreciate what is going on, along with the risks and opportunities associated with some of the new technologies, many of which haven't even been invented yet.

On the other hand, technology will offer untold opportunities. Technology will solve climate change and resource shortages, although in reality we will simply swap these for a set of new fears and anxieties.

Overall, then, I'm cynically optimistic. There are tough times immediately ahead, but I'm convinced that if we work together things will be all right in the end. There will obviously be problems, but it's worth remembering that there always have been. And there are wonderful ideas, discoveries and events over the horizon that we can't possibly imagine or comprehend. So while the future is unknown and unwritten, we can begin to see and trace its outline and to start preparing the first drafts.

On balance I think the future will be a pretty good place to live and if it isn't, we will only have ourselves to blame. If you think enough about the future you can change it.

5 things that won't change over the next 50 years

Things do not change, we change.
—Henry David Thoreau

We are continually told that change is the only constant. Change itself has changed. This is true, up to a point. Things evolve and we flatter ourselves if we think that anything remains static for ever. No man ever steps into the same river twice for it is not the same river and he is not the same man — as Heraclitus said in 500 BC, or something along those lines. One could argue that the really important things in life change very slowly or not at all and we are always overestimating the importance of new inventions and ideas at the expense of older ones. Consequently, the things that do change are perhaps not very important.

Here, then, are five things that I believe won't change over the next half-century. If this list doesn't float your boat, I suggest that you look at the seven deadly sins – lust, gluttony, greed, sloth, wrath, envy and pride – the basic rules of economics or a list of the higher human virtues.

An interest in the future and a yearning for the past

People have always been interested in the future. Indeed, the desire to look around the corner and over the garden fence is almost hard-wired into the human character. We are curious about what's out there and what's going to happen next because we want to avoid risk and we seek opportunity. This interest in the future will not change. In fact I'd predict that storytelling about the future will increase as change and uncertainty reach epidemic proportions. So is there any future in becoming a futurist? The answer (I'd predict) is yes, but only when imagination is backed up by rigorous analysis. Moreover, while machines are becoming competent at making numerical forecasts, we still need humans to ask the right questions and to interpret what the numbers really mean. In an age of uncertainty we will need people who can look out of windows and stare out to sea and calmly report back on what they think is out there.

A desire for recognition and respect   People have always craved recognition and respect. At the extreme this means a yearning for status and power, which in turn fuels a desire for the symbols of success. None of this will change in the future, although I expect that the types of power people crave and the objects they aspire to own will evolve. For example, having children (especially lots of children) may become a status symbol in some cultures, with a twin pram or baby buggy having the same social cachet as that of a Lexus today. Equally, not owning a watch or a cellphone may signify wealth by stealth — or at least signal that you don't need to work, which may be much the same thing. More likely, by the year 2050 time and space will have become the ultimate status symbols; and I don't mean space travel. The aspiration for status, recognition and respect isn't going away any time soon.

The need for physical objects, actual encounters and live experiences   Humans are a social species and the majority of us need physical contact with other people. This will not change in the future, although more of us will live alone and work alone. Indeed, the more life speeds up and becomes virtual, the more I'd expect people to want the opposite — physical interactions with other human beings — because a life lived remotely, or at a physical distance from others, is ultimately unbearable. People who live alone will crave the sensation of being held and touched, but so too will people in relationships who are so busy that they hardly ever see their partner. It will be a similar story with physical objects. The more that products and services become digitized and virtual, the more people will crave "real" reality — physical spaces and objects. Equally, we will covet the old ways of doing things, especially if the rest of our lives are dominated by the insubstantial, the intangible and the impermanent. Hence slow physical work and making simple things with your hands will flourish in the future.

Anxiety and fear   When the telephone was demonstrated in 1876, some people thought that the devil was on the line. The reaction to other new technologies like the automobile, the telegraph and even movies was similar. I have a framed poster at home dating from 1925 complaining about the speed of things and people: "Rushin' after money, rushin' after fame; Climbin', pushin', shovin', it's a dizzy game." Thus our current fears about the internet or virtual worlds have a historical precedent and it will be no different in the future. We will continue to invent things that make us uneasy and be unsettled and worried about the speed of change. We will therefore escape reality by going backwards in time (or forwards into the future), because historical visions of the past (and imagined versions of the future) will somehow feel safer and more certain. I expect that anxiety will accelerate and deepen too, in the sense that fear will be networked globally due to the level of connectedness. This blanket of fear will be comforting for some people because it will justify non-intervention. For the rest of us the only solution to this insecurity will be our enduring sense of hope and, ironically, our ability to change.

A search for meaning   According to Abraham Maslow's theory of human motivation, once our basic biological needs (food, water, sleep etc.) have been met we seek to satisfy a number of progressively higher needs. These range from safety through love and belonging to status and self-esteem. At the very top of Maslow's hierarchy of needs is self-actualization. Over the last 50 years or so an increasing number of people have reached the peak of this pyramid and have started searching for meaning; this will continue over the next 50. Implications? I'd expect an increase in spirituality and a search for experiences that transcend everyday life. So pilgrimages and rites of passage won't go away. I'd also expect that while some things will still need to be seen to be believed, more people will believe that things need to be believed to be seen.

Sources

I know what a few of you are thinking: where are your sources? The answer is: elsewhere. The sources of almost everything quoted in this book are a myriad of newspapers, magazines, reports and websites. However, to detail every single one of these would double the size of the book, so I've added a full list of sources, notes and recommended reading as hyperlinks at www.futuretrendsbook.com. If there's something specific that you would like to follow up on, I suggest that you start there and if that doesn't work, get in touch with me directly.

Further reading

If you like what you've read so far, you can find more of the same on my website at www.nowandnext.com. My quarterly trends report called *What's Next* is totally free of charge. Alternatively, if you would like to know more about some of the general themes highlighted in this book, I can recommend any of the following titles. Again, you can find a more extensive reading list on the book website, www.futuretrendsbook.com.

Scenario planning

Bressand, Albert, *Shell Global Scenarios to 2025*, Royal Dutch/ Shell, 2005.

Freeman, Oliver, *Building Scenario Worlds*, Richmond Ventures, 2004.

National Intelligence Council, *CIA Scenarios: Mapping the Global Future*, US Government Printing Office, 2002.

Schwartz, Peter, *The Art of the Long View: Planning for the Future in an Uncertain World*, Currency Doubleday, 1991.

van der Heijden, Kees, *Scenarios: The Art of Strategic Conversation*, John Wiley & Sons, 1996.

van der Heijden, Kees, *The Sixth Sense: Accelerating Organizational Learning with Scenarios*, John Wiley & Sons, 2002.

Current and future trends

Canton, James, *The Extreme Future*, Penguin, 2006.

Knowlson, T. Sharper, *Originality*, T. Werner Laurie, 1917.

Dixon, Patrick, *Futurewise*, Profile Books, 2003.

Hill, Sam, *60 Trends in 60 Minutes*, John Wiley & Sons, 2002.

Malone, Thomas W., *The Future of Work*, Harvard Business School Press, 2004.

Martin, James, *The Meaning of the 21st Century*, Eden Project Books, 2006.

Ministry of Defence, *The DCDC Global Strategic Trends Programme 2007–2036*, 2007.

Naisbitt, John, *Mind Set*, Collins, 2006.

Penn, Mark, *Microtrends*, Allen Lane, 2007.

Taylor, Jim & Wacker, Watts, *The 500-Year Delta*, Collins, 1997.

Toffler, Alvin, *Future Shock*, Pan, 1970.

Williams, Robyn, *What Next? And Other Impossible Questions*, Allen & Unwin, 2007.

Risk

Bernstein, Peter L., *Against the Gods: The Remarkable Story of Risk*, John Wiley & Sons, 1996.

Ernst & Young/Oxford Analytica, *Strategic Business Risk 2008: The Top 10 Risks for Business*, 2007.

Gardner, Dan, *Risk: The Science and Politics of Fear*, Virgin, 2008.

Taleb, Nassim Nicholas, *Black Swan: The Impact of the Highly Improbable*, Allen Lane, 2007.

General reading

Brand, Stewart, *The Clock of the Long Now*, Basic Books, 1999.

Brockman, John, *What Is Your Dangerous Idea?* Pocket Books, 2006.

Bywater, Michael, *Lost Worlds: What Have We Lost and Where Did It Go?* Granta Books, 2004.

Christensen, Clayton, *Seeing What's Next*, Harvard Business School Press, 2004.

Gleick, James, *Faster: The Acceleration of Just About Everything*, Random House, 1999.

Handy, Charles, *The Empty Raincoat*, Random House, 1995.

Handy, Charles, *The Hungry Spirit*, Random House, 1998.

Kaku, Michio, *Physics of the Impossible*, Doubleday/Allen Lane, 2008.

Kuhn, Thomas, *The Structure of Scientific Revolutions*, Institute of Religion and Public Life, 1962.

Maddox, John, *What Remains to be Discovered*, Touchstone, 1999.

Ralston Saul, John, *The Unconscious Civilization*, Penguin, 1997.

Seidensticker, Bob, *Future Hype*, Berrett-Koehler, 2006.

Wilson, Daniel, *How to Survive a Robot Uprising*, Bloomsbury, 2005.

Zeldin, Theodore, *Happiness*, Pan, 1990.

Zeldin, Theodore, *An Intimate History of Humanity*, Reed, 1994.

Acknowledgments

They say that if you steal an idea from someone it's called plagiarism, but if you steal ideas from several people it's called research. The thoughts and ideas of many people have influenced my thinking subconsciously over the years, so I would like to thank as many as my conscious mind remembers. People who have provided wise counsel and support (whether they know it or not) include Wendy Becker, Steve Bowbrick, Napier Collins, Andrew Crosthwaite, Ross Dawson, Victoria Fedorowicz, Oliver Freeman, Rune Gustafson, Charles Handy, Elizabeth Handy, Richard Hytner, Lynne Johnson, Helen Jones, T. Sharper Knowlson, Sally Lansdell, Adam Morgan, Richard Pearey, Heath Row, Mark Runnals, Jonathan Sands, Alan Sekers, Douglas Slater, Guy Smith, Patrick Smith, Elizabeth Stephenson, Georgie Vestey, Ron Zeghibe and Theodore Zeldin. Last but not least, I'd also like to thank Joss Evans for the idea and Russ Radcliffe and Nicholas Brealey for the wherewithal.

Index

'O' Garage 161
3D printers 54

accelerated education 55
accidents 150, 152–7, 164, 232
ACNielsen 119
adaptive cruise control 156
Adeg Aktiv 50+ 197
advertising 109–10, 111, 113
Africa 67, 86, 122, 165, 210, 231, 254, 258, 273
ageing 1, 10, 52, 66, 132, 140–41, 155, 178, 191, 197, 210, 214–15, 223, 225, 245, 262, 277, 279–80
airborne networks 54
allergies 186–7, 220, 222
Alliance Against Urban 4x4s 162
alternative energy 164
alternative medicine 229–30
amateur production 105¬–6
Amazon 32, 107–8
American Apparel 196
American Express 120–21
androids 53
Angola 70
anti-ageing drugs 217, 223
anti-ageing foods 178
anti-ageing surgery 2, 223
anxiety 10, 16, 30, 32, 121, 142, 169, 174, 187, 189, 214, 229, 242, 249, 266–7, 277–8, 282, 287
Apple 109, 123, 130–31, 148
Appleyard, Bryan 76
Argentina 199
Armamark Corporation 183
artificial intelliegence 22, 38, 42, 79,
124, 258, 268–9, 279, 282
Asda 129, 130
Asia 11, 67, 75, 86, 122, 165, 210, 262, 273
Asimov, Isaac 42
Asos.com 205
asthma 221
auditory display software 29
Australia 20–21, 69–70, 73, 138, 186, 228, 232, 254, 265
Austria 197
authenticity 32, 169, 184, 192 200
automated publishing machine (APM) 108
automotive industry 145–67

B&Q 262
baby boomers 39, 197
bacterial factories 54
Bahney, Anna 138
Bahrain 2
baking 27, 169, 185, 189
Bangladesh 2
bank accounts, body double 125
banknotes 29, 121
banks 22, 116, 127–131, 143
    virtual 127
Barnes and Noble 108
BBC 25, 113
Become 196
Belgium 224
benriya 28
Best Buy 212
biofuel 61
biomechatronics 54

biometric identification 28, 35, 50, 65, 85, 125
bionic body parts 53
Biosphere Expeditions 243
biotechnology 38, 282
blended families 20
blogs 97, 101, 102
Blurb 107
BMW 262
body double bank accounts 125
body parts
  bionic 53
  replacement 2, 178, 214
Bolivia 70
Bollywood 105
books 29, 99, 106–9
boomerang kids 138
brain transplants 217
brain-enhancing foods 178
Brazil 2, 81, 86, 164, 233, 238, 254, 273
Burger King 174
business 13, 258–75
Bust-Up 179
busyness 27, 185, 260

Calvin, Bill 43
Canada 60, 75, 226
car sharing 151, 166
carbon credits 164
carbon footprints 239
carbon taxes 73, 163
cars
  classic 159–60
  driverless 145–6
  flying 147, 156
  hydrogen-powered 12, 31, 148, 164
  pay-as-you-go 158–9
  self-driving 156
cascading failure 28
cash 119–20, 194
cellphone payments 122, 202
cellphones 3, 25, 35, 49, 51, 122, 147, 152
chicken, Christian 182
childcare robots 55
childhood 27, 33–4, 79–80

children's database 83
CHIME nations (China, India, Middle East) 2, 10, 78
China 2, 10, 11, 66–9, 72–8, 85, 118, 130, 132–3, 135, 154, 165–6, 211, 214, 234, 238, 244, 254–5, 258, 262, 277
choice 176–7
Christian chicken 182
Christianity, muscular 16, 70
cinema 104–6
Citibank 29, 125
citizen journalism 97–8, 101
City Car Club 159
Clarke, Arthur C. 56–7
Clarke's 177
classic cars 159–60
climate change 4, 11, 41, 57, 61, 65, 71, 73–5, 143, 146, 238, 241, 248, 281–2
climate-controlled buildings 238, 248
cloning 38
  human 23, 235
CNN 113
Coca-Cola 75, 211–12
co-creation 105–6, 113
coins 29, 121, 122
collective intelligence 43–5
Collins, Jim 271
Comme des Garçons 205
competition, in financial services 117–18
computers
  disposable 54
  intelligent 23, 41
  organic 54
  wearable 54
computing 3, 33, 41, 46, 79
connectivity 3, 10, 11, 15, 88, 219, 247, 258–9, 264, 279, 281
conscientious objection taxation 83
contactless payments 116, 143
continuous partial attention 51
convenience 116, 168–9, 174, 179, 201, 212
Coren, Stanley 232
corporate social responsibility 259, 265, 280

cosmetic neurology 236
Costa Rica 233
Craig's List 99
creativity 11, 269; *see also* innovation
credit cards 134–6, 143
crime 83–6
crime forecasting 83–4
crime gene 55, 83
Crowdstorm 196
Cuba 72
cultural holidays 243
culture 11, 17–37
currency, global 120
customization 54, 160, 211–12, 246
cyberterrorism 62, 85–6
Cyc 43

DayJet 246
death 223–5
debt 116–17, 133–7
defense 60, 83
deflation 132
democratization of media 98, 102,
    107
demographics 1, 10, 21, 66, 79, 191,
    259, 262–4, 279–80
Denmark 231
department stores 203
deregulation 11, 3
Destiny Health 142
Detroit Project 162
diagnosis 218
diagnosis, remote 214
digital evaporation 25
digital immortality 24–5
digital instant gratification syndrome
    191
digital Maoism 45
digital money 12, 29, 116, 119–20,
    122, 125, 131, 143, 181
digital nomads 20, 266
digital plasters 227
digital privacy 25, 91, 102
Dinner by Design 175
dirt holidays 222
Discovery Health 142
diseases 2, 214
disintegrators 55

Disney 112–13
disposable computers 54
divorce 33, 82
DNA 54–5, 172
DNA database 83
DNA testing, compulsory 83
do-it-yourself dinner shops 175–6
dolls 24
doorbells 32
downshifters 20
Dream Dinners 175
dream fulfillment 141
drink 168–90
driverless cars 145–6
drugs
    anti-ageing 217, 223
    performance-improving 267–8
Dubai 248, 251
dynamic pricing 246

E Ink 109
e-action 62
Earthwatch 243
Eastern Europe 273
eBay 196
e-books 29, 108, 109
economic collapse 2, 4, 69, 210, 277
economic protectionism 10, 15, 69,
    281
Ecuador 70
education 15, 18, 79–82, 280
    accelerated 55
    lifelong learning 263
Egypt 2
electronic camouflage 54
electronic surveillance 35
Elephant 230
email 18–19, 25, 51–2, 102
embedded intelligence 51, 145
emotional capacity of robots 38,
    58
energy 70, 73
    alternative 164
    nuclear 71
    solar 71
    wind 71
enhancement surgery 235
entertainment 34, 115

environment 4, 10, 11, 14, 61, 72–3,
    79, 146, 162, 164, 173, 189, 208–9,
    242–3, 255
epigenetics 55
escapism 16, 32–3
Estonia 82, 86
e-tagging 122–3
e-therapy 228
ethical bankruptcy 35
ethical investing 265
ethical tourism 243
ethics 22, 24, 39, 52, 75, 83, 125, 184,
    192, 202, 218, 224, 235–6, 242,
    259, 264–5, 280–81
Europe 11, 67, 69, 78, 88, 134, 165–6,
    172, 180, 182, 198
European Union 15, 132
euthanasia 224
Everquest 33
e-voting 62
extended financial families 137
extinction timeline 9

Facebook 91, 101
face-recognition doors 55
fakes 32
family loans 137
fantasy-related industries 32
farmaceuticals 169, 172
fast food 168, 173–4
fat taxes 180
fear 10, 34, 65, 143, 287
female-only spaces 199–200, 251
feminization 81
financial services 116–44
    trends 116–18
fish farming 171
flat-tax system 82–3
Florida, Richard 269
flying cars 156
food 66–7, 69, 75–6, 153, 168–90
food
    anti-ageing 178
    brain-enhancing 178   fast 168,
    173–4
    functional 169
    growing your own 168, 182, 185
    history 180–82

slow 168, 183
    trends 168–70
FoodExpert ID 172
food-miles 168, 183, 209
Ford 160, 202, 262–3
forecasting 47
    crime 83–4
    war 47
Forrester Research 125
fractional ownership 159, 166
France 97, 140, 161, 179, 188, 251
Friedman, Thomas 261–2
FriendFinder 32
Friends Reunited 22
functional food 169
Furedi, Frank 65

gaming 32–3, 67, 91, 105–6, 111, 123,
    157, 246
Gap 206
gardening 27, 141
GE Money 131, 138
gendered medicine 230–31
gene silencing 217
gene, crime 83
General Motors 148, 156
Generation X 39, 264
Generation Y 39, 91, 100, 131, 134–5,
    137, 191, 196, 259, 264
Genes Reunited 35
genetic enhancement 38, 46
genetic history 35
genetic modification 31, 172
genetic testing 217
genetics 3, 10, 43
genomic medicine 217
Germany 70, 140, 151, 161, 193–4,
    205–6, 245, 251, 262, 274
Gimzewski, James 218
global currency 120
global warming 4, 45, 74, 183, 220
globalization 3, 10, 15–16, 60, 64,
    69–70, 72, 78–9, 85, 94, 118, 132,
    136, 139, 161, 173, 179, 183–5,
    210, 219–20, 233–4, 247, 258,
    261–3, 278, 281
Google 22, 130
gout 221

government 14, 18, 60–89
GPS 3, 15, 26, 48, 85, 131, 141, 198, 223, 246, 268
Grameen Bank 128
gravity tubes 55
green taxes 73
Greenpeace 163
GRIN technologies (genetics, robotics, internet, nanotechnology) 3, 10, 11
growing your own food 168, 182, 185
Gucci 210
Gulf States 118, 244, 254

H&M 206
habitual shopping 201
Handy, Charles 261
Happily 199
happiness 60–61, 68–9, 139, 244
health 15, 79, 168–9
health monitoring 218, 222, 227
healthcare 2, 129, 137, 140–41, 145, 169–70, 173–4, 179–81, 214–37, 280; *see also* medicine
precision 220–23
trends 214–15
Heinberg, Richard 71
Helm, Dieter 73
Heritage Foods 185
hikikomori 18
hive mind 43
holidays 31, 113; *see also* tourism
holidays
at home 239
cultural 243
dirt 222
Hollywood 33, 105–6
holographic displays 54
Home Equity Share 138
home-based microgeneration 61
Hong Kong 251
hospitals 214, 227–9, 250
at home 214, 224, 226–8
hotels 19, 251
sleep 250
human cloning 23, 235
Hungary 233

hybrid humans 22
hydrogen power 61
hydrogen-powered cars 12, 31, 148, 164
Hyperactive Technologies 174
Hyundai 161

identities, multiple 35, 50
identity 61, 68
identity theft 85, 125
identity verification, two-way 125
India 2, 10, 11, 67–9, 73, 75–6, 78, 105, 118, 128, 132, 154, 165–6, 231, 233–4, 238, 244, 254, 258, 262
indirect taxation 83
Indonesia 2, 165
industrial robots 40
infinite content 90–91
information overlead 91, 150, 268; *see also* too much information
innovation 61, 78–9, 94, 166, 211, 224, 253, 260, 269–71, 274, 280, 282
innovation timeline 8
instant gratification 202
insurance 116, 131, 140–3, 145, 158, 181, 222, 236
pay-as-you-go 158
weather 248
intelligence implants 215
intelligence, embedded 51, 145
intelligent computers 23, 41
intelligent night vision 153–4
interaction, physical 22, 25, 91, 104, 112, 126–7, 204, 214, 229, 259, 286
interactive media 91, 99
intergenerational mortgages 133, 137–8
intermediaries 116, 128
internet 3, 10, 11, 17–18, 25, 65, 95, 102, 109–11, 117, 147, 226–7, 245, 254, 266, 272, 287
sensory 54
interruption science 51
iPills 226
Iran 2, 66
Ishiguro, Hiroshi 53

Islamic fanaticism 16
Italy 161, 188–9
iTunes 109, 123; *see also* Apple

Japan 1, 18, 26, 28–9, 52–3, 60, 77–8,
    108, 121–2, 125, 133, 137–8, 140,
    165, 176, 179, 182, 186, 188,
    198–9, 212, 226, 244, 248, 255,
    262, 274
journalism 90, 112
journalism, citizen 97–8, 101
joy-makers 55

Kaboodle 196
Kapor, Mitchell 43
Kenya 122
keys 28–9
Kramer, Peter 267
Kuhn, Thomas 264
Kurzweil, Ray 43
Kuwait 2

labor migration 273–4
labor shortages 3, 77–8, 262–4
Lanier, Jaron 45
laser shopping 201
leisure sickness 221
Let's Dish 175
Lexus 148
Libya 70
life-caching 24, 101–2
lighting 149, 151
Like.com 205
limb farms 235
limited editions 205–6
live events 92, 104, 286
localization 10, 15–16, 110, 121, 161,
    168, 179, 183, 185, 204, 209,
    211–12, 239, 254, 281
location tagging 85
location-based marketing 110
longevity 178–9, 191
Longman, Philip 68
low cost 191, 208–11
luxury 191, 210, 242, 244, 246, 249–50
machinamas 106
machine-to-machine communication
    54

marketing 109–10
    location-based 110
    now 110
    prediction 110
Marks & Spencer 199
Maslow, Abraham 287–8
Mayo Clinic 229
McDonald's 123, 159, 170, 174
McKinsey 270
meaning, search for 16, 243, 265, 273,
    287–8
MECU 125
media 90–115
    democratization of 98, 102, 107
    trends 90–92
medical outsourcing 233–4
medical tourism 2, 215, 233
medicine 178, 214–37; *see also*
    healthcare
    alternative 229–30
    gendered 230–31
    genomic 217
memory 215, 218, 225–6
memory loss 45
memory pills 217, 226
memory recovery 2, 214–15, 225
memory removal 29–30, 215, 226
Menicon 226
Meow Mix 205
Merriman, Jon 119
metabolomics 54
meta-materials 54
Metro 193–4
Mexico 2
micromedia 95
micro-payments 123, 143
Microsoft 130, 148
Middle East 10, 11, 67, 78, 86, 113,
    118, 122, 132, 165–6, 254
migration 3, 11, 66–7, 75, 79, 220,
    258, 273–4
    boomerang 20
    labor 273–4
Migros 204
military recruitment 66
military vehicles 149–50
mindwipes 55
Mitsubishi 188, 262

mobile payments 116, 143
Modafinil 218
molecular biology 217
monetization 112
money 116–44
    digital 12, 29, 116, 119–20, 122,
    125, 131, 143, 181
monitoring, remote 145, 159, 214,
    228
monolines 128, 130
mood sensitivity 39, 47, 145, 149,
    155, 177–8
Morgan Stanley 120
mortality bonds 141
Mozilla Corp. 272
M-PESA 122
MTV 99
multigenerational families 20
multiple identities 35, 50
Murdoch, Rupert 103
muscular Christianity 16, 70
My-Food-Phone 228
MySpace 22, 25, 44, 91, 101, 106

N11 nations (Bangladesh, Egypt,
    Indonesia, Iran, South Korea,
    Mexico, Nigeria, Pakistan,
    Philippines, Turkey, Vietnam) 2
nanoelectronics 54
nanomedicine 32
nanotechnology 3, 10, 23, 38, 42–3,
    48, 148, 173, 218, 229, 269, 282
napcaps 55
narrowcasting 103
NASA 25, 51
nationalism 16, 67, 69–70, 132, 173,
    281
natural resources 2, 4, 11, 61, 280–81
Nearbynow 212
Nestlé 185
Netherlands 224
NetIntelligence 266
networkcar.com 145
networks 28, 157, 271
    airborne 54
neural nets 47
neuronic whips 55
neuroscience 33, 46

Neville, Richard 56–7
New Economics Foundation 162
New Zealand 251, 254
newspapers 29, 96–102, 111, 113
Nigeria 2, 70
Nike 23
nimbyism 60
Nokia 99
Norelift 179
Northern Rock 132–3
Norwich Union 158
nostalgia 16, 31–2, 49, 160–61, 169,
    173, 189, 192, 285
now marketing 110
nuclear annihilation 10, 88
nuclear energy 71
nutraceuticals 169, 172

obesity 72, 180–82
oceanic thermal converters 55
oil 66, 69–71, 165
Oman 2, 254
organic computers 54
osteoporosis 221

Pakistan 2
pandemics 4, 10, 16, 57, 69, 121, 218,
    220, 277–9
parasite singles 138
passwords 50
    pictorial 50
pathogens 219
patient simulators 234
patina 31
patriotism 60, 64, 281
pay-as-you-go cars 158–9
pay-as-you-go insurance 158
payments
    cellphone 122, 202
    contactless 116, 143
    micro- 123, 143
    mobile 116, 143
    pre- 116, 143
PayPal 117, 130
Pearson, Ian 42
performance-improving drugs
    267–8
personal robots 40

personalization 19, 26, 54, 90–2, 94,
    96–7, 100, 102–3, 114, 131, 142,
    173, 194–5, 212, 230–31, 246, 251,
    253
Peru 70
Peters, Tom 263
Pharmaca 230
pharmaceuticals 2, 33, 214,
    223
Philippines 2, 201, 273
Philips 108
Philips, Michael 218–19
photographs 102
physical interaction 22, 25, 91, 104,
    112, 126–7, 204, 214, 229, 259,
    286
physicalization 91–2, 95–6, 100, 104,
    114
pictorial passwords 50
Pink, Daniel 268
plagiarism 80
polarization 15–16, 252
politics 60–89
    regional 60
    trends 60–62
pop-up retail 205
pornography 31
portability 168, 173–4
power shift eastwards 2, 10–11, 78
Prada 194–5, 205
precision agriculture 171–2
precision healthcare 220–23
prediction marketing 110
pre-payments 116, 143
privacy 3, 15, 39, 48, 85, 145, 156–8,
    194, 222, 235, 267, 277
    digital 25, 91, 102
Procter & Gamble 99, 263
Prosper 117, 128
protectionism 64, 132, 209
    economic 10, 15, 69, 281
provenance 168, 183
proximity indicators 32
PruHealth 142
psychological neoteny 50
public transport 162
purposeful shopping 201

Qatar 2
quality 90–91, 92, 95, 103
quantum mechanics 54
quantum wires 54
quiet materials 54

radio 111
randominoes 55
ranking 34, 80, 102, 110, 127, 196
Ranking Ranqueen 176
reality mining 49
Really Cool Foods 175
recession 132–6, 191, 211
recognition 36, 286
refrigerators 187–8
regeneration 219
regional politics 60
regionality 168, 182–4
regulation 117, 130, 136
REI 196
Reid, Morris 87
religion 16, 56
remote diagnosis 214
remote monitoring 145, 159, 214, 228
reputation 34–5
resistance to technology 49
resource shortages 11, 15, 139, 146,
    169, 185, 239, 282
resources, natural 2, 4, 11, 61, 70–71,
    136, 280–81
respect 36, 286
restaurants 176–8
retail 20–21, 191–213, 280
    pop-up 205
    stealth 204
    theater 203
    trends 191–2
Revkin, Andy 74
RFID 3, 24, 48, 15, 119, 142, 172, 175,
    182, 186, 194
rickets 221
risk 15, 117, 127, 131, 133, 142–3,
    153, 158, 163, 181, 247, 281–2, 285
Ritalin 218
road pricing 157
Robertson, Peter 47
robogoats 53
robot department store 198

Robot Rules 42
robotic
    assistants 52, 195
    concierges 252
    financial advisers 124–5
    lobsters 53
    pest control 55
    soldiers 39, 53, 58
    surgery 35, 39, 235
robotics 3, 10, 39, 42–3, 224, 258,
    268–9, 279
robots 39, 52–4, 124, 223, 235
    childcare 55
    emotional capacity of 38, 58
    industrial 40
    personal 40
    security 198
    therapeutic 39, 52
Russia 2, 66, 69, 72, 77, 86, 118, 165,
    218, 238, 254, 277

safety 32, 149–7, 163–4, 172, 182, 186
Sainsbury's 204
Salt 177
satellite tracking 157–8
Saudi Arabia 2, 66
Schwartz, Barry 176
science 13, 16, 38–59, 282
    interruption 51
    trends 38–40
scramble suits 55
scrapbooking 25, 102
Sears Roebuck 130
seasonality 168, 183–4
Second Life 124, 196–7
securitization 117, 133
security 16, 31
security robots 198
self-driving cars 156
self-medication 228
self-publishing 97, 107–8
self-reliance 35, 72
self-repairing roads 55
self-replicating machines 23, 42
Selfridges 203
sensor motes 15, 48, 186
sensory internet 54
Sharia-based investment 118

Shop24 198
shopping 191–213
    habitual 201
    laser 201
    malls 200–4
    purposeful 201
    slow 202
    social 196
short-wave scalpels 55
silicon photonics 54
simplicity 160–61, 169, 176, 191, 207
Singapore 227
single-person households 19–20,
    191–2, 197–8, 210, 231, 280, 286
sky shields 55
sleep 150–1, 178, 214, 217, 232–3,
    249
sleep debt 90, 250
sleep hotels 250
sleep surrogates 55
slow food 168, 183
slow shopping 202
smart devices 26–7, 28, 32, 35, 42, 48,
    54, 55, 155, 195, 196
smart dust 3, 15, 48, 186
smartisans 20
Smartmart 198
snakebots 53
social networks 91, 101, 104, 126,
    196, 245
social shopping 196
society 13, 15¬–16, 17¬–37
    trends 15–16
Sodexho 183
solar energy 71
Sony 108
South Africa 81, 142, 228
South America 78, 254
South Korea 2, 97, 121–2
space ladders 54
space mirrors 45
space tourism 255
space tugs 55
speed 155, 191, 198, 231, 278–9
spirituality 16, 22, 265, 280, 288
spot knowledge 45
spray-on surgical gloves 55
St James's Ethics Centre 265

stagflation 132
starch-based plastics 61
stealth retail 204
stealth taxation 83
Sterling, Bruce 53
storytelling 192
Strayer, David 152
street signs 153–4
stress 32, 90, 221, 229, 231–2, 242–3,
    249, 251–3, 258, 260, 266–8
stress-control clothing 55
Stylehive 196
Sudan 70
suicide tourism 224
Super Suppers 175
supermarkets 128–9, 174–6, 178,
    181–2, 184, 193–4, 201, 204,
    207–8, 215
surgery 2, 31
    anti-ageing 2, 223
    enhancement 235
Surowiecki, James 43
surveillance 35, 39
sustainability 4, 71, 171, 183–5, 192,
    264, 271, 280–81
Sweden 81
Switzerland 159, 199, 204
synthetic biology 54

Taco Bell 174
Tactical Numerical Deterministic
    Model 47
tagging, location 83, 85
Taiwan 78
talent, war for 258, 262; see also labor
    shortages
Target 205
Tasmania 251
Tata Motors 165
taxation 82–3
    carbon 73, 163
    conscientious objection 83
    fat 180
    flat 82–3
    green 73
    indirect 83
    stealth 83
Tchibo 206

technology 3, 14–16, 18, 22, 26, 28,
    32, 38–59, 71–2, 79–80, 90, 113,
    125, 140–41, 145, 148, 151, 153,
    156–8, 160, 168, 172, 185–8, 197,
    210, 215, 223, 228–9, 234, 241,
    245, 249–50, 252, 258–9, 263,
    266–70, 278–9, 282
    refuseniks 30, 49, 91
    trends 38–40
telemedicine 214, 224, 228
telepathy 29
teleportation 54
television 21, 90, 102, 111, 113
terrorism 64, 88, 102, 143, 248–9,
    251, 277–8
Tesco 99, 128–9, 175, 195, 204, 208,
    212
Thailand 233, 273
therapeutic robots 39, 52
thermal imaging 218
things that won't change 10, 285–8
ThisNext 196
Tik Tok Easy Shop 198
time scarcity 30, 90, 96, 168, 174–6,
    207, 239
time shifting 90, 104, 110
time stamps 48
timeline, extinction 9
timeline, innovation 8
timelines 7
tired all the time 232
too much choice (TMC) 29, 191,
    207–8
too much information (TMI) 29, 49,
    51, 191, 215; see also information
    overload
tourism 238–57
    ethical 243
    medical 2, 215, 233
    space 255
    suicide 224
    tribal 246
Tourism Concern 243
tourist quotas 238, 255
Toyota 46–7, 148
traceability 185
transparency 3, 15, 136, 259, 265,
    281

transport 15, 145–67, 280
    public 146, 162
    trends 145–7
travel 2, 3, 11, 141, 238–57
    trends 238–40
trend maps 6–7
trends 1, 5–7, 10, 13
trends
    financial services 116–18
    food 168–70
    healthcare 214–15
    media 90–92
    politics 60–62
    retail 191–2
    science and technology 38–40
    society 15–16
    transport 145–7
    travel 238–40
    work 258–60
tribal tourism 246
tribalism 15–16, 60, 120–21, 173, 182,
    209, 244
trust 79, 126, 130, 132, 136, 182, 192,
    259, 265–6
tunnels 162
Turing test 43
Turing, Alan 42
Turkey 2, 233
two-way identity verification 125

UAE 2
UFOs 56
UK 19–20, 69, 73, 81, 83, 87–8, 94,
    96–7, 99, 121–2, 125, 130, 132–5,
    140–42, 154, 158–9, 161–2, 166,
    175, 185–6, 189, 195, 199, 203–5,
    224, 243, 251–2, 261–2, 267, 271
uncertainty 16, 30, 34, 50, 163, 189,
    232, 247, 282, 285
Unilever 185
University of Chicago 231–2
urbanization 11, 18–19, 75, 81, 146,
    219
US 1, 11, 19–21, 23, 53–4, 60, 64, 66,
    69, 72, 74, 77–80, 83, 85–7, 96–7,
    100, 122–6, 128, 132–5, 137, 140,
    142, 153, 158, 160–62, 165, 175,
    180–3, 185, 194–5, 198, 200, 202,
    205, 207, 209, 211–12, 223–4,
    226–34, 244, 246, 251–2, 258,
    262–3, 265–7, 270, 274
user-generated content (UGC) 44, 91,
    96, 272

vending machines 198
Venezuela 66, 70
verbal signatures 125
VeriChip 119
video on demand 90
Vietnam 2, 273
Vino 100 107
Virgin Atlantic 245
virtual
    adultery 33
    banks 127
    economy 123–4
    protests 62
    reality 67
    sex 32
    stores 195–7
    vacations 32, 245
    worlds 148, 202, 239, 245, 254,
    287
Vocation Vacations 243–4
Vodafone 130
voice recognition 39
voice-based internet search 54
voicelifts 2, 223
voluntourism 243
Volvo 155
voting 3, 65, 87–8

Walgreens 230
Wal-Mart 99, 129–30, 204, 208–9,
    212, 230, 265
war 65–6, 69
war for talent 258, 262; *see also* labor
    shortages
war forecasting 47
water 66–7, 71, 74–6
wearable computers 54
weather 61
weather insurance 248
Weinberg, Peter 118
wellbeing 2, 173, 178, 189
white flight 20

Wikipedia 44, 98
Wilson, Edward O. 71
wind energy 71
wisdom of idiots 45
Wizard 138
work 258–75
    trends 258–60
work/life balance 61, 68, 244, 26o,
    272
worldphone 19

xenophobia 16, 60

YouTube 44, 97, 101, 106

Zara 205–6
Zipcar 158
Zopa 117, 127